Improving the Medicare Market

Adding Choice and Protections

Committee on Choice and Managed Care: Assuring Public
Accountability and Information for Informed Purchasing
by and on Behalf of Medicare Beneficiaries

Stanley B. Jones and Marion Ein Lewin, *Editors*

Office of Health Policy Programs and Fellowships

INSTITUTE OF MEDICINE

NATIONAL ACADEMY PRESS
Washington, D.C. 1996

NATIONAL ACADEMY PRESS • 2101 Constitution Avenue, N.W. • Washington, D.C. 20418

NOTICE: The project that is the subject of this report was approved by the Governing Board of the National Research Council, whose members are drawn from the councils of the National Academy of Sciences, the National Academy of Engineering, and the Institute of Medicine. The members of the committee responsible for the report were chosen for their special competences and with regard for appropriate balance.

This report has been reviewed by a group other than the authors according to procedures approved by a Report Review Committee consisting of members of the National Academy of Sciences, the National Academy of Engineering, and the Institute of Medicine.

The Institute of Medicine was chartered in 1970 by the National Academy of Sciences to enlist distinguished members of the appropriate professions in the examination of policy matters pertaining to the health of the public. In this, the Institute acts under both the Academy's 1863 congressional charter responsibility to be an adviser to the federal government and its own initiative in identifying issues of medical care, research, and education. Dr. Kenneth I. Shine is president of the Institute of Medicine.

Support for this project was provided by The Robert Wood Johnson Foundation, The Commonwealth Fund, the Kansas Health Foundation, and The Pew Charitable Trusts. The views presented are those of the Institute of Medicine Committee on Choice and Managed Care and are not necessarily those of the funding organizations.

Library of Congress Cataloging-in-Publication Data

Improving the medicare market : adding choice and protections /
    Committee on Choice and Managed Care : Assuring Public Accountability
    and Information for Informed Purchasing by and on Behalf of Medicare
    Beneficiaries, Office of Health Policy Programs and Fellowships,
    Institute of Medicine ; Stanley B. Jones and Marion Ein Lewin,
    editors.
        p. cm.
    Includes bibliographical references and index.
    ISBN 0-309-05535-0
    1. Medicare. 2. Aged—Medical care—United States—Finance.
    3. Managed care plans (Medical care)—United States. I. Jones,
    Stanley B. II. Lewin, Marion Ein. III. Committee on Choice and
    Managed Care : Assuring Public Accountability and Information for
    Informed Purchasing by and on Behalf of Medicare Beneficiaries.
    RA413.7.A4I47   1996
    362.1'0425—dc20   96-42908
                                             CIP

Additional copies of this report are available from the National Academy Press, 2101 Constitution Avenue, N.W., Box 285, Washington, D.C. 20055. Call 800-624-6242 or 202-334-3313 (in the Washington Metropolitan Area). **http://www.nap.edu.**

The serpent has been a symbol of long life, healing, and knowledge among almost all cultures and religions since the beginning of recorded history. The image adopted as a logotype by the Institute of Medicine is based on a relief carving from ancient Greece, now held by the Staatlichemuseen in Berlin.

iii

Preface

As part of the ongoing transformation of the U.S. health care system, there is mounting pressure to reform the $180 billion Medicare program to make it more efficient and to secure its future viability. A centerpiece of current public- and private-sector efforts to restructure the nation's biggest social program and to reduce Medicare expenditure growth focuses on expanding health plan options for beneficiaries, with an emphasis on managed care arrangements. A number of studies and surveys attribute the recent slowing rate of spending on health benefits by large employers to the growth of managed care programs.

Although only 10 percent of the Medicare population is currently enrolled in managed care plans, these risk contract programs now appear to be attracting more Medicare beneficiaries. Enrollment more than doubled between 1987 and 1995 and is now growing at more than 25 percent a year.

As major efforts to shift Medicare patients into managed care plans move forward, many experts and patient advocates are concerned whether the necessary information and protections are in place to enable Medicare patients to select an appropriate health plan wisely and to ensure that this group continues to have access to high quality health care. The potentially daunting scope and speed of the transition by elderly Americans into what for most beneficiaries remains uncharted waters makes the need for high-quality, trustworthy information and accountability particularly critical. Only by laying a sound infrastructure in which individuals can make informed purchasing decisions and in which competition is based on quality performance can the public confidence needed to move Medicare beneficiaries safely and responsibly into a marketplace for choice and managed care be ensured.

Within this context of historical change and major legislative proposals by the 104th Congress to restructure the Medicare program, the Institute of Medicine was asked to appoint a committee that would provide guidance to policy makers and decision makers on ensuring public accountability, promoting informed purchasing, and installing the necessary protections to help Medicare beneficiaries to operate effectively, safely, and confidently in the new environment of greater health plan choice. The Robert Wood Johnson Foundation generously took the lead in funding this project, and was joined by The Commonwealth Fund, the Kansas Health Foundation, and The Pew Charitable Trusts, which also provided funding.

In the fall of 1995, a committee of 10 individuals was appointed to conduct a 12-month study on ensuring public accountability and informed purchasing for Medicare beneficiaries, performing the following tasks:

- to commission background papers from experts and practitioners in the field that review the literature and synthesize aspects of the leading issues and current policy proposals as they pertain to ensuring public accountability and informed purchasing in a system of broadened choice;
- to guide, develop, and convene an invitational symposium to (1) examine what is known (or not known) about ensuring public accountability and informed purchasing in the current Medicare program and other health plans, (2) recommend how public accountability and informed purchasing can be ensured for Medicare beneficiaries in managed care and other health plan choices, and (3) discuss options and strategies that can be used to help government and the private sector achieve the desired goals in this arena; and
- to produce a report that will include the commissioned

background papers, a summary of the symposium discussion, and recommendations on the major issues that need to be addressed to ensure public accountability and the availability of information for informed purchasing by and on behalf of Medicare beneficiaries in managed care and other health care delivery options.

The committee met twice during the course of this study. In carrying out its charge, the committee recognized that the science-based and peer-reviewed literature in the major areas of the committee's scrutiny is sparse since the field is young and continues to evolve at an unprecedented pace. The state-of-the-art information in this area resides primarily among a large number of private and public purchasers and various other organizations and agencies. With that in mind, the committee constructed a 2-day symposium primarily around real-world experts who could comment on and respond to the available research findings and to current Medicare reform proposals from their well-recognized experiences. Given the committee's broad charge and the many issues that potentially fall under the rubric of ensuring public accountability and informed purchasing in an environment of choice and managed care, the committee had to set some priorities and parameters and provide some caveats regarding its work agenda. These are detailed in the body of the report.

The report is divided into three chapters and 12 appendixes. Chapter 1, an overview, provides the background, context, and parameters of the study. Chapter 1 also outlines how the committee defined and approached its charge and work agenda. Chapter 2 presents highlights from testimony heard at the invitational symposium held on February 1 and 2, 1996, and summarizes the major points made by the authors of the commissioned papers, by the invited respondents, and at the discussion that followed the panel presentations. As a summary, however, this section cannot do adequate justice to the rich and valuable data and information included in the eight commissioned papers found in Appendixes E to L. The information found in the papers contributed significantly to the committee's findings and recommendations.

Acknowledgments

This study could not have succeeded without the help, guidance, and generosity of a number of organizations and many individuals. This is especially true for a study such as *Improving the Medicare Market: Adding Choice and Protections*, where new research findings, information, and assessments continue to be developed on almost a weekly basis as part of the ongoing transformation of the U.S. health care system. Whereas it is not possible to mention by name all of those who contributed to the study as it moved from conception to completion, the committee wants to express its gratitude to a number of groups and individuals for their special contributions.

Deep appreciation is extended to The Robert Wood Johnson Foundation for major funding of this activity and to The Commonwealth Fund, the Kansas Health Foundation, and The Pew Charitable Trusts for generous additional support. The committee thanks these sponsors, not only for the support that enabled the Institute of Medicine to undertake this timely and important assignment, but also for their encouragement and interest.

Getting "up to speed" for a new study is always a challenging exercise, particularly when a study is focused on a dynamic and evolving field and has to be completed within a relatively short time frame. A number of organizations and individuals with special interest, recognized expertise, and key responsibilities pertinent to the committee's charge provided invaluable background information and important perspectives.

At the Health Care Financing Administration, thanks go to Bruce C. Vladeck, Kathleen M. King, Jeffrey Kang, Judy Sangle, Deborah Ball, Debbie Thomas, Celeste Newcomb, and several staffers in the Office of Managed Care. Helen Smits did an outstanding job of briefing the committee at its first meeting. Harvey Brook also served as a very helpful resource expert in the early stages of the committee's deliberations.

Janet L. Shikles, Carlotta Joiner, and Sarah F. Jaggar of the U.S. General Accounting Office were enormously helpful in keeping the committee informed about GAO activities related to the themes of this report. Margaret O'Kane and Cary Sennett from the National Committee on Quality Assurance gave generously of their time and expertise to inform the committee on NCQA's activities related to quality and accountability.

The committee greatly appreciated the help and contributions of Lauren B. LeRoy, John F. Hoadley, and Anne L. Schwartz of the Physician Payment Review Commission. Laura A. Dummitt from the Prospective Payment Assessment Commission deserves our sincere thanks as well. Irene Fraser of the Agency for Health Care Policy and Research (AHCPR) was very helpful in sharing with study staff current projects at AHCPR that could inform the committee's task and work agenda.

Shoshanna Sofaer of the George Washington University Medical Center not only played an important role in the study's major symposium, but also provided the committee with invaluable additional guidance and key readings. Catherine M. Dunham from The Robert Wood Johnson Foundation offered important information about the special needs of vulnerable populations in an environment of managed care and enhanced choice. Bettina Experton of Humetrix shared with the committee a number of important study findings on the special needs of the frail elderly in managed care arrangements. Herbert Nickens and Lois Bergeisen of the Association of American Medical Colleges contributed to the committee's understanding of the role of minority physicians in improving care for the underserved.

Michael Hash from Health Policy Alternatives contributed to the success of this project in important ways, given his well-respected knowledge of government programs and the workings of the Congress and executive branch. The committee also acknowledges with gratitude Kenneth Cohen of the U.S. Senate Special Committee on the Aging who, throughout the process, helped keep the committee and study staff current on the ongoing changes to the Medicare reform provisions of the Balanced Budget Act of 1995.

The committee is thankful for the guidance and contributions of Simeon Rubenstein of the Group Health Cooperative of Puget Sound, Deborah Lipson of the Alpha Center, Trish Newman from the Kaiser Family Foundation, Robert B. Friedland of the National Academy on Aging, Michael E. Gluck of the National Academy of Social Insurance, and Louis F. Rossiter from the Medical College of Virginia.

The committee also extends many thanks to Judy Miller Jones and Larry Lewin, not only for the support they gave to their spouses during the duration of this project, but also for lending their own valuable expertise and insights.

Sincere thanks go to all of the participants in the February 1 and 2, 1996 symposium who gave so generously of their time and expertise to help inform and guide this study (Appendix C). An added note of thanks go to Marc A. Rodwin and Lucy Johns for their contributions not only during the workshop but before and after as well. In addition, the committee wishes to express heartfelt appreciation to the authors of the eight commissioned papers (Appendix D). The well-researched and highly informative background papers not only enhanced the committee's understanding of the many dimensions of this complex issue but also represent notable additionals to the literature in this field.

Linda Loranger deserves many thanks for contributing to the write-up of the February symposium and we are indebted to Michael Hayes for his careful editing of the report.

The committee wants to give special thanks to the dedicated and hard-working staff at the Institute of Medicine. Study director Marion Ein Lewin's professionalism and expertise in health policy coupled with her excellent writing skills advanced the progress of the report through its several reviews and revisions. Valerie Tate Jopeck, who served as research assistant, worked closely with the study director on various aspects of the study. She took primary responsibility for coordinating the committee's briefing materials and ably orchestrated the operation of the February 1996 symposium. Program assistant Richard Julian is also to be commended for his diligent administrative support. We are especially grateful to them.

Other IOM staff provided very valuable guidance, both in the areas of substance and process, particularly Kathleen N. Lohr, former director of the Division of Health Care Services, and deputy director Marilyn J. Field. They were always available to answer questions and to offer excellent advice. The committee extends its appreciation as well to Karen Hein for her ongoing interest in, and enthusiastic support of, this study effort. Mona Brinegar and Nancy Diener ably kept us on budget. At a difficult time Claudia Carl graciously and competently helped us to negotiate the complex logistics of the IOM/NAS report review process. Michael Edington guided the report through the editing and production process with skill and aplomb. Sally Stanfield, Francesca Moghari, and Estelle Miller of the National Academy Press were generous with their creativity and expertise.

Finally, the committee would like to thank the chair, Stanley B. Jones, for his outstanding work and deep commitment to the purposes of this project. His tireless dedication to the development of an "un-vanilla" IOM report made participating in this activity both more meaningful and enjoyable. He, in turn, wishes to thank the hardworking, and particularly cooperative and dedicated committee members.

IOM Committee on Choice and Managed Care

Contents

Improving the
Medicare Market

Executive Summary

America's health care system is being transformed at an unprecedented pace. As part of deficit reduction and the call for smaller government, public programs are being downsized, reorganized, and privatized. This call for smaller government comes in the wake of a dramatic revolution that continues to take place in the private health care sector, characterized by the move to managed care, increased vertical and horizonal integration, and new partnerships and relationships among insurers, providers, and purchasers in an increasingly competitive marketplace.

All of these changes and new dynamics have placed a special focus on the need to reform the Medicare program to make it more efficient and to secure its future viability. As the government's second biggest social program, Medicare expenditures grew from $34 billion in 1980 to an estimated $183.8 billion in 1995, representing an annual growth rate of 11.7 percent (Physician Payment Review Commission, 1996). With the inexorable upward trend in Medicare expenditures and the aging of the baby boom generation, deepening concern is being expressed about the future solvency of the program and its drain on the federal budget (Board of Trustees, 1996). The U.S. Congress is now intent on slowing Medicare growth and has become con-

1

vinced that interventions that go beyond the traditional strategies of reducing provider payments or asking beneficiaries to
pay more are needed. It is widely believed that more attention
must be focused on controlling the volume of services used by
the elderly to slow the growth in program expenditures.

Strategies to reform and preserve Medicare focus on rede-
signing elements of the 31-year-old program to reflect some of
the major financing and organizational changes revolutionizing
the provision of health care services in the private sector. Chief
among these changes has been a major influx of the population
under age 65 into managed care, viewed by many researchers
and policy specialists as holding the potential for providing more
appropriate, quality services at costs lower than those of fee-for-
service plans. A number of studies and surveys attribute the
slowing rate of spending on health benefits by large employers
over the past 2 years to the growth of managed care programs.

Until recently, enrollment of the Medicare population in
managed care programs has lagged the enrollment in such programs in the private sector: about 10 percent of all Medicare
beneficiaries are enrolled in managed care, whereas more than
70 percent of the population under age 65 are enrolled in such
programs.[1] After existing for nearly a decade, the current Medicare risk contract program now appears to be attracting more
beneficiaries. Enrollment more than doubled between 1987 and
1995, with the annual growth rate reaching about 25 percent
between 1993 and 1994 (U.S. General Accounting Office, 1996).

The pressing need to reduce Medicare's rate of growth and to
create a more competitive, market-oriented environment for
health delivery is resulting in a major emphasis on moving beneficiaries away from the current fee-for-service system, in which
the vast majority of the Medicare population continues to receive care, into a broad range of managed care and other delivery options, including health maintenance organizations with a
point-of-service option, preferred provider options, unrestricted
private fee-for-service plans that have utilization review, a network of contracted providers, plans that combine insurance with

---

[1]Enrollment in managed care is growing at approximately 2 percent per
year.

a high deductible with medical savings accounts, and plans offered by provider-sponsored organizations. In recent years the greatest growth in managed care arrangements for the population under age 65 has been in preferred provider organization and point-of-service-type networks. The existing fee-for-service Medicare program, which consists of a traditional indemnity insurance arrangement, would remain available.

As major efforts move forward to shift Medicare patients into managed care plans, many experts and patient advocates are concerned whether the necessary information and protections are in place to enable Medicare patients to select an appropriate health care plan wisely and to ensure that this group continues to have access to high-quality care.[2] The potentially daunting scope and speed of the transition by elderly Americans into what for most beneficiaries remains uncharted waters makes the need for high-quality and trustworthy information and accountability particularly critical. Only by laying a sound infrastructure in which individuals can make informed purchasing decisions and in which competition is based on quality performance can there be the public confidence needed to move Medicare beneficiaries safely and responsibly into a marketplace for choice and managed care.

Among the 37 million Medicare beneficiaries are those with limited financial resources, those with very serious disabling conditions, and those for whom catastrophic medical expenses are commonplace. Medicare spending averaged about $4,000 for beneficiaries in 1993. For the 10 percent of beneficiaries with the highest health care costs, Medicare spent an average of more than $28,000 per beneficiary. Medicare paid no benefits on behalf of the healthiest 20 percent of beneficiaries (Henry J. Kaiser Family Foundation and Institute for Health Care Research and Policy, Georgetown Unviersity, 1995). Understanding this variation in expenditures is particularly important in any discussion of expanding capitated managed care coverage

---

[2]The Institute of Medicine's 1991 report, *Medicare: New Directions in Quality Assurance* defines quality of care as, "the degree to which health services for individuals and populations increase the likelihood of desired health outcomes and are consistent with current professional knowledge."

for Medicare. If capitation payments are not appropriately adjusted for health status, over- or underpayments can be quite serious. The incentives to enroll only healthier enrollees or to encourage less healthy enrollees to disenroll may be formidable.

Unlike many employed individuals, who have the help of their employers in screening and evaluating their health plan options, most Medicare beneficiaries must rely on their own information and judgment to select wisely. Yet, a recent study found a higher prevalence of inadequate functional health literacy skills, skills needed to function in the health care environment, among the elderly (Williams et al., 1995). For elderly individuals who have the skills required to select health plan options, they often are unable to make effective choices because the variation and array of coverage are confusing (McCall et al., 1986; Jost, 1994). Although the availability of useful and reliable information is critical for consumer choice, such information is still in a stage of infancy.

Whether or not current Medicare reform legislation eventually becomes law, private industry and the Health Care Financing Administration (HCFA) are poised to lend a big boost to the managed care market for the elderly, a market already showing signs of rapid expansion. In 1994 health maintenance organization enrollment by Medicare beneficiaries was one of the health care industry's three fastest-growing market lines, in addition to enrollment in the Medicaid program and open-ended products. HCFA reports that 70,000 Medicare beneficiaries are enrolling in managed care plans each month.

The current national debate over "bringing the market" to Medicare and offering choice in health plans with an emphasis on managed care arrangements stimulated the Institute of Medicine to appoint a committee that would provide guidance to policy makers and decision makers on ensuring public accountability, promoting informed purchasing, and installing the necessary protections to help Medicare beneficiaries to operate effectively, safely, and confidently in the new environment of greater health plan choice.

Three tasks framed the committee's charge:

• to commission background papers from experts and practitioners in the field that review the literature and synthesize aspects of the leading issues and current policy proposals as they pertain to ensuring public accountability and informed purchasing in a system of broadened choice;

• to guide, develop, and convene an invitational symposium to (1) examine what is known (or not known) about ensuring public accountability and informed purchasing in the current Medicare program and other health plans, (2) recommend how public accountability and informed purchasing can be ensured for Medicare beneficiaries in managed care and other health plan choices, and (3) discuss options and strategies that can be used to help government and the private sector achieve the desired goals in this arena; and

• to produce a report that will include the commissioned background papers, a summary of the symposium discussion, and recommendations on the major issues that need to be addressed to ensure public accountability and the availability of information for informed purchasing by and on behalf of Medicare beneficiaries in managed care and other health care delivery options.

The study was initiated in the fall of 1995 with the expectation that Medicare legislation providing broader beneficiary choice would pass the U.S. Congress before the study was completed. The committee used the Medicare reform provisions of the Balanced Budget Act of 1995 (H.R. 2491) as a template for its work agenda. Although, President Clinton vetoed the final bill, the committee believes that the bill's Medicare reform provisions still provide a useful and relevant framework for reform.

In carrying out its charge, the committee recognized that the science-based and peer-reviewed literature on the major areas of the committee's scrutiny is sparse since the field is young and continues to evolve at an unprecedented pace. The state-of-the-art information in this arena resides primarily among a number of large private and public purchasers that currently define the field and various other organizations and agencies (i.e., the National Committee on Quality Assurance, HCFA, the Physician Payment Review Commission, the Foundation for Accountability, and the Agency for Health Care Policy and Research) that have a major interest in and programs directed to this area. With that in mind, the committee constructed a symposium primarily around real-world experts who could comment on and respond to the available research findings and to the current congressional Medicare reform proposals from their well-recognized experiences. The committee also was primarily interested in learning about current best practices in the public and private sectors as they relate to developing infrastructures for public accountability, informed purchasing, and competition based on performance.

In considering its work and statement of task, the committee had to be mindful of the relatively short time frame within which this report had to be completed and the limited resources available to support the commissioned papers/research syntheses and the symposium activity. Given the committee's broad charge and the many issues that potentially fall under the rubric of ensuring public accountability and informed purchasing in an environment of choice and managed care, the committee believed that it was important and essential to set some priorities, parameters, and caveats regarding its work agenda. They are as follows:

1. The task of the committee was not to judge the value of managed care as a vehicle for providing more appropriate, cost-effective care to Medicare beneficiaries or reducing the rate of escalation in the costs of the Medicare program over time. The committee operated under the assumption that managed care plans will continue to grow and develop and to be made available to the Medicare population. Several members of the committee, however, expressed concern that any balanced appraisal by the elderly population of the potential of managed care to provide better care may be made more difficult for two important reasons. One, current proposals to restructure Medicare are being viewed by many elderly as a means of financing deficit reduction and achieving other political objectives. Two, in the case of all areas of health in which fundamental change are being proposed, the media tends to focus on areas of discord and contention, contributing perhaps to additional anxieties among the already risk-averse elderly.

2. In looking at the issue of public accountability and the availability of information for informed purchasing, the committee's major focus was the consumer (Medicare benefi-

ciary) rather than plans, clinicians, or group purchasers. Much of the current information relating to performance and quality has been developed for these groups and may not be useful or relevant to the Medicare population.

3. The committee was asked to focus its attention on the issue of choice and the number and range of health plans, not the inherent merit or value of individual types or forms of plans to be offered (i.e., preferred provider organizations versus medical savings accounts versus unrestricted fee-for-service indemnity coverage).

4. Although the committee recognizes the great diversity of the Medicare population, this report focuses primarily on the "mainstream" Medicare beneficiary. The committee realizes that severely disabled individuals and dually-eligible beneficiaries (Medicare and Medicaid recipients) may need additional protections with regard to public accountability and informed purchasing. It was not possible within the scope of this particular study to reflect adequately on the special and additional information and accountability requirements that may be needed by these groups as they enter a more market-oriented delivery environment.

5. Many of today's elderly are particularly apprehensive about managed care and are concerned about their ability to make informed choices among health plan options. The committee heard evidence that the move to a choice paradigm with an emphasis on managed care represents greater challenges and problems for the current generation of Medicare beneficiaries, particularly the older cohort. With the increasing role of managed care, there is every expectation that future Medicare beneficiaries will have had considerable experience with this new delivery structure and therefore will be better informed and more comfortable consumers of managed care.

6. The committee did not focus on the issue of risk selection, although it acknowledges that it is a major problem that must be addressed.

7. Although the issues of fraud and abuse, estimated by the U.S. General Accounting Office to be in the range of 10 percent of Medicare health care costs, are a significant problem in the

Medicare program, they were outside the mandate of the present study.

8. The committee focused much of its work on learning from model programs and major purchasers in the private sector, with the full realization that Medicare as a government social insurance program requires, in many important respects, a different response. The committee also heard considerable testimony from public purchasers including state-based organizations and the Health Care Financing Administration.

9. In defining the parameters and vehicles that can be used to promote public accountability and informed purchasing, the committee recognizes the importance of maintaining the necessary flexibility to respond in a timely, appropriate fashion to a dynamic and evolving marketplace.

The committee's major charge and responsibility was to provide direction and guidance on how to promote public accountability and informed purchasing by and on behalf of Medicare beneficiaries in a new market-oriented environment characterized by choice and managed care. The committee was cognizant that in the new health care marketplace, Medicare beneficiaries as consumers or customers will be given both greater freedom and more responsibility for choosing their health plans and for making many of the important decisions associated with purchasing their health care and judging its value, adequacy, and responsiveness. Given the breadth and scope of its charge, the committee recognizes that many of the issues and topics that it addressed will benefit from additional review and analysis as better data and research findings become available.

It should also be noted that the committee was carefully formulated to reflect a balance of expertise particularly relevant to its charge. It included two experts from health plans, two individuals from the world of large purchasers—one public and one private, two consumer advocates with special expertise in elderly consumers in the health care marketplace, an expert on state insurance laws and regulations, a geriatrician, and an economist who has written extensively on the issue of opening choice and the structure of choice under market conditions.

The report is divided into three chapters and 12 appendixes. Chapter 1, an overview, provides the background, context, and parameters of the study. Chapter 1 also outlines how the committee defined and approached its charge and work agenda. Chapter 2 presents highlights from testimony heard at the invitational symposium held on February 1 and 2, 1996, and summarizes the major points made by the authors of the commissioned papers, by the invited respondents, and at the discussion that followed the panel presentations. As a summary, however, this section cannot do adequate justice to the rich and valuable data and information included in the eight commissioned papers found in Appendixes E to L. The information found in the papers contributed significantly to the committee's findings and recommendations.

With these caveats and ruminations, the committee formulated its recommendations, which are summarized below and described in greater detail in Chapter 3.

RECOMMENDATION 1. All *Medicare choices*[3] that meet the standard conditions of participation and that are available in a local market should be offered to Medicare beneficiaries to increase the likelihood that beneficiaries can find a plan of value. Traditional Medicare should be maintained as an option and as an acceptable "safe harbor" for beneficiaries, especially those who are physically or mentally frail.

RECOMMENDATION 2. Enrollment and disenrollment guidelines, appeals and grievance procedures, and marketing rules should reflect Medicare beneficiaries' vulnerability and lack of understanding of traditional Medicare and Medigap insurance, and their current lack of trust in important aspects of alternative health plans.

RECOMMENDATION 3. The committee recommends that special and major efforts be directed to building the needed consumer-oriented information infrastructure for Medicare beneficiaries. This resource should be developed at the na-

---

[3]For the purpose of this report, the term *Medicare choices* is an umbrella term for alternative health plans (including managed care) as well as traditional Medicare and Medigap plans.

tional, state, and local levels, with an emphasis on coordination and partnerships. Information and customer service techniques and protocols developed in the private sector should be used to guide this effort utilizing the best technologies available currently or projected to be available in the near term.

RECOMMENDATION 4. The federal government should require all *Medicare choices* to be marketed during the same open season to promote comparability and to enable beneficiaries to adequately assess and compare the benefits and prices of the various options.

RECOMMENDATION 5. The committee is concerned about the increasing restrictions on physicians (and the potential conflict of interest of physicians) when they act in their professional role as advocates for their patients and carry out their contractual responsibilities and receive economic incentives as health plan providers. The committee favors the abolition of payment incentives or other practices that may motivate providers to evade their ethical responsibility to provide complete information to their patients about their illness, treatment options, and plan coverages. So-called anticriticism clauses or gag rules should be prohibited as a condition of plan participation.

RECOMMENDATION 6. The federal government should hold *Medicare choices* accountable by requiring them to meet comparable conditions of participation as a Medicare option and by monitoring and reporting on their compliance with these conditions.

RECOMMENDATION 7. Serious consideration should be given and a study should be commissioned for establishing a new function along the lines of a Medicare Market Board, Commission, or Council to administer the *Medicare choices* process and hold all *Medicare choices* accountable. The proposed entity would include an advisory committee composed of key stakeholders, including purchasers, providers, and consumers.

1
Overview

THE MEDICARE PROGRAM

Medicare is the single largest payer in the U.S. health care system, purchasing about 19 percent of all personal health care services. The program pays for 30 percent of U.S. expenditures for hospital services, 21 percent of expenditures for physician services, and 40 percent of expenditures for home health care services (Congressional Budget Office, 1995c). In 1995 the Medicare program paid $178 billion, 11 percent of the total federal budget, to cover 37 million individuals. Medicare is the nation's largest single business-type operation and is larger than General Motors, the largest private company in the United States (Fortune, 1995).

Medicare provides coverage to 33 million elderly individuals (those over age 65), 4 million disabled individuals, and about 210,000 people with end-stage renal disease (Prospective Payment Assessment Commission, 1995). The Medicare population has nearly doubled since the program began, growing from 19.5 million in 1967 to 37 million in 1995. This increase reflects the aging of the population and the rising number of disabled beneficiaries. The oldest old (ages 85 and older), disabled individuals under age 65, and those with end-stage renal disease are

Medicare's fastest-growing groups. During the 1990s, the number of Medicare beneficiaries has been growing at 1 to 2 percent annually (Physician Payment Review Commission, 1996).

Medicare Part A provides coverage for inpatient hospital, home health, hospice, and limited skilled nursing facility services. Medicare Part A is financed from the Hospital Insurance Trust Fund, paid for primarily through a payroll tax on employers and employees. Beneficiaries are responsible for deductibles and copayments. The Congressional Budget Office forecasts that Part A spending will increase by 10.2 percent in 1995, with annual growth rates of between 7.5 and 10 percent projected for the rest of the decade (Congressional Budget Office, 1995b). A recent report by the trustees of the Social Security and Medicare trust funds forecast that unless changes are made, the Hospital Insurance Trust Fund will run out of money by 2001 (Board of Trustees, 1996).

Medicare Part B coverage is optional and helps pay for covered beneficiaries' physician services, medical supplies, and other outpatient treatments and is financed by a combination of general tax revenue (about 75 percent of program costs) and enrollee premiums (about 25 percent of program costs). In addition to their premiums, beneficiaries are responsible for copayments and deductibles. According to the Congressional Budget Office, Medicare Part B spending is expected to increase by 10.9 percent in fiscal year 1995, and to average 12 to 13 percent annual rates of increase through the remainder of this decade (Congressional Budget Office, 1995b).

The distribution of Medicare expenditures for different services has shifted over time, partially because of greater reliance on ambulatory rather than inpatient medical care. Between 1980 and 1995 Medicare spending for inpatient hospital services declined from 66 to 44 percent, whereas spending for home health services increased from 1 to 8 percent. In the same time period spending for post-acute-care services—skilled nursing facility, home health, and hospice services—increased from 3 to 13 percent.

As it is presently structured the Medicare program provides incomplete protection; for example, it provides poor catastrophic coverage, no coverage for outpatient prescription drugs, and high deductibles and copayments for hospitalization costs. The Medicare benefit package is less generous than about 85 percent of the employer-based plans primarily because of comparatively high deductibles and copayments (Iglehart, 1992). The program covers less than half of all health care costs incurred by elderly individuals and even less of all health care costs incurred by the oldest old, who require more nursing home care. Although the Medicare benefit package has remained reasonably constant over the years, enrollees' out-of-pocket medical care costs represent an increasing share of their incomes. In 1994 out-of-pocket spending on acute-care services and premiums averaged 21 percent of the incomes of all elderly individuals, moving to 30 percent on average for the poor elderly and people over age 80 (Moon and Mulvey, 1996).

Most elderly beneficiaries (89 percent) have supplemental coverage to fill in the gaps that Medicare does not cover. More than one-third of these individuals receive such insurance from a former employer, whereas another one-third buy supplemental insurance (Medigap) for themselves. Eleven percent lack supplemental insurance altogether, and 12 percent of Medicare beneficiaries are protected from some or most out-of-pocket health care costs by the Medicaid program. Since 1988 state Medicaid programs have been required to pay Medicare Part B premiums and cost-sharing for all qualified Medicare beneficiaries (QMBs) whose incomes are less than 100 percent of the federal poverty threshold and whose assets are below a certain level. For low-income beneficiaries whose incomes are between 100 and 120 percent of the federal poverty level, Medicaid pays for Medicare Part B premiums only. Individuals must apply for Medicaid in their state to be eligible. Less than half of the eligible QMB population has applied for Medicaid payments (Neumann et al., 1995).

MEDICARE MANAGED CARE

Since the early 1970s the federal government has supported the voluntary enrollment of Medicare beneficiaries in managed care programs through a number of demonstration projects. The 1982 Tax Equity and Financial Responsibility Act, which became operational in 1985, gave Medicare beneficiaries the option to enroll in federally-qualified health maintenance organizations (HMOs) and competitive medical plans, all of which offer Medicare-covered benefits and the majority of which also offer coverage of cost sharing and supplemental services that replace Medigap policies.[1] Beneficiaries may choose to enroll in an HMO when they become eligible for Medicare or at other times that Medicare HMOs offer open enrollment. Plans must have at least one 30-day open season each year and may offer additional open enrollment periods. Furthermore, they must allow enrollment at other times to beneficiaries who have been disenrolled because of contract termination or nonrenewal by another managed care plan. Medicare beneficiaries can disenroll from their plans at the end of any month.

The Health Care Financing Administration's (HCFA's) managed care program has different types of contracts. Until recently, the only private health plans (risk contracts or risk plans) available to Medicare beneficiaries were HMOs, under which plans receive capitated payments for the beneficiaries whom they enroll. In general enrollees who select a risk plan are required to use the plan's network of providers and to agree to obtain all covered services through the plan, except in emergencies.

Capitation payments to the plans are based on an estimate of local fee-for-service costs and are established for each county at 95 percent of the adjusted average per capita cost (AAPCC) for Medicare fee-for-service beneficiaries. HCFA adjusts the AAPCC for enrollees' demographic characteristics such as age, sex, Medicaid eligibility, and residence in an institution such as a nursing home. The "risk adjustment" attempts to prevent HMOs from benefiting from favorable selection of health risk, which occurs when HMOs enroll beneficiaries who are healthier (and therefore less costly to care for) than those in the fee-for-service sector. In 1995 AAPCC monthly rates ranged from a low

---

[1]Only beneficiaries who are eligible for Medicare because of old age or disability may choose to enroll in an HMO. Beneficiaries who are eligible for Medicare because of end-stage renal disease are not eligible unless they already were HMO enrollees at the time that they were certified to be eligible for Medicare because of end-stage renal disease. Also, beneficiaries choosing to receive care in a Medicare-certified hospice are not eligible for HMO enrollment.

of $177.32 to a high of $678.90 (U.S. General Accounting Office, 1996).

Under current law risk contract HMOs can retain profits up to the level earned on non-Medicare business. Profits that exceed this amount must be returned to enrollees either in out-of-payment reductions or enhanced benefits. On the basis of guidelines issued in October 1995, selected risk contracts will now be able to include a point-of-service option, upon HCFA's approval, which will allow beneficiaries to use providers outside a plan's network. HCFA expects that the point-of-service benefit may encourage more beneficiaries to join managed care plans.

Plans also can enter into cost contracts under which they are paid on a fee-for-service basis for the reasonable costs of services provided to their enrolled Medicare beneficiaries.[2] Medicare beneficiaries in cost contract HMOs may seek care outside of the HMO at Medicare's expense—a benefit that is not available under risk contracts.

Medicare SELECT, another plan option, offers a network-based supplemental insurance (Medigap) policy that provides coverage for Medicare cost sharing. Medicare SELECT was created as a demonstration project in 1990 to offer beneficiaries in up to 15 states a new Medigap insurance option. In 1995 it was authorized to expand to all states. It could be made permanent in 1998.

Under its demonstration authority, HCFA also has operated a number of social HMO (SHMO) pilot projects with the purpose of providing a broad spectrum of acute- and long-term-care services to the frail elderly under a managed care system. In these types of projects HMOs receive higher reimbursements in exchange for providing home-based custodial care. The SHMO demonstrations also receive Medicaid funding.

In 1995, HCFA announced a new demonstration project called Medicare Choices, designed to offer flexibility in contracting requirements and payment methods for health plans and other organized delivery systems that wish to participate in

---

[2] A variant of the traditional cost contract is the health care prepayment plan (HCPP). Under HCPP contracts, managed care organizations are retroactively reimbursed services covered under Medicare Part B.

Medicare. Its broader purpose is to test beneficiaries' response to a range of health care delivery system options and to evaluate their suitability for Medicare.

The Medicare Managed Care Population

Although risk contracts make up the bulk of the Medicare managed care market and have accounted for most of the program's growth (with 197 risk contracts serving 3.4 million beneficiaries as of March 1, 1996), Figure 1-1 and Table 1-1 show that enrollment is concentrated in a few states and a few large HMOs. About 55 percent of Medicare HMO enrollees live in California and Florida and represent approximately 36 and 19 percent of the beneficiaries in those two states, respectively (Office of Managed Care, Health Care Financing Administration, 1996). Similarly, 10 large HMOs enroll 44 percent of all Medicare beneficiaries. As of August 1995, 31 states had no or insignificant enrollment in Medicare risk contract HMOs (U.S. General Accounting Office, 1996).

States with the highest concentrations of Medicare enrollees have one or both of two characteristics: they contain mature health care markets in which managed care has become a dominant mode of health care delivery for the population under age 65, and they are in areas of the country with high AAPCCs (U.S. General Accounting Office, 1996). As shown in Figure 1-2, to attract Medicare beneficiaries, participating HMOs are increasingly turning to the use of additional incentives: charging elderly enrollees zero premiums as well as offering popular benefits such as routine physicals, eye and ear examinations, and immunizations. About half of the HMOs offer outpatient prescription drug coverage. Over the past 3 years the number of HMOs charging Medicare beneficiaries no premiums for the services provided increased from about 26 to about 49 percent (U.S. General Accounting Office, 1996).

A number of recent studies indicate that changes in employment-based health care coverage for retirees is another factor contributing to the recent rapid rate of growth of Medicare beneficiary enrollment in HMOs (Interstudy, 1995; U.S. General Accounting Office, 1996). The rising cost of health care coverage for retirees is forcing a growing number of firms to drop or

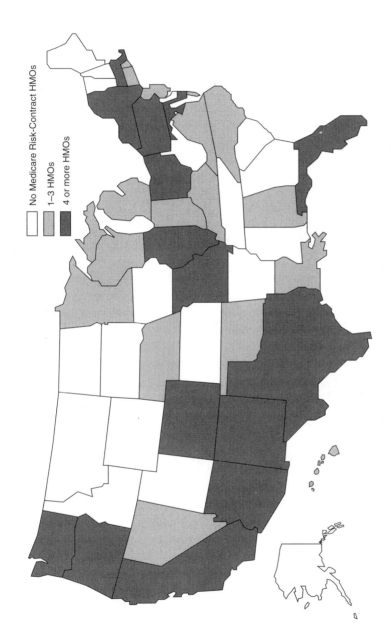

FIGURE 1–1 Number of Medicare risk contract HMOs, by state, August 1995. SOURCE: U.S. General Accounting Office, 1996, p. 25.

TABLE 1–1 State and Territorial Enrollment in Medicare and the Percent of Beneficiaries Enrolled in Managed Care Plans[a] (Data as of January, 1996)

STATE	Medicare Enrollees (% of national total)	National Rank	Medicare Managed Care Enrollees[b]	Percent of State's Medicare Population Enrolled in a Managed Care Plan
Alabama	645,000 (1.7)	19	12,952	2
Alaska	34,000 (0.09)	52	0	0
Arizona	604,000 (1.6)	21 (tie)	184,742	31
Arkansas	424,000 (1.1)	31 (tie)	0	0
California	3,653,000 (9.8)	1	1,302,713	36
Colorado	424,000 (1.1)	31 (tie)	92,757	22
Connecticut	504,000 (1.3)	26	15,259	3
Delaware	101,000 (0.27)	48	0	0
District of Columbia	78,000 (0.21)	50	11,568	15
Florida	2,630,000 (7.03)	3	487,906	19
Georgia	837,000 (2.2)	12	2,954	0.35
Hawaii	151,000 (0.4)	43	50,092	33
Idaho	150,000 (0.4)	44	0	0
Illinois	1,622,000 (4.3)	7	117,585	7
Indiana	825,000 (2.2)	14	12,446	2
Iowa	475,000 (1.3)	29	9,300	2
Kansas	384,000 (1.03)	34	9,484	2
Kentucky	589,000 (1.6)	23	5,420	1
Louisiana	583,000 (1.6)	24	34,311	6
Maine	203,000 (0.54)	38	0	0
Maryland	604,000 (1.6)	21 (tie)	19,631	3
Massachusetts	936,000 (2.5)	11	105,667	11
Michigan	1,353,000 (3.6)	8	8,260	1
Minnesota	632,000 (1.7)	20	118,500	19
Mississippi	399,000 (1.07)	33	0	0
Missouri	835,000 (2.2)	13	50,958	6
Montana	131,000 (0.35)	45	0	0
Nebraska	250,000 (0.67)	36	3,684	1
Nevada	195,000 (0.5)	39	50,690	26
New Hampshire	157,000 (0.4)	42	0	0
New Jersey	1,173,000 (3.1)	9	43,846	4
New Mexico	212,000 (0.57)	37	31,915	15
New York	2,647,000 (7.08)	2	252,511	10

•

TABLE 1–1 Continued

STATE	Medicare Enrollees (% of national total)		National Rank	Medicare Managed Care Enrollees[b]	Percent of State's Medicare Population Enrolled in a Managed Care Plan
North Carolina	1,033,000	(2.8)	10	4.043	0.39
North Dakota	103,000	(0.28)	47	731	0.71
Ohio	1,671,000	(4.5)	6	46,803	3
Oklahoma	489,000	(1.3)	27	18,006	4
Oregon	470,000	(1.3)	30	157,645	34
Pennsylvania	2,075,000	(5.6)	5	182,885	9
Puerto Rico	481,000	(1.3)	28	0	0
Rhode Island	169,000	(0.45)	41	18,425	11
South Carolina	512,000	(1.4)	25	0	0
South Dakota	117,000	(0.3)	46	0	0
Tennessee	774,000	(2.1)	16	0	0
Texas	2,091,000	(5.6)	4	167,080	8
Utah	188,000	(0.5)	40	30,558	16
Vermont	83,000	(0.22)	49	708	1
V.I./Guam/ American Samoa	18,000	(0.05)	53	0	0
Virginia	822,000	(2.2)	15	5,121	1
Washington	690,000	(1.8)	18	104,804	15
West Virginia	330,000	(0.88)	35	7,726	2
Wisconsin	763,000	(2.0)	17	11,387	1
Wyoming	61,000	(0.16)	51	0	0
United Mine Workers[c]	n/a		n/a	81,545	n/a
TOTAL	37,382,000	(100)		3,872,618	10

[a]Enrollee data (19,186) for Social Health Maintenance Organizations (SHMOs) are included in the total Medicare Managed Care enrollees. Totals do not necessarily equal the sum of rounded components.

[b]Medicare Managed Care Enrollees include: TEFRA Risk, Cost, SHMOs, and Health Care Prepaid Plans.

[c]United Mine Workers is a separate entity within Health Care Prepaid Plans (HCPP).

SOURCES: HCFA/Office of Managed Care/Bureau of Data Management and Strategy and U.S. Department of Commerce/Bureau of the Census.

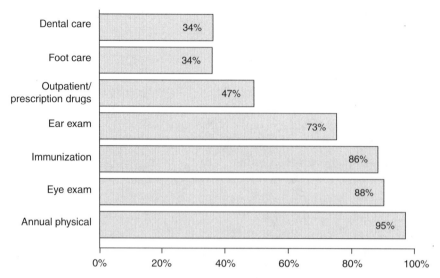

FIGURE 1–2 Percent of Medicare managed care risk contract plans that offer additional benefits. SOURCE: Medicare Chart Book prepared by The Henry J. Kaiser Family Foundation and The Institute for Health Care Research and Policy, Georgetown University, 1995, p. 18. Reprinted with permission of the Henry J. Kaiser Family Foundation.

redefine this benefit by adding greater cost-sharing provisions for beneficiaries. This trend is making HMO enrollment more attractive to elderly beneficiaries, given that a growing number of plans offer more extensive coverage without deductibles or coinsurance.

Medicare beneficiaries often face a difficult tradeoff between lower cost HMO risk plans or staying with their own physician. This is more obvious in low penetration areas of the country where fewer physicians join HMO networks. Although some research studies indicate that out-of-pocket costs remain the major determinant in deciding what plan an elderly beneficiary will join, other focus groups and survey findings indicate that a portion of the elderly population places even a higher value on the ability to remain with their doctor and their network of specialists and are willing to pay additional dollars in order to do so. Health care is a major priority and preoccupation for many elderly individuals and the value of continuing their relationship with trusted and known providers is often a higher consideration than gaining access to the most affordable plan (personal communication July 22, 1996, Randall Brown, Senior Fellow, Mathematica Policy Research, Inc.).

RESTRUCTURING MEDICARE AND THE CONTEXT FOR THE IOM STUDY

Early conversations about having the Institute of Medicine (IOM) conduct a study on accountability and informed purchasing for Medicare beneficiaries in an environment of broader choice and managed care began against a background of rising concern about the pressing need to dramatically reduce the rate of growth in entitlement spending and focused congressional interest in transforming the Medicare program to give beneficiaries the same health plan choices that have shown promise for holding down costs in the private sector. In the fall of 1995 the U.S. House Committee on Ways and Means of the 104th Congress first introduced the Medicare Preservation Act of 1995 (H.R. 2425). The Act contained provisions to expand the types of health plans to be offered to the elderly beyond traditional fee-for-service and HMOs to include point-of-service plans, provider service networks, and medical savings accounts. The bill contained financial incentives for the elderly to leave traditional Medicare and enroll in managed care plans, provisions that were largely eliminated in the Medicare provisions of the Balanced Budget Act of 1995 (H.R. 2491), which was vetoed by the President on December 6, 1995.

Congressional proposals to expand Medicare health plan options (MedicarePlus) stipulated that health plans contracting with Medicare be required to meet minimum standards in a number of areas, including solvency, quality assurance, service capacity, and consumer protections. In most cases plans would need to be licensed to bear insurance risk under state laws. MedicarePlus plans would provide benefits to beneficiaries in about the same manner as Medicare HMOs do today. The plans would receive capitated payments from the Medicare program for each beneficiary whom they enrolled. Plans would be responsible for providing at least the level of benefits that the current Medicare program provides, plus any additional benefits that the plan offered. Plans could modify the manner of cost sharing, as long as the total cost sharing did not exceed the cost-sharing guidelines for the fee-for-service program.

To further encourage and facilitate the move to managed care, the legislation provided for a structured enrollment process and the requirement that beneficiaries be provided with more information about their options. A coordinated annual enrollment period would occur each year, during which beneficiaries would be able to change plans if they so desired. To assist beneficiaries in executing their choices, the congressional proposals required the Secretary of the U.S. Department of Health and Human Services to ensure that beneficiaries receive adequate information about their coverage options.

Activities at HCFA

In 1995 HCFA announced the Medicare Choices demonstration project, which would allow non-HMO managed care plans such as provider networks and POS plans to enroll Medicare patients for the first time, using a variety of payment mechanisms. The project was intended to test beneficiaries' responses to a range of health care delivery system options and to evaluate the suitability of those options for Medicare. The request for proposals explicitly encouraged a range of organizations, in addition to traditional HMOs, to submit applications, and it solicited applications from organizations in markets where Medicare managed care participation was relatively low (Health Care Financing Administration, U.S. Department of Health and Human Services, 1995). The HCFA solicitation produced inquiries from 400 managed care plans in 47 states. HCFA asked 52 plans to submit applications and in April 1996 announced 25 final candidates.

Although there is general agreement for the need to reduce Medicare spending and even on the potential merit and value of providing Medicare beneficiaries with the same array of health plan options available to the population under age 65, questions continue to be raised about the scope and pace of change being proposed and whether the necessary infrastructure for providing information, protections, and accountability are in place to enable Medicare beneficiaries to move safely and responsibly into what is for the vast majority of them a new frontier of health care delivery for this population: managed care. Although managed care has become the norm for the employed population, for most elderly individuals it represents uncharted waters, even with today's dramatic growth in the level of Medicare HMO enrollment.

HOW IS THE MEDICARE MARKET DIFFERENT?

Demographics

Although Medicare has uniform eligibility and financing requirements and all elderly beneficiaries have access to the same basic benefit package, individuals served under the program are extremely diverse in terms of sociodemographic characteristics and health needs. As a group Medicare beneficiaries are older and sicker than patients who have traditionally used managed care plans (Vladeck, 1995).

Among the Medicare-eligible population, 46 percent are ages 65 to 74, 31 percent are ages 75 to 84, and 12 percent are ages 85 and older (Henry J. Kaiser Family Foundation, 1995). Four and a half million of the Medicare-eligible population are persons under age 65 with disabilities or individuals with end-stage renal disease. Figure 1-3 illustrates that 57 percent of Medicare beneficiaries are women, 43 percent are men, and 84 percent of beneficiaries are white. Medicare beneficiaries, like the general population, tend to reside in urban areas (74 percent for Medicare beneficiaries versus 79.7 percent for the total U.S. population) (Henry J. Kaiser Family Foundation and Institute for Health Care Research and Policy, Georgetown University, 1995; Bureau of the Census, 1995).

The oldest old (ages 85 and over), persons under age 65 with disabilities, and individuals with end-stage renal disease have been Medicare's fastest-growing populations. The 31.2 million people in the United States over the age of 65 in 1990 is expected to grow to 52 million by the year 2020. In the same period, the very old, those age 85 and older, will more than double in size, from 3.1 million to 6.5 million people.

Although there is a perception that Medicare beneficiaries are relatively better off than their younger counterparts, three-quarters of older people have annual incomes of less than

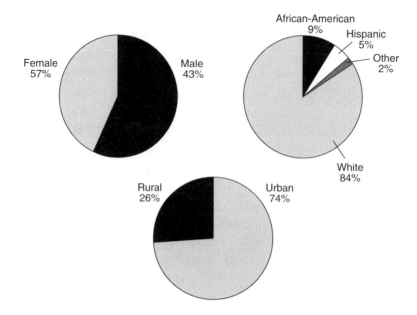

FIGURE 1-3 Distribution of Medicare population by gender, race, and residence, 1992. SOURCE: Medicare Chart Book prepared by The Henry J. Kaiser Family Foundation and The Institute for Health Care Research and Policy, Georgetown University, 1995, p. 4. Reprinted with permission of the Henry J. Kaiser Family Foundation.

$25,000, as shown in Figure 1-4. In 1992 about 83 percent of Medicare program spending was on individuals in this income group. Eighteen percent of the Medicare population have annual incomes of between $25,000 and $50,000, and 5 percent have annual incomes greater than $50,000.

Recent reports indicate that many elderly may buy into managed care because of its lower price and affordability (U.S. General Accounting Office, 1996). Financially, they may not have any viable alternative even when they have credible grievances or are dissatisfied with managed care. This places a special burden on developing public accountability parameters to ensure adequate performance and access standards.

Both the aged and disabled groups have relatively high levels of education, with over 50 percent of each group having graduated from high school or attended college. The median number of school years completed among the population age 65

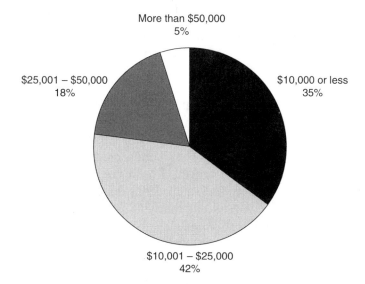

More than $50,000
5%

$25,001 – $50,000
18%

$10,000 or less
35%

$10,001 – $25,000
42%

FIGURE 1–4 Distribution of elderly beneficiaries, by income, 1992. SOURCE: Medicare Chart Book prepared by The Henry J. Kaiser Family Foundation and The Institute for Health Care Research and Policy, Georgetown University, 1995, p. 2. Reprinted with permission of the Henry J. Kaiser Family Foundation.

or older has risen steadily in the past 20 years (Adler, 1995). Obscured in these statistics, however, are the sizeable number of elderly individuals with inadequate functional literacy skills. A recent study to assess the ability of patients to perform the wide range of literacy tasks required to function in the health care environment found a higher prevalence of inadequate functional health literacy skills among elderly individuals than among individuals in younger age groups (Williams et al., 1995).

Health Status and Risk Selection

Data from the Medicare Current Beneficiary Survey indicate that almost half of the aged Medicare beneficiaries (45.8 percent) rate their health as excellent or very good, a proportion that is "remarkably stable" across age groups. On the other hand, only 17 percent of the disabled rate their health as excellent or very good, whereas 57.8 percent rate their health as fair or poor (Adler, 1995, p. 175). A Henry J. Kaiser Family Foundation survey reports that 30 percent of Medicare beneficiaries rate their health as fair to poor (Henry J. Kaiser Family Foundation, 1995). Self-assessed health has been shown to be a reliable predictor of future health care utilization.

Similar to the rest of the population, a small proportion of all Medicare beneficiaries consumes a significant share of total Medicare spending: 10 percent of the beneficiaries account for 70 percent of program expenditures. Per capita spending for the elderly, however, is roughly four times that for the rest of the population. Annual per capita Medicare spending averaged about $4,000 for beneficiaries in 1993. For the 10 percent of beneficiaries with the highest health costs, Medicare spent an average over $28,000 per beneficiary. Medicare paid no benefits on behalf of the healthiest 20 percent of beneficiaries (Henry J. Kaiser Family Foundation and Institute for Health Care Research and Policy, Georgetown University, 1995). As the Medicare market becomes more competitive, protections must be put into place to ensure that plans do not engage in practices that discriminate against high-risk patients.

Much of the literature suggests that Medicare beneficiaries enrolled in HMOs have tended to be healthier than those enrolled in the traditional Medicare program, although a more recent study indicates that the Medicare HMO population is becoming more broadly based and that its overall health status mirrors that of the non-HMO population (Price Waterhouse LLP, 1996). Nevertheless, the concern that HMOs may limit access to necessary care remains. Although conventional fee-for-service care is thought to promote the excessive utilization of medical services, there is concern that providers may overreact to the financial incentives to limit utilization, leading to reduced access to needed services by the elderly (Clement et al., 1994).

The potential for risk selection in Medicare health plans is a particularly serious concern. Some plans may draw beneficiaries whose health care costs are expected to be low (favorable selection); others may attract beneficiaries with complex medical problems and whose health care costs are expected to be high (adverse selection) (Physician Payment Review Commission, 1996). The problem of risk selection is greater under Medicare both because beneficiaries enroll as individuals and because variability in health care expenditures among elderly and disabled enrollees is far greater than those among the general population (Aaron and Reischauer, 1995). In addition, opportunities for biased selection are shaped by the rules and practices of the present market. For example, the current ability of Medicare beneficiaries to change health plans every month, unlike the typical annual open enrollment seasons for employees, enhances the opportunities for biased selection, as does the ability of an HMO to decide whether or not to enter the Medicare market and the type of contract options it will make available to beneficiaries (Miller and Luft, 1994).

A number of studies have shown that the elderly generally suffer from a lack of understanding about basic health care coverage and therefore are not equipped to operate effectively in an environment of broader choice. Consumers are unable to make effective choices because the variation and array of coverage are confusing (McCall et al., 1986; Jost, 1994). The availability of state-of-the-art information is critical for consumer choice (and voice), but such information for the Medicare population is still in a stage of infancy.

Information Dissemination

Unlike the population under age 65, Medicare beneficiaries have had relatively little exposure to diverse managed care models and have been shown to be more apprehensive and concerned about managed care than their younger counterparts (The Robert Wood Johnson Foundation, 1995). Much of this concern and apprehension is linked to the possibility that beneficiaries, in joining a managed care plan, will no longer be able to stay with their current physician (Frederick/Schneiders, 1995).

The lack of familiarity with managed care underscores the importance of providing beneficiaries with information that will enable them to make informed choices. Numerous studies, however, have shown that Medicare beneficiaries are poorly informed about what the traditional Medicare program covers and have very limited understanding of what managed care is or what the specific benefits of a particular managed care plan are (Sofaer, 1993; McCall et al., 1986; Rice, 1987; Davidson, 1988).

Medicare beneficiaries are not particularly distinguished from other consumers in their lack of understanding of their insurance coverage; such information has been shown to be not important to most people until they become sick (Mechanic, 1989; Pemberton, 1990). Older individuals, however, process information differently than young adults, finding more difficulty understanding information when it is new or complicated (Davidson, 1988). Surveys indicate that it takes more time and that it is more resource intensive to educate the elderly than younger individuals about their health care choices. Elderly beneficiaries like to have information presented to them in a variety of formats and have a particular preference for face-to-face interactions. Materials and approaches used to inform the employed population about their health care options may not be well suited to the elderly population.[3]

THE COMMITTEE'S CHARGE

The current debate over offering Medicare beneficiaries more choice in health plans as a vehicle for reform and deficit reduction stimulated the Institute of Medicine to appoint a committee that would provide guidance to policy makers and decision makers on ensuring public accountability by and on behalf of Medicare beneficiaries in a system of expanded choice and with a growing role for managed care.

Three tasks framed the committee's charge:

• to commission background papers from experts and practitioners in the field that review the literature and synthesize aspects of the leading issues and current policy proposals as they pertain to ensuring public accountability and informed purchasing in a system of broadened choice;
• to guide, develop, and convene an invitational symposium to (1) examine what is known (or not known) about ensuring

------

[3]These observations were initially detailed in a background paper prepared by Anne Schwartz of the Physician Payment Review Commission entitled, "Providing Information about Insurance Options to Medicare Beneficiaries," and were subsequently incorporated into the Commission's 1996 Annual Report.

public accountability and informed purchasing in the current Medicare program and other health plans, (2) recommend how public accountability and informed purchasing can be ensured for Medicare beneficiaries in managed care and other health plan choices, and (3) discuss options and strategies that can be used to help government and the private sector achieve the desired goals in this arena; and

• to produce a report that will include the commissioned background papers, a summary of the symposium discussion, and recommendations on the major issues that need to be addressed to ensure public accountability and the availability of information for informed purchasing by and on behalf of Medicare beneficiaries in managed care and other health care delivery options.

DEFINITIONS AND STUDY APPROACH

Definitions

At its first meeting the committee spent considerable time discussing the context of its charge and establishing some working definitions of *choice and managed care*, *public accountability*, and *informed purchasing by and on behalf of Medicare beneficiaries*. Each of these deserves a note of clarification for the purpose of this report.

Choice and Managed Care

The committee's original name was, "Medicare Managed Care: Assuring Public Accountability and Informed Purchasing for Beneficiaries." At its first meeting the committee felt strongly that responsibility for public accountability and informed purchasing should not be limited to the new plans that would be offered to beneficiaries but should pertain equally to the traditional Medicare program. Although the committee acknowledged that the traditional Medicare program remains very popular among the elderly, it should not be excluded from the measures of accountability and performance that will be required of managed care plans. *Choice* for the purpose of this report refers to all of the health plan options (e.g., traditional

Medicare and other indemnity plans, medical savings accounts, and Taft-Hartley-sponsored plans) not only managed care arrangements.

The committee recognized that there is not a universally accepted definition of managed care. As the managed care industry continues to evolve, the boundaries between different types of plans will become increasingly blurred. Therefore, for the purpose of this report the committee selected to define *managed care* broadly to include the following:[4]

> Any product or arrangement that seeks to coordinate or control the use of health services by its enrolled members. Arrangements can involve a defined delivery system or providers with some form of contractual arrangement with the plan. Types of plans can range from simple PPOs to more tightly structured HMOs.

Public Accountability

A 1994 IOM study, *Defining Primary Care: An Interim Report*, defined the term *accountability* as the quality or state of being responsible or answerable. Accountability also has been defined to mean "subject to the obligation to report, explain or justify" (Random House, 1983).

For the purpose of this report, the committee discussed the difference between "accountability" and "consumer protections" and suggested that accountability for services could be viewed as the equivalent of ensuring the safety of products through consumer protections. Consumer protections are usually mediated on a case-by-case basis, whereas accountability usually implies a broader concept to include responsibility to a group and to a larger public.

During the committee's deliberation the article, "What is

---

[4]For purposes of comparison, the Physician Payment Review Commission, in its 1996 Annual Report to Congress, defines managed care as follows: "Any system of health service payment or delivery arrangements where the health plan attempts to control or coordinate use of health services by its enrolled members in order to contain health expenditures, improve quality, or both. Arrangements often involve a defined delivery system of providers with some form of contractual arrangement with the plan" (Physician Payment Review Commission, 1996, p. 394).

Accountability in Health Care?" was published (Emanuel and Emanuel, 1996). The article reflects the notion that occasionally a single word comes to dominate discussions about a topic and becomes a "keyword." Such a keyword can serve as a "shorthand expression for an entire view; and persons with diverse perspectives affirm its perspective" (Emanuel and Emanuel, 1996, p. 229). In the current health policy dialogue, *accountability* has become a keyword.

In health care the matrixes of accountability (the who, what, and how) have traditionally been shared by three different domains: the professional, political, and economic domains. Part of the rationale for the present IOM activity was the concern on the part of some stakeholders that under a more market-oriented Medicare program, the locus of accountability may shift markedly from the public to the largely untested private sector. Such a shift in accountability would have special relevance for elderly individuals, who in the past have relied on providers and government to provide the necessary assurances and protections.

For the purpose of this report the committee selected to define *public accountability* as accountability to the public, defining *public* as beneficiaries in the first instance, but also the larger public as interested parties and taxpayers, and to define government as the elected representatives of the citizenry.

Although public accountability may mean different things to different people, most would accept the basic premise that managed care (choice) plans should be held accountable to both Medicare beneficiaries and the public at large: to Medicare beneficiaries because of the contractual arrangements between managed care plans and their Medicare enrollees and to the general public because it pays (through Medicare taxes, Part B premiums, and general revenues) for the care that is provided.

Considering the mandate of this report, the committee discussed some additional elements of public accountability and determined that these should include the following:

• requirements for disclosure and the dissemination of relevant and useful information,

• the capacity to assess and report whether contracted services are performed responsibly and effectively,

• requirements as a public program financed by taxpayer dollars to see that the needs of individuals are balanced against the wise use of collective resources, and

• a special level of responsibility as the purchaser of health care for elderly beneficiaries, many of whom are vulnerable.

Informed Purchasing by and on Behalf of Beneficiaries

If there is little dissension over the need for public account-ability and informed purchasing, the question of how to ensure it is far more contentious. Some will argue that market compe-tition and informed purchasing are the best guarantees of ac-cess to high-quality services. Others argue for a strong federal regulatory and oversight role and advocate for extensive regula-tions in a number of areas including marketing, access, quality, appeals and grievances, data collection, and solvency. Others propose a middle ground that would permit a greater role for the market, with its potential to be more efficient and innova-tive and as a better expression of consumer wants and desires, yet leave to government the role of limiting the number of mar-ket entrants to those that meet certain minimum standards of performance and that offer certain minimum protections. Each of these three models (market, directed, and assisted) results in a different matrix of accountabilities.

Without adequate, reliable, comparable, and timely infor-mation, it is not possible to exercise informed choice. At its first meeting, the committee discussed the problem that even under the best of circumstances, some elderly people, particularly ex-tremely frail and cognitively impaired individuals, would not be able to exercise choice on their own. The committee was struck by a report from the Alina Health Plan, a major HMO in Minne-sota serving a large Medicare population, which reported that for almost half of the plan's elderly enrollees, major decisions about medical care are made not by the enrollees but by a spouse, a family member, or a caretaker (Mastry, 1995). The committee wanted the title of its activity to reflect the reality that for a significant part of the Medicare population, the re-sponsibility of informed purchasing will need to be delegated in some manner. This has implications for how the information infrastructure is developed and disseminated for this group.

Several members of the committee noted that the term *beneficiary* may be inappropriate in a more market-oriented health care system. In today's competitive choice environment, beneficiaries will be regarded increasingly as consumers and customers who can vote with their feet and who will need to be satisfied. The thrust of this report focuses on identifying accountability systems, resources, and the knowledge base that will help beneficiaries to become informed and effective consumers, even as it applies to traditional Medicare.

Study Approach

In considering the best way to accomplish its task, the committee arrived at a number of approaches and conclusions that shaped its agenda.

- The committee's focus was on beneficiaries/consumers (rather than plan managers, clinicians, or payers of care). The committee used the analogy of wholesale and retail information that had been well-described in a recent paper by Lynn Etheredge (Etheredge, 1995). The success of the choice paradigm will require Medicare beneficiaries to act as consumers and individual purchasers and to move from having a passive role to having an active voice, a new role and responsibility that succeeds only if information and standards of accountability that are directly relevant, meaningful, and accessible to them are developed. Until now most of the information on quality and performance has been developed for private group purchasers, managers, clinicians, and some public payers.
- The present study was initiated with the expectation that Medicare legislation providing broader beneficiary choice would pass the U.S. Congress before the study was completed. The committee used the Medicare provisions of H.R. 2491, the Balanced Budget Act of 1995, as a template for its work agenda and for the focus and structure for its deliberations. Although, President Clinton vetoed the final bill, the committee believes that the bill's Medicare reform provisions still provide a useful and relevant framework for reform.

- The science-based and peer-reviewed literature on public accountability and informed purchasing for Medicare beneficiaries under a market-oriented choice paradigm is sparse since the field is young and continues to evolve at an unprecedented pace. The state-of-the-art information in this arena resides primarily among a number of large private and public purchasers that currently define the field and various other organizations and agencies such as the National Committee on Quality Assurance (NCQA), HCFA, the U.S. General Accounting Office, the Physician Payment Review Commission (PPRC), the Foundation for Accountability, and the Agency for Health Care Policy and Research, which have a major interest in and programs directed to this area. With that in mind, the committee developed a symposium primarily around real-world experts who could comment on and respond to the commissioned papers, to other relevant and available research findings, and to the Medicare reform proposals from their well-recognized experiences.

- The committee was primarily interested in learning about current best practices in the public and private sectors as they relate to public accountability, informed purchasing, and competition based on excellence. There was a caution that the term *best practices* should be reserved for interventions that had been tested and evaluated on the basis of quality and cost-effectiveness and that the term *promising interventions* or *models* might be more accurate.

- The committee was fortunate to be able to commission eight papers—including five literature reviews and two case studies that review the state-of-the-art and consider a continuum of organizational and policy options for assuring public accountability and informed purchasing—written by national experts. These papers cover the most critical aspects of ensuring public accountability and informed purchasing for Medicare beneficiaries in an environment of choice.

    — To frame the symposium dialogue and the committee's later deliberations, the committee asked Lynn Etheredge to write a paper proposing a conceptual framework for ensuring public accountability and informed choice from the perspective of beneficiaries by looking at how and where the various loci of responsibilities would be placed in the continuum of three alternative potential models: letting the market prevail (market model), letting government decide what is best (directed model), or providing a larger role for the market but leaving to government the responsibility of weeding out the bad apples (assisted model). Each model requires a different matrix of accountability and informed purchasing.

— A paper by Elizabeth Hoy, Elliott Wicks, and Rolfe Faland reviews current best practices for structuring and facilitating consumer choice of health plans, looking at model programs developed by leading private and public purchasers.

— A third paper, by Joyce Dubow, focuses particularly on the special considerations required to move Medicare beneficiaries as a more vulnerable cohort into managed care arrangements.

— A paper by Susan Edgman-Levitan and Paul Cleary reviews the literature on what information consumers want and need and their ability to assess issues of quality and accountability.

— Carol Cronin's paper summarizes what is known about how to most successfully reach and educate beneficiaries about choice.

— A paper by Patricia Butler focuses on the effectiveness of current federal and state regulatory activities designed to satisfy and protect consumers in managed care plans.

— Two case studies were also commissioned. The committee was aware of several U.S. General Accounting Office studies indicating that HCFA needed to improve its HMO monitoring processes and, furthermore, that as currently staffed and organized, HCFA may not be well structured to respond to the complex, rapidly changing health care system and would need to develop a new set of tools and authorities to operate as an effective purchaser of risk contracts (Cunningham, 1996; U.S. General Accounting Office, 1995a-f; Special Committee on Aging, U.S. Senate, 1995). The committee commissioned a paper to summarize HCFA's recent efforts directed at improving and streamlining its data collection and performance monitoring as well as to review HCFA's recent investments in beneficiary and customer communications. A case study of the California Public Employees' Retirement System (CalPERS) was also commissioned. CalPERS is frequently referred to as a model of group purchasing in a competitive environment on the basis of performance and consumer satisfaction measures.

• The symposium agenda, a list of the participants, and a list of the commissioned papers are provided in Appendixes B, C, and D, respectively. The symposium was organized as an expert hearing with an emphasis on fact finding from the perspective of published research, current practices, and well-regarded firsthand expertise from the field.

In considering its work and statement of task, the committee had to be mindful of the relatively short time frame within which this report had to be completed and the limited resources available to support the commissioned papers/research syntheses and the symposium activity. Given the committee's broad charge and the many issues that potentially fall under the rubric of ensuring public accountability and informed purchasing in an environment of choice and managed care, the committee believed that it was important and essential to set some priorities, parameters, and caveats regarding its work agenda. They are as follows:

1. The task of the committee was not to judge the value of managed care as a vehicle for providing more appropriate, cost-effective care to Medicare beneficiaries or to reducing the rate of escalation in the costs of the Medicare program over time. The committee operated under the assumption that managed care plans will continue to grow and develop and to be made available to the Medicare population. Several members of the committee, however, expressed concern that any balanced appraisal by the elderly population of the potential of managed care to provide better care may be made more difficult for two important reasons. One, current proposals to restructure Medicare are being viewed by many elderly as a means of financing deficit reduction and achieving other political objectives. Two, in the case of all areas of health in which fundamental changes are being proposed, the media tends to focus on areas of discord and contention, contributing perhaps to additional anxieties among the already risk-averse elderly population.

2. In looking at the issue of public accountability and the

availability of information for informed purchasing, the committee's major focus was the consumer (Medicare beneficiary) rather than plans, clinicians, or group purchasers. Much of the current information relating to performance and quality has been developed for these groups and may not be useful or relevant to the Medicare population.

3. The committee was asked to focus its attention on the issue of choice and the number and range of health plans, not the inherent merit or value of individual types or forms of plans to be offered (i.e., preferred provider organizations [PPOs] versus medical savings accounts versus unrestricted fee-for-service indemnity coverage).

4. Although the committee recognizes the great diversity of the Medicare population, this report focuses primarily on the "mainstream" Medicare beneficiary. The committee realizes that severely disabled individuals and dually-eligible beneficiaries (individuals who enrolled in both Medicare and Medicaid) may need different and additional protections with regard to public accountability and informed purchasing. It was not possible within the scope of this particular study to reflect adequately on the special and additional information and accountability requirements that may be needed by the disabled and the dually eligible as they enter a more market-oriented delivery environment.

5. Many of today's elderly are particularly apprehensive about managed care and are concerned about their ability to make informed choices among health plan options. The committee heard evidence that the move to a choice paradigm with an emphasis on managed care represents greater challenges and problems for the current generation of Medicare beneficiaries, particularly the older cohort. With the increasing role of managed care, there is every expectation that future Medicare beneficiaries will have had considerable experience with this new delivery structure and therefore will be better informed and more comfortable consumers of managed care.

6. The committee did not focus on the issue of risk selection, although it acknowledges that it is a major problem that must be addressed.

7. Although the issues of fraud and abuse, estimated by the

U.S. General Accounting Office to be in the range of 10 percent of Medicare health care costs, are a significant problem in the Medicare program, they were outside the mandate of the present study.

8. The committee focused much of its work on learning from model programs and major purchasers in the private sector, with the full realization that Medicare as a government social insurance program requires, in many important respects, a different response. The committee also heard considerable testimony from public purchasers including state-based organizations and HCFA.

9. In defining parameters and vehicles to promote public accountability and informed purchasing, the committee recognizes the importance of maintaining the necessary flexibility in order to respond in a timely, appropriate fashion to a dynamic and evolving marketplace.

The committee's major charge and responsibility was to provide direction and guidance on how to promote public accountability and informed purchasing by and on behalf of Medicare beneficiaries in a new market-oriented environment characterized by choice and managed care. The committee was cognizant that in the new health care marketplace, Medicare beneficiaries as consumers or customers will be given both greater freedom and more responsibility for choosing their health plans and for making many of the important decisions associated with purchasing their health care and judging its value, adequacy, and responsiveness. Given the breadth and scope of its charge, the committee recognizes that many of the issues and topics that it addressed will benefit from additional review and analysis as better data and research findings become available.

It should also be noted that the committee was carefully formulated to reflect a balance of expertise particularly relevant to its charge. It included two experts from health plans, two individuals from the world of large purchasers—one public and one private, two consumer advocates with special expertise in elderly consumers in the health care marketplace, an expert on state insurance laws and regulations, a geriatrician, and an economist who has written extensively on the issue of opening choice and the structure of choice under market conditions.

2
Symposium Summary

STRUCTURING ACCOUNTABILITY FOR MEDICARE: LOOKING AT A CONTINUUM OF OPTIONS[1]

One of the federal government's major reasons for encouraging growth in Medicare managed care is to give Medicare beneficiaries a choice of health plans that people in the private sector already enjoy. Widening choice for Medicare beneficiaries, however, involves oversight and protection trade-offs. The challenge is how to develop a structure for accountability and consumer choice in a changing health care market.

The health care market emerging today is significantly different from that of the fee-for-service system with which most Medicare beneficiaries are familiar. In the fee-for-service system, consumers have relied to an extent on the professionalism of providers and on government standards in making their choices. Premium costs generally have not played a key role in the elderly's health care purchasing decisions.

A new paradigm is forming, however, in which efforts are being made to restructure the Medicare program around mar-

---

[1]Unless otherwise noted, the material in this section is based on a presentation by Lynn Etheredge.

39

TABLE 2-1 Health Plan Choices for Private-Sector Employees, 1993

Number of Health Plans Offered per Establishment	Weighted by Number of Establishments (%)	Weighted by Number of Employees (%)
1	76	48
2	16	23
3	5	12
4	2	6
5 or more	1	11

SOURCE: Preliminary tabulations from the 1993 Robert Wood Johnson Foundation Employer Health Insurance Survey conducted by the RAND Corporation (courtesy of Stephen Long).

kets. In this new system, government attempts to structure the market by encouraging competition, consumers have an array of health care options to choose from, and health plans share responsibility for accountability with the government. This accountability is reinforced by the power of the consumer to choose and to change plans. In the Medicare-restructuring proposals developed by the 104th Congress and the Clinton Administration, elderly beneficiaries would have choices beyond the current fee-for-service, traditional Medigap, and risk-based HMO options. These choices will include preferred provider organizations (PPOs), unrestricted fee-for-service health plans, and high-deductible plans combined with medical savings accounts. Under the new paradigm most Medicare beneficiaries would have more health plan choices than the majority of today's private-sector employees (Table 2-1).

To ensure accountability and informed purchasing for beneficiaries in a restructured Medicare program, a continuum of structural and oversight options can be considered. These range from (1) a more active government role, to (2) strengthening the role of the consumers so that they are better equipped to exercise choice, to (3) strengthening professional influences and advancing the science base for clinical effectiveness and outcomes. Each of these directions involves trade-offs.

More Active Government Role

Options for a more active government role in helping Medicare enrollees include raising the standards for entry into the Medicare health plan market. As the regulator of Medicare managed care, HCFA currently institutes fairly tight health plan entry requirements and other specific rules to ensure that "bad actors" do not enter the HMO risk market, such as the 50-50 rule, which ensures that a plan already has experience providing services.[2] Medicare also requires that for a risk-based contract, at least 5,000 of the plan's prepaid capitated members must be enrollees from the private sector. The minimum requirement drops to 1,500 for rural HMOs. Some Medicare reform proposals have sought to reduce these minimum requirements to increase the number of plans that would be available to enter the Medicare market.

As an alternative, under the Federal Employees Health Benefit Plan (FEHBP) the federal government contracts with all health care plans that meet participation requirements, and consumers make their own coverage decisions (Butler and Moffitt, 1995). This more inclusive purchaser approach may cause confusion among some beneficiaries, since they have had little experience with managed care plans and there is evidence that they may need assistance evaluating information. To alleviate some confusion and anxiety, the federal government could consider another option, that of assuming a more active purchasing role. As a large purchaser, the federal government could adopt some of the best practices of current large employers or purchasing alliances, which often negotiate actively with plans and require certain quality and service performance guarantees. In this capacity government could force competition among plans and then choose a subset of plans that offer the best choices for enrollees. This approach would afford Medicare

---

[2]The 50-50 rule requires that for all HMOs in which Medicare beneficiaries enroll, at least half of the members must consist of non-Medicare and non-Medicaid beneficiaries. This is meant to provide assurance that Medicare HMOs do not constitute a perhaps second class of care for the elderly and disabled populations. A number of analysts believe the HMO accreditation requirements developed by NCQA may make the 50-50 rule less essential.

beneficiaries the greatest protections. The farther government moves along the continuum of tightening controls and acting as a purchasing agent, however, the greater the likelihood of loss of flexibility and competitiveness in the market, and thereby a reduction in the number and types of health plan choices.

In discussing the role of government in holding the system accountable, a fundamental question that arises is whether this is government purchasing or, in fact, purchasing by elderly beneficiaries. For example, is the government a patron allowing some choice on the part of its clients, or is the government effectively providing people with vouchers and providing beneficiaries with the freedom to decide how to use those vouchers?[3]

The unique leverage of a $180 billion program such as Medicare needs to be considered, however. By virtue of its sheer size and as a public purchaser, the federal government has the power to profoundly influence the market and to drive health plans from the market by setting conditions of participation extremely high and then deciding the plans with which it wants to do business. Historically, government has not acted in this capacity.

Strengthening the Role of Consumers

Strengthening the role of consumers would require providing them with sufficient relevant information about health plans to help them decide whether to join a managed care plan and, if so, how to choose a plan that meets their needs. To provide better information, one must understand what information consumers want, how they want to obtain that information, and what kinds of information they should know.

Here, opportunity may lie in strengthening ombudsperson-type organizations. Today, many employee benefits offices serve an ombudsperson function in which they assist employees with complaints or other health plan issues that may arise. Senior

---

[3]At the symposium, Mark Pauly indicated that the level of choice afforded Medicare beneficiaries is affected by whether or not Medicare beneficiaries are viewed as owning the benefits awarded to them.

citizens' groups and counseling organizations could serve such a function.

In the case of Medicare, a network of ombudsperson offices operating in areas with significant Medicare health plan enrollments could provide assistance to Medicare beneficiaries trying to decide which health plan to enroll in and could also help those who have complaints about their health plans. The ombudsperson's duties could range from investigating patient complaints, to monitoring marketing presentations, to helping beneficiaries obtain needed services. HCFA currently supports health insurance counseling programs funded through federal grants to states. Although generally well-respected, these programs tend to be small and underfunded operations.

Strengthening Professional Influences

Along the professionalism continuum, further effectiveness and outcomes research could be encouraged and funded to bolster the scientific clinical basis for managing care and establishing guidelines that would narrow variations among procedures and practices. Other options that might be considered and reflected in proposed legislation are requirements that health plans meet high government standards in order to be accredited organizations for participation as a Medicare health plan. Another option would be for Medicare to develop best-practice benchmarks and other management purchasing techniques that promote high standards for competing health care plans.

Three Key Issues

Three areas will affect the debate on where to place accountability:

1. What agencies do elderly citizens trust to protect their interests and to hold the system accountable?

2. How strong is the information base and how adequate are consumer skills?

3. In the new environment, can professionalism continue to be relied on to help the elderly exercise choice wisely and appropriately?

Trust

In recent times the public's trust in many institutions has plummeted (Washington Post, 1996). Americans have lost confidence in the federal government and virtually every other major national institution. The public does not appear to trust insurance companies, health plans, or businesses. So the following question can be asked: In an era of growing cynicism, what sector and what institutions can be relied on to maintain protections and to be accountable?

Patients as Consumers

Evidence indicates that many among the elderly and disabled populations have difficulty choosing among health plans. Questions regarding how well the elderly population is equipped to choose a health plan in today's market, as well as in the future, when the market will have been fine-tuned, will prove to be important in determining accountability. Although the next generation of elderly will be more familiar with managed care arrangements, the vast majority of current Medicare beneficiaries face a very steep learning curve.

Professionalism

Many health care analysts argue that professional judgments on medical care should be relied on to determine what care is necessary and appropriate. There is evidence, however, as suggested by Wennberg,[4] that wide variations in major medical procedures exist across the country. Given these variations and the lack of clinical evidence supporting the use of many procedures, can the public rely on members of the medical profession to tell them what a good plan is or who is practicing good

---

[4]The *Dartmouth Atlas of Health Care in the United States*, created by a team of researchers led by epidemiologist John E. Wennberg, is a comprehensive study detailing the geographic distribution of health care resources in the United States. Released in January 1995, the study indicates that wide variations in health care services, procedures, and cost reimbursements exist across the country.

medicine? The role of professionalism is further challenged in today's health care marketplace by the increasing use of capitation payments, which creates incentives on the part of providers to limit the number or the cost of health care services being delivered.[5]

Ensuring That Traditional Medicare Remains a Viable Option

Since Medicare beneficiaries in general are apprehensive about change, steps need to be taken to ensure that the traditional Medicare fee-for-service system remains a viable option for them. The 30-year-old Medicare program could benefit from some changes so that it becomes as much a competitor as managed care organizations in the new health care system.

Symposium participants advised the committee that the Medicare fee-for-service system should be held up to the same standards as any new Medicare managed care option. In an environment where there is increasing pressure on managed care systems for accountability, there needs to be comparable accountability in fee-for-service plans. If the quality and service indicators in both fee-for-service and managed care plans are the same, then both types of plans will be comparable. This will also allow Medicare beneficiaries to make a better informed choice.

One symposium presenter expressed the view that in 10 or 20 years it is unlikely that both fee-for-service and managed care systems will be options at similar prices.[6] The incentives for both of these systems are so diverse that it would be difficult to be a physician or hospital operating simultaneously in each environment. Furthermore, there is great potential for adverse risk selection. If health plans attract the healthier Medicare enrollees, the sicker, more costly population will remain in the traditional Medicare fee-for-service system. The costs within that system would escalate and beneficiaries may find themselves facing higher costs, as well as reduced numbers of physi-

---

[5]Material presented by Robert Berenson.
[6]Material presented by Robert Berenson.

cians willing to provide services to them. In that environment physicians themselves are in a position to risk select since they can determine which patients may fit better in a risk arrangement or a traditional Medicare fee-for-service plan.

To avoid adverse risk selection, attention needs to be given to better risk adjusters, and an even greater focus must be placed on educating Medicare beneficiaries about their choices. HCFA currently has at least a dozen risk adjuster projects in development, including predictive and concurrent models.

STRUCTURING CHOICE: A LOOK AT MODEL PROGRAMS[7]

An assessment of the leading purchasers that currently offer their employees a choice of health plans shows that these organizations take a variety of approaches to how they structure choice for their workers and the processes that they put in place to facilitate choice. The thresholds of participation that they set for health plans also vary a great deal. In some instances many plans in the marketplace may meet the threshold criteria, and in other instances only a very few may be able to meet the criteria.

Purchasing coalitions or cooperatives help expand the limited choices that are typically available to workers employed in small businesses. These alliances generally provide their members with extensive, comparable information that enables them to make informed choices. Many purchasing coalitions go a step further, however, in that they negotiate with health plans for the best premiums and options and then select a number of plans on this competitive basis, in effect eliminating the need for their members to be as discriminating as they might otherwise have to be.

Often such organizations develop additional criteria to assist them in deciding which plans they will offer to their enrollees. The objective of some organizations is to offer plans with a variety of benefit structures, including fee-for-service plans in

---

[7]Unless otherwise noted, the material in this section is based on presentations by Elizabeth Hoy and Richard E. Curtis.

addition to managed care alternatives. If an organization chooses only to offer managed care plans to its members, it may offer plans with different options and benefit levels. These organizations also differ greatly in the degree to which they negotiate price.

However, evidence from a variety of these leading purchasers and purchasing alliances—such as Xerox, Edison International, the Health Insurance Plan of California, the Connecticut Business and Industry Association, and the Cooperative for Health Insurance Purchasing in Denver, Colorado—demonstrates that they all place importance on the practice of creating a level field on which individuals can compare health plans. The comparable information provided by these organizations usually includes details on plans' benefit designs and features, the different types of plans that are being offered, the geographic areas they cover, and other specific information.

The information provided can be either extensive, as in the case of Xerox, in which the company provides a report card about participating plans, to minimal, as in the case of the Cooperative for Health Insurance Purchasing in Denver, which offers a single trifold brochure with comparative charts. Some organizations go as far as providing superdirectories that list and describe every provider in the community and the plans in which they participate, together with such information as the languages spoken in the office and board certification of a plan's physicians.

Even with the best information on price, plan performance, and benefits covered, however, consumers can still find it difficult to compare plans and coverage. This is why many purchasing organizations have adopted standardized benefit designs for plans.

Many purchasers set a basis for the comparison of plans' benefit design that can be either broad or specific. For example, some organizations define different copayment levels and detail the inclusions and exclusions in various health plans. On the other side of the spectrum, Xerox, for example, does not define, line for line, the covered services in their plans' benefit designs, but requires that participating plans cover all medically necessary services. The company provides criteria for the range of services, facilities, and treatments that should be available.

These organizations also try to create a level playing field by providing enrollees with an objective source of information, such as a customer service center, structuring an open enrollment process, and providing comprehensive information on which people can base their choices. Finally, they hold health plans accountable for their performance, often by establishing certain standards or performance criteria during the contracting process. The plans must submit data and information to the purchasing organization or the employer, and that information is used to evaluate a plan's performance. Often, an independent party is hired to evaluate consumer satisfaction and to review grievances.

Case Study of CalPERS[8]

The California Public Employees' Retirement System (CalPERS) has close to 1 million members and offers an example of a government agency that has been able to take a strong purchasing role while ensuring quality. When CalPERS first began the process of negotiating with health plans, CalPERS considered restricting the number of plans that would be available to its members. The theory was that a multitude of health plans was not necessary if four or five could do the job. Upon further assessment, however, all legally licensed plans that met the standards set forth for quality and fiscal solvency were invited to participate.

CalPERS decided not to use its power in the marketplace to set tight controls on the market. Instead, CalPERS set high standards, focused on providing information to consumers, and let the health plans in the market compete. The agency uses a number of proactive procedures and checks and balances to ensure accountability by:

  • requiring all health plans to be licensed to do business by the California Department of Corporations;
  • gathering data from the plans on cost, performance and service, as well as externally driven data;

---

[8]Material provided by Tom J. Elkin.

- verifying provider access, to ensure that there are adequate numbers of providers to serve members of specific geographic areas;
- requiring a standard benefit design that uses a standard definition for each benefit;
- collecting and publishing performance and cost data in quality report cards, incorporating Health Plan Employer Data and Information Set (HEDIS) data;
- managing and monitoring customer service through an ombudsperson program; and
- monitoring and tracking complaints and grievances and how they are resolved.

This information enabled CalPERS to provide comparisons among plans and to negotiate better premiums. It also put the agency in a position to determine which plans it wished to continue doing business with in the future.

Evidence from Minnesota and Edison International on Structuring Choice for Retirees[9]

Evidence from Minnesota and Edison International demonstrates that factors other than comparability of health plan benefits must be considered when structuring choice for retirees. Experience in these areas indicates that any entity dealing with this population must be prepared to devote considerably more time and resources to providing this group with information. For example, materials must be tailored to retirees to ensure that they can understand the information being conveyed. This includes printing materials in larger type and often targeting written materials to the appropriate reading level.

Multiple communications vehicles are necessary for this group, including open enrollment sessions, videotapes, toll-free telephone numbers, mailings, presentations, and one-on-one meetings. Other tools such as up-to-date directories listing the primary care physicians participating in a plan and plan options are also helpful.

---

[9]The material in this section is based on remarks by Kathleen P. Burek and Barbara L. Decker.

Retirees are frequent users of health care. The status of
their health and health care in general are major focuses in
their lives. For many, medical care is part of a social experience. Given this, they require that a great deal of time explaining and reviewing these issues be devoted to them.

Issues of cost are a major factor in exercising choice for the
Medicare population. A survey of retirees in Minnesota found
that retirees were not willing to make any changes in their
insurance coverage if it meant an increase in costs. At the same
time they did not want any benefits reductions.

ARE MEDICARE BENEFICIARIES DIFFERENT?[10]

Medicare beneficiaries are extremely diverse. They include
the "young old," who are vibrant and healthy, and those who are
in greater need of health care services, many of whom suffer
from chronic diseases. Although the members of this population
are diverse, in general they can be classified as "vulnerable" for
a variety of reasons, including their greater need for health care
services and the higher health care costs that they incur.[11]

The needs of the Medicare population are different from the
needs of many of those already enrolled in managed care organizations. Although managed care organizations traditionally
have focused on prevention and acute-care services—targeted to
a relatively healthy membership—the elderly are more often in
need of chronic care or services for the disabled. In 1989 the
most prevalent chronic conditions for people over age 65 were
arthritis, hypertension, hearing impairment, heart disease, cataracts, deformity or orthopedic impairment, chronic sinusitis, diabetes, visual impairment, and varicose veins (U.S. Senate Special Committee on Aging et al., 1991).

---

[10]Unless otherwise noted, the material in this section is based on presentations by Joyce Dubow, Peter Fox, and L. Gregory Pawlson.

[11]There are different interpretations of vulnerability in the Medicare population. The definition highlighted in the text is based on views by Joyce
Dubow. The National Academy of Aging identifies vulnerable groups to include frail elders, older women, minorities, rural elders, and the growing numbers of oldest old individuals (National Academy on Aging, 1995).

The Medicare population is also diverse in terms of its experience with and expectations of managed care. Particularly for older beneficiaries (ages 75 to 85), in most markets managed care is a foreign concept, a system that they have never dealt with and may not understand. Medicare beneficiaries in their 60s, however, are more likely to have had experience with the managed care system through their workplace. That level of experience will continue to grow since managed care is now the dominant mode of delivery of health care services for the population age 65 and under.

How Medicare Enrollees Have Fared in HMOs

Given the different needs of the Medicare population, the question is: How have Medicare beneficiaries fared so far in the managed care delivery system? Since the incentives that exist in managed care differ from those in the fee-for-service system, there are concerns that managed care organizations may be more focused on efficiency and profits than on developing a system of care that meets the needs of the elderly. In general, HMOs save money by reducing the use and intensity of health care services. Some researchers note that the use of managed care systems may be the best way to ensure coordinated care for this population.

To date managed care organizations have had little experience providing services to the Medicare population or treating older and sicker patients: just 10 percent of Medicare beneficiaries are enrolled in managed care risk plans. That is beginning to change, however. From 1995 to 1996 the number of Medicare beneficiaries enrolled in managed care risk plans grew by 26 percent. Each month close to 70,000 new Medicare beneficiaries enroll in a managed care plan. It is a market in which HMOs are beginning to concentrate their resources. As of February 1996, 189 plans nationwide had Medicare risk contracts, and approvals for another 48 plans were pending before HCFA. Eliminating the 50-50 rule and the requirement that there be 5,000 commercial enrollees before a plan can get a Medicare risk contract would spur further growth. Most employers these days are not very interested in contracting with new HMOs, and when they do, they want to make sure that a broad market area is covered. This makes new entry within the 50-50 requirement very difficult.[12]

HMOs with large numbers of Medicare beneficiaries are concentrated in a few geographic areas, a trend that is changing. Of the 10 percent of Medicare beneficiaries who have enrolled in managed care plans, more than 50 percent have been enrolled in risk-based HMOs in just two states, California and Florida. Another 11 percent are enrolled in HMOs in Arizona and New York. Within the total Medicare population, 16 percent reside in California and Florida combined and 8.5 percent live in New York and Arizona combined (unpublished data provided by the Office of the Actuary, Health Care Financing Administration, May 30, 1996).

The studies that have investigated how well vulnerable populations fare in managed care plans have produced mixed conclusions. Most of the discussion around this particular topic continues to take place in a "fact-free" environment.[13]

HMOs differ significantly in their ability to meet the needs of the elderly. Some do not differentiate between elderly and nonelderly enrollees in terms of service delivery. Others have implemented services specifically targeted toward seniors. These include screening for frailty, geriatric assessment, specialized case management, and enhanced primary care for long-term nursing home populations. Some managed care plans offer additional services and benefits not covered by traditional Medicare such as respite care, home inspections, physical adaptations for the home, relationships with community-based social service programs, support programs for people who are newly widowed, and group clinics for people with chronic illnesses.

Several studies have found that whereas overall satisfaction and outcomes for beneficiaries in fee-for-service plans and HMOs are similar, HMO enrollees appear to be relatively less satisfied with quality of care[14] and physician-patient interactions and

---

[12]Point made by Peter D. Fox.

[13]Point made by Peter D. Fox.

[14]The Institute of Medicine's 1991 report *Medicare: New Directions in Quality Assurance* defines quality of care as, "the degree to which health services for individuals and populations increase the likelihood of desired health outcomes and are consistent with current professional knowledge."

more satisfied with costs in managed care plans compared to indemnity plans (Miller and Luft, 1994). Take the following example of joint pain and chronic arthritis, which are common conditions for many Medicare beneficiaries. A study comparing Medicare beneficiaries with chest and joint pain in risk HMOs with their counterparts in fee-for-service plans found that those in the HMO were less likely to be referred to a specialist and less likely to receive follow-up care. Although the outcomes were similar, the HMO enrollees experienced less alleviation of joint pain (Clement et al., 1994).

Other studies indicate that HMOs are not as proficient in some areas. A study conducted by Shaughnessy et al. in 1994 found that most home health care outcomes for individuals in fee-for-service plans were better than those for individuals in HMOs. HMO costs for home health care were significantly lower than the home health care costs incurred by fee-for-service plans. The approach taken by many HMOs was one of maintenance as opposed to rehabilitation or restoration.

Several studies, however, indicate that HMOs do some things very well. For example, the Group Health Cooperative of Puget Sound practices population-based medicine, an approach to providing clinical care, especially for patients with chronic conditions. The plan identifies enrollees by such characteristics as age, sex, health status, health complaints, and disease diagnoses. Once the subgroups have been identified, specific services and programs are developed for them.

Most of the studies assessing how Medicare enrollees have fared in managed care plans have involved staff and group model HMOs, which are different from the current and emerging independent practice associations, PPOs, and provider service networks. Several key studies have looked at a variety of HMOs, however (Miller and Luft, 1994; Brown et al., 1993b). The managed care environment and health care delivery models will continue to change and evolve. Given this, the fact that managed care has had little experience with the elderly, and the fact that there is little conclusive evidence on how managed care organizations manage and coordinate care for the frail elderly, there may be a need for studies to determine areas in which managed care does result in real improvements for the elderly population. There may be a need to identify and carve out populations with special needs within the larger Medicare managed care infrastructure.[15]

Steep Learning Curve and Disenrollment

Despite a lack of clear evidence as to the effectiveness of managed care in dealing with the Medicare population, it is clear that enrollment in Medicare managed care plans is growing, and there is no evidence that this growth is going to subside. In this area, the Medicare program is on a steep learning curve. As experience with managed care grows and the learning curve begins to flatten out, current problems may be worked through. However, new problems may arise if the pressure to reduce overall Medicare program costs leads to rationing or significantly affects plan and provider behavior.[16]

Until there is more documented experience, the Medicare population needs to be assured that they can disenroll from a managed care plan if they are not satisfied. The freedom to disenroll is especially important for the members of this population since they are unfamiliar with managed care and do not have experience dealing with this system. In the long run, such assurances of easy and rapid disenrollment may not be necessary since many new Medicare enrollees will already have had experience with managed care.

Although Medicare enrollees can now disenroll from any plan on a monthly basis, there is still concern on the part of some beneficiaries that they cannot see another doctor at all (or only with an additional charge) or leave a plan immediately if they are dissatisfied. Furthermore, there is now discussion of changing the provision to call for an annual lock-in period.

One way to curb disenrollments is to focus on providing enrollees with as much information as possible up front so that enrollees understand how the plan works, what their expected costs will be, the benefit structure, how out-of-plan care is handled, and what situations constitute an emergency. The

---

[15]Point made by L. Gregory Pawlson.

[16]Point made by L. Gregory Pawlson.

plan's responsibilities and the members' rights need to be fully outlined in terms that are easily understood. For example, it has been proven that any written information is most effective if it is at a sixth-grade reading level.[17] This education process needs to occur before an enrollee joins a specific health plan. Studies indicate that the plans with the lowest rates of rapid disenrollment spend a great deal of time educating potential new enrollees up front.[18]

According to analysts, high disenrollment rates indicate a likely misunderstanding of a plan's features (Rossiter et al., 1989). If a misunderstanding has occurred, HCFA now permits retroactive disenrollment for people who misunderstood the HMO lock-in requirements and received needed care from an out-of-plan provider. Retroactive disenrollment, especially in cases involving beneficiaries with cognitive impairments, can be an especially important feature. In this case HCFA will pay the charges for services provided during the unintentional HMO enrollment. HCFA is also in the process of creating a system that would allow Medicare beneficiaries to disenroll through an on-line HCFA computer service instead of having to go through the HMO.[19] There have been reports that consumers have run into difficulty or delays when trying to process their disen-rollment with the plans themselves (U.S. Senate Special Com-mittee on Aging, 1995).

According to a speaker at the symposium, health plans have strong incentives to educate new enrollees as much as possible. The cost of marketing is so high that plans cannot afford a high rate of disenrollment. The average cost of acquiring one new member can be in excess of $500.[20] HMOs are also keenly aware of the fact that the best advertising is word of mouth and personal recommendations, so they would want to avoid any negative impressions caused by too many disenrollments. Con-sumer choice and competition are meaningless if the consumer is confused.[21]

---

[17]Point made by Elizabeth Hoy.

[18]Point made by Helen Darling.

[19]Material presented by Kathleen M. King.

[20]Point made by Peter D. Fox.

[21]Point made by Shoshanna Sofaer.

WHAT INFORMATION DO MEDICARE
BENEFICIARIES WANT AND NEED?[22]

Before Medicare beneficiaries can make an educated decision regarding managed care, they first must understand the Medicare fee-for-service program. Then they need to know how managed care works. Without a clear understanding of how both of these delivery systems operate, Medicare beneficiaries will be ill-equipped to make informed decisions about their own health care. Once they understand the various benefits or characteristics of each program, they can move to the task of choosing among the myriad plans and benefit packages available to them.

Numerous studies indicate that adults of all ages have a poor understanding of their health insurance coverage until the time that they become ill and need services (Mechanic, 1989; Pemberton, 1990). Many elderly beneficiaries do not know that Medicare is a program run by the federal government, and many are not aware that managed care is an option. HCFA currently mails each Medicare beneficiary a brochure approximately 3 months before the new enrollee's 65th birthday. The brochure explains the Medicare program, Medigap insurance, managed care options, and other private insurance coverage that might be available to the beneficiary. Anyone interested in more information on managed care can also request a copy of the *Medicare Handbook* and another HCFA brochure entitled "Medicare Managed Care Plans," which discusses how managed care works, enrollment issues, how to select doctors and hospitals, the advantages and disadvantages of HMOs, and disenrollment and appeals procedures (Cronin, 1996). Beneficiaries can also call a toll-free telephone number to see if an HMO exists in their area.

Despite these sources of information, many people still are not clear on how the program operates. Several studies indicate that Medicare beneficiaries have a limited understanding of their benefits. They are more aware of the services most often used, such as physician care and prescription drug coverage, but

---

[22]Unless otherwise noted, the material in this section is based on presentations by Susan Edgman-Levitan, Shoshanna Sofaer, and Lucy Johns.

are less aware of infrequently used services like hospital and nursing home care.

In addition to not fully understanding Medicare, most people—not just Medicare beneficiaries—do not understand the concept of managed care and all of its variations. It is difficult to make decisions about managed care when consumers do not know the difference between their managed care options and their fee-for-service options.

Comparisons between the two systems are even more difficult given that little information about care in the fee-for-service system is available to consumers. Under the fee-for-service system, the consumer (patient) selects a physician or service. If that consumer is not happy with the choice or if the physician provides less than satisfactory care, it falls to the consumer to take appropriate action. In the case of a growing number of HMOs, there are concerted efforts to assess quality and to help enrollees understand the meaning of quality by presenting report cards on measures particularly relevant to elderly beneficiaries. This information and other indicators that consumers find useful in evaluating health plans would be just as helpful to them in evaluating physicians in the fee-for-service system.[23]

The Importance of Comparability

Without a clear picture of how managed care works there is great potential for dissatisfaction with managed care.[24] Managed care represents a new paradigm for doing business, and consumers need to be educated about the potential benefits of this new system. It has to be made clear that managed care should not be regarded as the current fee-for-service system but with a richer benefit package and the same freedoms. The simplified paperwork, added benefits including prescription drug coverage, and reduced out-of-pocket costs come at a price. In exchange for these benefits, enrollees may be limited as to the physicians whom they can see or the services that will be covered.

---

[23]Point made by Marcia A. Laleman.
[24]Point made by Marcia A. Laleman.

Understanding how this new paradigm works will also help
Medicare enrollees understand that their current fee-for-service
primary care physician may operate differently in a managed
care network. They may not get the same degree of individual
attention from their customary physician working in a network.
The incentives for the physician under a fee-for-service system
are different from those for the physician under an HMO, in
which the goal of the HMO is to make certain not only that
coordinated, appropriate care is given but also that costs are
controlled.[25]

Information That Interests Medicare Enrollees: Specific Plan Information[26]

In general, Medicare beneficiaries are most interested in
information about how their plan works, how much it will cost
them, if their physician is in the plan, and what benefits are
covered. As shown in Table 2-2, the types of information in
which Medicare enrollees are interested range from information
on quality, to service, to accessibility and choice. In terms of
hospital care, they want to know if their preferences will be
respected, how much information they will be given, how well
their care will be coordinated, if they will receive emotional
support, how their physical comfort needs will be met, and what
will happen to them when they leave the hospital and return
home.

In terms of ambulatory care, their concerns are centered
around issues of access. Will they have access to the physician
whom they choose or to specialists when needed? Will they be
able to afford that physician's services? How long does it take
someone to answer the phone, and how long does it take to get
an appointment? They also want to know what will happen
when they get to the doctor's office. How much information will
they receive? What will the testing procedure be? And what
follow-up activity can be expected?

Medicare beneficiaries are also interested in the overall quality of care and how satisfied they will be with the services pro-

---

[25]Point made by Diane Archer.
[26]Material presented by Susan Edgman-Levitan.

TABLE 2-2 Typology of Information Likely to Be of Interest to Medicare Beneficiaries

Structural Information
- Premiums and copayments
- Ratings of the hassle factor associated with paperwork
- Brief summary of contractual arrangements with providers: incentives to reduce utilization
- Medical/loss ratio of plan
- Comparable information for fee-for-service plans
- Description of grievance and disenrollment process

Benefit Package
- Description of standard benefit package
- Coverage for special concerns of the elderly: prescriptions, foot care, home care, long-term care, other supplemental coverage

Quality
- Accreditation status
- Percentage of board-certified physicians
- Patient reports and ratings of care for all members and for members over age 65
  — Member services, including member support, choice of doctor and hospital, prior approval process, restrictions on referrals for specialty care
  — Access: appointment waiting times, visit waiting times
  — Access to and choice of primary care physicians and specialists
  — Communication/interpersonal skills
  — Coordination of care
  — Information and education
  — Respect for patient preferences
  — Emotional support
- HEDIS and other technical measures appropriate for a Medicare population: mammography rates, cholesterol screening

SOURCE: Susan Edgman-Levitan and Paul D. Cleary. "What Information Do Consumers Want and Need: What Do We Know About How They Judge Quality and Accountability." Paper prepared for the IOM study Choice and Managed Care: Assuring Public Accountability and Information for Informed Purchasing by and on Behalf of Medicare Beneficiaries.

vided. Several areas of specific concern include prescription drug coverage, foot care, home care, and long-term-care issues and what happens to their coverage when they, for example, move to Florida for the winter.

More importantly, however, the Medicare population wants to know how others like themselves—with the same conditions and of the same socioeconomic status—fare within a given health plan. For example, they want to know the quality of care that someone with arthritis can expect within a certain plan and will likely not be as concerned with that plan's outcomes in obstetrics.

Whether a Medicare beneficiary gives any credence to the information provided has a great deal to do with who is providing the information. The Medicare population is highly cynical about who provides them with information; they do not trust health plans, providers, or insurance companies. They are also skeptical of employers and government. According to several focus group studies, they appear to trust family, friends, and neighbors, as well as independent sources of information such as the American Association of Retired Persons (AARP) or senior citizens' counseling groups. The opinions and experiences of family and friends are very important in helping seniors determine whether they should join an HMO.

Full Disclosure[27]

Although Medicare beneficiaries may express interest only in the specific information that they deem relevant to their current health conditions or service preferences, there is a great deal of information that they may not know exists and that could have an impact on their decisions when choosing between fee-for-service and managed care plans or when choosing a particular managed care plan.

To ensure informed choice there is a certain level of information that should be made available to all consumers, whether or not they have expressed an interest in obtaining such information. This information runs the spectrum from quality-of-care

---

[27]Point made by Lucy Johns.

"report cards," to the incentives driving doctors within health plans, to financial solvency information involving a plan, to disenrollment rates in a given area. Beneficiaries need to understand a plan's responsibilities and their rights as members—not only their rights to appeal decisions but also their rights to access to quality care in a timely manner.

Furthermore, although plans may provide a wide range of information, they may not be providing comprehensive information. In other words, they may not elaborate on areas that are often open for interpretation by the consumer. For example, in the California marketplace, officials are concerned that plans are not providing enough information to members regarding what exactly constitutes emergency care, how much coverage enrollees can expect when they seek care outside of an area covered by their plan (if they need care when traveling), and under what circumstances enrollees can negotiate referrals to specialists.[28]

There are questions regarding just how much information consumers need. Some consumer advocates argue for the provision of data on the satisfaction of people who have been involved in a grievance process or the satisfaction rates for those who suffered major medical illnesses. Others argue for consumer information on profits or compensation for chief executive officers. Although some say that this level of information could be irrelevant and overwhelming for the consumer, others argue that interested consumers are capable of processing this kind of information (Rodwin, 1996). Medicare consumers want, need, and have a right to a variety of information. If consumers do not understand some of the information provided, insurance counseling groups, such as the ones operated by United Seniors Health Cooperative, can help them understand and interpret it.[29]

Other areas of disclosure involve the performance of a health plan in terms of both quality and service. Although plans generally provide extensive information on covered benefits, costs, and required copayments, little information is available to con-

---

[28]Comment by Lucy Johns.
[29]Comment by Priscilla Itzcoitz.

sumers regarding quality. Without information regarding quality it is difficult for consumers to determine the value of their benefits. Several participants observed, however, that quality may be assessed differently by consumers than by clinicians and purchasers and that more work needs to be done to develop indicators that are particularly relevant and useful to individual elderly consumers.

Information regarding disenrollment rates, appeals and reversal rates, board certification, the training and experience of a plan's doctors, and a detailed participating provider list are also important. Provider lists can be misleading, however. Often, lists include physicians whose panel of patients may be closed or who can accommodate only a few new patients. Some providers are dropped from plans after open enrollment periods end. Some plans may list certain centers as participating providers, but they may only cover such services as open heart surgery at one of these centers and nothing else. This is referred to as the *marquee effect*.

Beneficiaries and advocates for the elderly express concern that physicians in managed care plans may be in a conflict-of-interest situation in which they are wearing two hats: patient adviser and manager of care and costs. Given the increasing numbers of physicians taking on this dual role and the fact that many Medicare beneficiaries rely on their physicians for advice and protection, Medicare beneficiaries may need to know of noncriticism clauses or "gag rules" between plans and providers. So-called gag rules prevent physicians from criticizing or questioning a plan's rulings. There is concern that physicians may not advise their patients about procedures if those procedures or treatments are not covered by the plan.[30]

---

[30]U.S. Healthcare as well as a number of other health plans recently have dropped provisions in their physician contracts that relate to limitations to speak freely with patients. At least six states have enacted legislation preventing health plans from utilizing "gag rules," or anticriticism provisions, which prevent a physician from disclosing financial incentives that may affect patient care. In addition, a bill has been introduced in Congress, H.R. 2976, the "Patient Right to Know Act" that bars restrictions on physician-patient communication in HMO contracts. As of the third week of July, 1996, the bill had nearly 100 cosponsors.

HOW DO YOU GET THE INFORMATION OUT EFFECTIVELY?[31]

A thorough review of the literature indicates that Medicare beneficiaries use all types of media and do so often. Television is the most widely used medium among adults age 55 and older. Eighty-four percent of adults over age 50 read a newspaper daily, and 70 percent are magazine readers. Perhaps one of the least-used media is radio, with just 20 to 25 percent of the adult radio-listening audience consisting of those over age 55.

The Medicare population is not homogeneous, however, and should not be stereotyped. Education, age, income, and living arrangements all affect the types of media that people use. Someone with more education is more likely to use a variety of media than someone who did not complete high school.

In marketing, focus groups have determined the value of segmenting messages according to groups of people who demonstrate consistent attitudes, values, and behaviors. Among Medicare enrollees, focus groups have identified four different groups: proactive adults who seek information, faithful patients who do what the doctor tells them, optimists who think they will never get sick, and the disillusioned who do not trust anyone.

In addition to media, there are myriad other sources of information: handbooks and guides produced by public agencies such as HCFA; libraries; information kiosks; videotapes; on-line computer services such as Senior Net or Retirement Living Forum; community meetings; information, counseling, and assistance (ICA) programs; non-profit organizations such as AARP; one-on-one counselors; private organizations; employers; and physicians.

It has been found that forums in which Medicare beneficiaries can have one-on-one personal contact carry the most weight and influence with this group. A series of 15 focus groups conducted in the fall of 1993 for the Kaiser Family Foundation found that the biggest problems with Medicare had to do with communication and coverage (Frederick/Schneiders, 1995). In

---

[31]Unless otherwise noted, the material in this section is based on a presentation by Carol Cronin.

another series of focus groups, participants indicated that they would like to be able to call a toll-free telephone number to obtain answers to their questions by a knowledgeable operator (Mellman, Lazarus & Lake, 1994). Although Medicare beneficiaries trust and turn to family and friends for information, this group wants unbiased information from all other sources. Studies have found that seniors overwhelmingly express interest in obtaining information about health plans through one-on-one counseling, personal presentations, or group presentations where they would have the opportunity to ask questions afterward (Research Triangle Institute, 1995).

Given that health plans often are the source for much of the information that beneficiaries receive regarding these plans, a distinction needs to be made between marketing and education. There needs to be a place where a Medicare beneficiary can go for unbiased, objective information, preferably where a beneficiary can talk to someone in person or via the telephone.

Role for Information Facilitating Organizations

Since Medicare beneficiaries expressed a preference for receiving unbiased information through sources other than the health plans themselves or even through employers or government, symposium participants indicated the usefulness of third-party organizations. These third-party organizations could include organizations that focus solely on education or groups that combine an education function with their selected purchasing power, such as voluntary purchasing cooperatives.

Information, Counseling, and Assistance Programs[32]

Since 1992 HCFA has funded ICA programs to help Medicare beneficiaries obtain unbiased information about public and private health insurance alternatives. Through individual counseling, group seminars, and written materials, the programs provide information about Medicare, supplemental insurance products, long-term-care insurance, managed care plans, and

---

[32]Material provided by Diane Archer.

eligibility for Medicaid and other public programs. Program staff are also trained to help participants complete claims forms and file appeals. Currently, all states have ICA programs, which are staffed through a combination of paid staff and volunteers.

Funding for these organizations, however, has always been limited and is an area of concern. Communications programs require substantial resources. One potential source of funding for these centers or similar counseling programs would be the Medicare program itself, in which consumer education funds could be deemed a priority.

Nonprofit Counseling Organizations

Other organizations, such as the United Seniors Health Cooperative, operate counseling programs to educate seniors about their health care options. The health insurance counseling program for United Seniors receives calls and letters from seniors all over the country.[33]

ENROLLEE SATISFACTION AND CONSUMER PROTECTIONS[34]

National surveys on consumer satisfaction in Medicare HMOs have been conducted, but the information they offer is limited, and there are concerns that they are not useful indicators of the quality of care that an HMO provides.

An early study comparing the satisfaction of Medicare beneficiaries in HMOs with that of beneficiaries in traditional fee-for-service plans showed that a high percentage—about 80 percent—of both groups were "very satisfied" with their health care overall (Rossiter et al., 1989). In general, satisfaction surveys of HMO members indicate that they are more satisfied than their counterparts in fee-for-service plans with the out-of-pocket expenses and the reduced paperwork in managed care plans. They are less satisfied with access to care, referrals to specialists, and physician choice.

---

[33]Material presented by Priscilla Itzcoitz.

[34]Unless otherwise noted, the material in this section is based on a presentation by Patricia Butler.

Approximately 20 percent of those who participate in satisfaction surveys report being dissatisfied.[35] A number of separate studies not focused specifically on the Medicare population
indicate that people who are chronically ill or who have poor
health status are more likely to report dissatisfaction with their
HMOs, indicating that they have trouble obtaining services and
getting referrals to specialists (The Robert Wood Johnson Foundation, 1995). People who were disabled or who have end-stage
renal disease have also reported being much less satisfied with
their ability to obtain access to needed services and specialists
(Office of Inspector General, U.S. Department of Health and
Human Services, 1995a). They also reported that they waited
longer for appointments than they did when they were in fee-
for-service plans and that their physicians were less likely than
physicians in fee-for-service plans to explain what they were
doing. Enrollees in managed care plans have expressed a variety of concerns about obtaining access on the telephone, long
waiting times for appointments, and physicians who do not
spend enough time with patients and who do not appear to be
sympathetic.

Surveys of managed care plan enrollees indicate that dissatisfaction with plans often arises from a lack of understanding
about how the plan operates or the services that it covers. The
most common areas for confusion involve the limits of the network, such as restrictions on out-of-plan use, requirements for
obtaining referrals, and payment for services from non-plan providers as well as emergency care that is obtained out of plan.

Satisfaction ratings are subjective, however, and are of limited value. Focus group studies conducted by the Picker Institute indicate that many consumers are not interested in overall
satisfaction information, because they do not know how to interpret it or what biases it reflects. Ratings would be more useful
if they were combined with reports on care, in which the person
describes the actual care received or notes exactly how much

---

[35]According to Medicare data for 1994, 90 percent of those who chose an
HMO remained enrolled in HMOs. Six percent left for reasons not related to
quality or satisfaction (e.g., moving outside the plan's service ares). Only 4
percent changed to fee-for-service coverage.

time he or she had to spend in a waiting room. This detailed information allows for greater comparisons rather than simply providing information on whether one person's personal expectations were met.[36]

The Agency for Health Care Policy and Research through its Consumer Assessment of Health Plans Study is working to identify the different types of consumer satisfaction information that should be made available and how that information should be distributed. The project's goal is to develop appropriate consumer satisfaction instruments and then to make certain that the information collected is comparable across health plans. The project will consider what literacy level the information should be targeted to and the level of cognitive skills people need to process the comparative information.

From another perspective, in 1994 the PPRC undertook a survey using data from the Medicare Current Beneficiary Survey to look at Medicare beneficiaries' general perceptions of access to and satisfaction with care. The study and its supplements address beneficiary perceptions of access to care and include information on utilization of services, health insurance coverage, access to health care services, satisfaction with care, expenditures, and demographic data, among other issues (Physician Payment Review Commission, 1996). As a follow up to the study, PPRC has contracted with Mathematica Policy Research, Inc. to develop and conduct a survey to monitor beneficiary access to and satisfaction with services in the Medicare managed care program.

Disenrollment

Current evidence indicates that the disenrollment rate among Medicare beneficiaries in Medicare risk contracts is about 5 percent. A 1993 survey conducted by the Office of the Inspector General of the U.S. Department of Health and Human Services showed that Medicare beneficiaries most often cited the following four reasons for leaving an HMO:

---

[36]Material presented by Susan Edgman-Levitan.

- not liking the choice of primary HMO doctors,
- premiums and copayments were too expensive,
- dislike of going through the preliminary HMO doctor to get medical services, and
- desire to use the doctor that the beneficiary had before joining the HMO (Office of the Inspector General, U.S. Department of Health and Human Services, 1995b).

According to the report of the Office of the Inspector General, beneficiaries who are more likely to disenroll perceive that an HMO is more interested in containing costs than providing the best possible care. Those more likely to disenroll also reported problems obtaining access to care.

A 1989 study comparing Medicare HMO enrollees with enrollees in fee-for-service plans found that about 18 percent of the Medicare HMO enrollees disenrolled within a year and a half. More than a quarter of those who disenrolled within 3 months misunderstood the nature and limitations of the HMO. About half of those disenrolling expressed dissatisfaction with the care and the lack of physician continuity (Rossiter et al., 1989).

There is evidence that some dissatisfied enrollees do not leave HMOs simply because they cannot afford to. A recent Office of the Inspector General report found that although 84 percent of enrollees had no plans to leave their HMOs, 16 percent (an estimated 150,000 beneficiaries) either planned to leave or wanted to leave but felt that they could not. They cited the following reasons: the HMO was the only way to afford the health care that they needed, medicine was too expensive outside the HMO, they could not afford non-HMO doctors, they could not afford private health insurance, and they were not eligible for Medicaid (Office of the Inspector General, U.S. Department of Health and Human Services, 1995b).

Consumer Protections

The potential for quality coordinated care for the Medicare population is good if a variety of safeguards can be established for consumer protection. A critical safeguard is supplying consumers with trustworthy information that enables them to make informed choices about managed care. There is also evidence that information does make a difference.[37]

Beyond that, safeguards can be established in several areas, including the setting of standards that address marketing, grievance and appeals procedures, disenrollment allowances, definitions of emergency care, geographic access, and referral processes. Standards such as the 50-50 rule already incorporated in the Medicare program are one form of protection.

Standards

Many states already apply licensure and standards requirements, yet licensure requirements have not necessarily been found to guarantee quality or afford consumers protection. HCFA officials, however, point to the effectiveness of standards at helping to improve quality of care, citing the standards that are now applied to nursing homes. Symposium participants indicated that standards and regulations, such as those applied to the nursing home industry, might be necessary in the Medicare managed care market to avoid abuses. If standards are set too low or if oversight and enforcement actions are weak, abuses and scandals such as those in Florida with Medicare managed care could arise.[38]

Standardization may help consumers to make better choices in a complex and increasingly competitive health care market. As an example, the federal government overhauled the Medigap

---

[37]At the symposium, Shoshanna Sofaer referred to a study that she conducted in 1986, the Health Insurance Decision Project. The project provided Medicare beneficiaries with information to help them compare traditional Medicare, a variety of Medigap policies, and Medicare HMOs. The information provided in the study led those participating to drop duplicative coverage—which was a large problem in the Medigap market at that time—to spend less on premiums and led more of them to join managed care organizations. The project demonstrated that information can make a difference in behavior.

[38]In 1992 and 1993, the General Accounting Office found serious quality problems (i.e., delay in treatment, treatment not competent or timely, denial of access) in many of the risk contract HMOs in the Florida Medicare market. The Florida market contains 19 percent of all Medicare HMO enrollees (U.S. General Accounting Office, 1995b).

insurance program in 1990 by creating a system of standardizing plans, labeled A through J, approved for marketing to Medicare beneficiaries. This reduced major disreputable marketing practices but brought about a hodgepodge of clumsily written plans whose features were virtually impossible for Medicare beneficiaries to comprehend (Kramer et al., 1992). Since the managed care market for Medicare beneficiaries is growing rapidly, there is potential for confusion, especially since managed care itself is also changing and more plans are offering variations, such as point-of-service options. One symposium participant suggested that national standards for Medicare—whether fee-for-service or managed care plans—would ensure that the care that Medicare beneficiaries receive from state to state does not vary. This would also ensure that they receive the same standard of care as they enter Medicare from a private system and if they move from a fee-for-service system to a managed care system.[39]

Marketing

Marketing and education should be viewed as two separate functions. The purpose of marketing is to get people to enroll in a plan, and the purpose of consumer education is to give consumers the information they need to make a choice. Although marketing may provide some useful information, the fundamental intent of marketing is different from that of unbiased education. Since Medicare beneficiaries lack knowledge about Medicare and the choices available to them, it is important to safeguard Medicare beneficiaries against potential marketing abuses.

Although Medigap insurance currently allows door-to-door marketing, symposium participants expressed concern that door-to-door marketing by Medicare managed care plans should not be allowed since the elderly, more than any other group, rely on personal, one-on-one interactions for most of their information. The potential for providing misleading information can be great in a private setting, as indicated by past door-to-door marketing experiences with the Medicaid program.

---

[39]Point made by Ellen R. Shaffer.

Banning all undesirable marketing practices might not be feasible because of First Amendment issues. There are ways to mitigate potential problems, however. Some voluntary purchasing cooperatives use agents and brokers to address the small group and individual markets. They train and certify the agents and brokers who are licensed to sell their product before they are permitted to sell the product. The purchasing cooperative provides the information that the agents and the brokers use, and the information is bound together so that agents or brokers cannot pull out only the information that they would like the consumer to see. This packet of information outlines all the health plan options that a consumer has.[40]

The purchasing cooperatives also review and approve any marketing materials that participating plans wish to distribute. Furthermore, the compensation for agents is structured so that an agent's commission does not vary according to which plan a consumer chooses. The amount of the commission also is disclosed to the payer.

To ensure that Medicare beneficiaries are not dependent on the information provided through marketing, it is important that they have access to other sources of unbiased information. Competing against the marketing resources of commercial companies, however, may prove to be an issue. Although HCFA may spend $10 million on consumer education and all of the states combined may spend the same amount, health plans devote far greater amounts to marketing activities.

Grievance and Appeals Procedures

The majority of appeals filed with HCFA by Medicare beneficiaries are over disputes over payment for services provided by nonplan providers and emergency care (Network Design Group, 1995). Studies have documented problems with access to rehabilitative services, especially following hospitalization. HMOs may deny authorization for short-term skilled nursing facility services, home health care, and physical, speech, or occupational therapy, even though these services are covered un-

---

[40]Material presented by Richard E. Curtis.

der Medicare when they are deemed medically necessary or will improve a person's functional status. Disputes may arise if an HMO has a more narrow definition of medical necessity.

In the case of managed care, expedited grievance and appeals procedures are important. Under the fee-for-service system, grievances and disputes generally occur after a service has been rendered and the health plan is refusing to cover the service. Under the managed care system, the dispute generally occurs before a service or specialty referral is rendered. In some instances a denial of care could prove to be life-threatening. In some cases by the time that an appeal is decided in favor of an enrollee, a service such as short-term rehabilitation may no longer be of benefit to the patient.

Medicare beneficiaries need to be informed about their appeal and grievance options before they enroll in a health plan. They should understand the different classifications of and processes for (1) an information request, (2) registering a complaint, (3) filing a grievance, and (4) making an appeal. A 1994 survey of Medicare risk plans showed that 25 percent of beneficiaries did not know that they had the right to appeal their HMO's denial to provide or pay for services (Office of the Inspector General, U.S. Department of Health and Human Services, 1995b).

The Changing Role of HCFA[41]

Medicare has traditionally acted more as a bill payer than a private-sector purchaser. In the past HCFA has made little effort to inform Medicare enrollees of their choices regarding health care providers, treatment options, or competing private health plans. There have been several exceptions, including the disclosure of nursing home inspections, public listing of high-mortality hospitals, mailings containing preventive care information, and some use of centers of excellence arrangements.

HCFA is taking a more active role in trying to expand consumer choice by focusing on information needs and treating

---

[41]Unless otherwise noted, this section is based on a presentation by Judith D. Moore.

beneficiaries as their primary customers. The agency is in the process of revising its Medicare handbook and establishing an on-line help service for beneficiaries. The Office of Managed Care is also working on charts comparing both managed care and fee-for-service Medicare. The charts, which have been tested with focus groups, will be issued in three phases, with the first phase comparing benefits.[42]

Symposium participants indicated that HCFA could take a number of steps to help safeguard the interests of Medicare beneficiaries, including the establishment of uniform, national standards for plans, in addition to requiring external reviews of quality. HCFA could also take on greater quality assurance responsibilities.

HCFA currently conducts primarily paper reviews of the organizations with which it has contracts, in addition to biannual, on-site reviews of every managed care organization. As part of this process HCFA reviews the operational areas of a plan, including enrollment and disenrollment, information systems, quality assurance, appeals, and provider payments. This review process has not been able to stop problems. Often, what is written on paper is not necessarily accurate. For example, in the 1980s abuses occurred when plans signed enrollees, yet no providers were available to provide care.

HCFA is also paying greater attention to quality indicators and is working with NCQA to modify HEDIS to incorporate measures more germane to the Medicare population. As part of that project, HCFA plans to provide side-by-side comparisons using basic administrative data, consumer satisfaction data, and eventually, quality data. The information will be published and available on the Internet.

In another major initiative to improve the accountability of HMOs, HCFA, along with the U.S. Department of Defense and FEHBP, has joined a group of large employers through the Foundation for Accountability to develop performance measures that will assist purchasers and consumers in choosing health plans.

Historically, HCFA has been successful at obtaining and analyzing volumes of data, but it has been less successful at

---

[42]Material presented by Kathleen M. King.

making those data available to consumers and has also been reluctant to use those data to sanction plans that were not performing satisfactorily (U.S. General Accounting Office, 1995b). Although HCFA does have the authority to freeze enrollment or to discontinue a contract, it is difficult to take action when a plan may be serving thousands of enrollees. Nevertheless, HCFA could benefit from transitioning to a more efficient administrative model.[43]

The collection of information on quality, such as HEDIS and performance measures, is one way to hold plans accountable. In negotiating contracts, purchasing organizations are able to build certain quality and performance measures standards into the contracts. Measuring quality is a new science, however, and there are questions as to whether the current quality measurements are the most appropriate ones. How such measures will need to be translated and modified to be truly useful to consumers in exercising choice is also an issue. For example, low-birthweight measurements on report cards can be affected by socioeconomics, education, and nutrition, not just the care that is received through a health plan. But in the absence of any other measurements, symposium participants agreed that HEDIS and the quality measurements offered by NCQA represent a promising start.

State-Federal Partnerships

The entire oversight role, however, does not need to fall to HCFA. Although the federal government sets standards for federally qualified HMOs, competitive medical plans, Medicare risk contracts, and Medicaid HMOs, states also have as part of their insurance regulations laws that require minimum operating standards for managed care firms.

However, one symposium presenter challenged the notion of federal-state partnerships in this arena, preferring to use the analogy of two different train tracks that sometimes run in parallel lines but that often cross each other.[44] The original HMO act was directed to the general population, and now new laws

---

[43]Comment by Garry Carneal.
[44]Comment by Lynn Shapiro Snyder.

and protections must be put into place to ensure accountability for different groups with different requirements—elderly, chronically ill, and poor individuals—not to mention rules and regulations for the new managed care entities that continue to evolve. Efforts must be made to ensure that all of these new regulations achieve the desired result and do not become duplicative, too complex, and too burdensome.

Another presenter reminded the symposium that one size does not fit all when it comes to regulations.[45] For example, Utah's population, infrastructure, and political culture are very different from those of Florida. In many parts of the country the federal government is viewed as "Mean Joe Green, where you gather up the whole back field and throw them out until you find the guy with the ball." Another way this approach has been described relates to the old grandmother who yells out to her grandchildren, "Put on your coat, I'm cold." In defining the role of government, one needs to assess who should be protected and what they need to be protected against.

PROPOSED LEGISLATIVE CHANGES TO THE MEDICARE RISK PROGRAM: A "REPORT CARD"

From the perspective of Medicare beneficiaries and with a focus on issues of accountability and informed purchasing, the committee asked David Kendall to reflect on the various themes and findings that had been highlighted during the symposium and how those related to the Medicare reform provisions introduced as part of the Balanced Budget Act of 1995 and the Clinton administration's proposal. How much of what had been said and suggested during the symposium was reflected in the various provisions? What were the areas of concordance, and where were there substantial differences? What areas or issues, if any, were highlighted at the symposium but not addressed in the various proposals?

To fulfill his assignment, David Kendall presented a report card on eight major aspects of the Congressional Medicare reform provisions of the Balanced Budget Act of 1995 and the

---

[45]Material presented by Dixon F. Larkin.

Clinton administration's proposal for reform: (1) benefits/plan types, (2) licensing (regulatory oversight), (3) enrollment, (4) consumer information, (5) purchasing style, (6) plan payments, (7) communications/education strategy, and (8) chronic care/disclosure. Kendall assessed each of these areas from the perspective of whether the legislation had adopted one of three approaches: government knows best, leave it to the market, or government policy is to correct market deficiencies. In the process of developing the report card Kendall used prior focus groups (with other audiences), together with the commissioned papers and conference presentations to identify the eight key issues required for informed policy making. The results are listed in Tables 2-3 and 2-4.

According to the report cards, the U.S. Congress and the Clinton administration have taken a regulatory (government knows best) approach to setting the conditions of participation. This approach requires plans to comply with a hefty range of rules and regulations regarding access, provide adequate ser-

TABLE 2-3 Medicare Legislation Report Card: Medicare Reform Provisions of the Balanced Budget Act of 1995 (H.R. 2491)

Issue	Government Knows Best	Leave It to the Market	Government Policy Is to Correct Market Deficiencies
Benefits/plan type		X	
Licensing	X		
Enrollment			X
Consumer information			X
Purchasing style	X		
Plan payments	X		
Communications / education strategy		X	
Chronic care / disclosure		X	
Total (%)	37	37	25

TABLE 2-4 Medicare Legislation Report Card: The Clinton Administration's Proposal

Issue	Government Knows Best	Leave It to the Market	Government Policy Is to Correct Market Deficiencies
Benefits/plan type	X		
Licensing	X		
Enrollment			X
Consumer information			X
Purchasing style	X		
Plan payments	X		
Communications/ education strategy		X	
Chronic care/ disclosure		X	
Total (%)	50	25	25

vice, be fiscally solvent, and adhere to internal as well as external quality assurance requirements. Similarly, payments to plans are not based on competitive bidding or contracting, but continue to use government-set payments, based on modifications to the current AAPCC system and, in the case of the congressional legislation, based on further national per capita growth limits.[46]

With regard to purchasing style, both proposals support the FEHBP approach in which the federal government offers all plans that meet the conditions of participation and do not permit more selective and active purchasing based on performance, a strategy used by many employers to ensure accountability and value.

Both proposals would generally let the market prevail in the range of plan choices to be offered to beneficiaries. The Clinton administration's proposal, however, would not allow medical

---

[46]HCFA is currently testing a number of competitive pricing approaches under its demonstration authority.

savings accounts or private fee-for-service plans to be offered. In addition, both proposals rely on the market, not the government, to develop a public education strategy to familiarize beneficiaries with the opportunity and responsibility for informed decision making. The proposals rely on the plans to disclose financial incentives to providers and methods for making coverage and utilization decisions, issues that may be of special relevance for those with major or chronic illnesses.

Both proposals use government policy to correct market deficiencies in the enrollment process. They would structure enrollment to discourage beneficiaries from switching between levels of coverage based on anticipated health costs, a problem known as adverse selection. Congress would phase in over 2 years an annual open enrollment period with a 12-month lock-in to prevent continuous enrollment and disenrollment. (New enrollees in managed care plans would have a 90-day grace period for disenrollment.) The Clinton administration's proposal would shift the responsibility for enrollment from the health plans to the Office of the Secretary of the U.S. Department of Health and Human Services to discourage adverse selection and "cherry-picking" caused by direct selling. Both proposals would correct market deficiencies as well in the area of consumer information. They both contain a number of rules and requirements regarding information on benefits, premiums, and quality indicators that would allow Medicare beneficiaries to make comparisons.

The overall "scores" from the report cards on each proposal's philosophical approach (as indicated in Tables 2-3 and 2-4) are remarkably similar despite the sharp rhetoric from each side on their differences. The difference in scores is attributable only to the inclusion of medical savings accounts and private fee-for-service plans in the legislation passed by Congress and vetoed by the President. Although much rhetoric has been sounded regarding letting the market prevail, the legislation preserves a significant role for government in most aspects of the Medicare reform provisions.

In keeping with the "report card" theme, three areas of the Congressional legislation were identified as "needing improvement." First, the Balance Budget Act's provisions provide little enlightened thinking about getting consumers more actively engaged in decision making with an emphasis on reliable, comparable, and objective information. The "communications" and "education" provisions of the bill rely heavily on marketing as a vehicle for getting information to beneficiaries and not enough on building an infrastructure for helping consumers to make informed, responsible choices. Second, the bill does not demand sufficient requirements for disclosure on how financial and coverage decisions are made by individual health plans. This issue has particular importance for beneficiaries, many of whom suffer from chronic conditions. Third, the legislation falls short in setting standards for competition based on quality and performance rather than on costs.

3
Findings and Recommendations

RECOMMENDATION 1

All *Medicare choices*[1] that meet the standard conditions of participation and that are available in a local market should be offered to Medicare beneficiaries to increase the likelihood that beneficiaries can find a plan of value. Traditional Medicare should be maintained as an option and as an acceptable "safe harbor" for beneficiaries, especially those who are physically or mentally frail.

Number and Type of Health Plans to Be Offered

Findings

Medicare beneficiaries are currently offered traditional Medicare, Medigap policies, and, in many areas of the country, a growing number of alternative health plans. New initiatives in Medicare and proposed reforms of the Medicare program would

---

[1]For the purpose of this chapter, the term *Medicare choices* is an umbrella term for traditional Medicare, Medigap insurance, and alternative health plans (including managed care).

broaden the number and range of alternative health plans offered.

For most Medicare beneficiaries the range of options and the responsibility for choosing among those options are likely to be significantly greater than those currently available to a large percentage of the working population. Unlike private employers, which have the power to limit the number and types of plans offered, current Medicare practice and proposed reforms would allow any plan that meets specified conditions of participation to sell coverage to Medicare beneficiaries.

Although the committee was cautioned that a large number of choices may increase the confusion for Medicare beneficiaries, it may also increase the ability of Medicare beneficiaries to find a plan that they like, for example, a plan that includes their chosen doctor, that offers valued additional coverage, or that provides convenient access to services. The fear of not being able to continue to see a chosen caregiver has been shown to be a major reason why elderly individuals are reluctant to move into managed care arrangements. Competition among a larger number of health plans will likely produce more innovation on the part of health plans to find ways to be more responsive to the wants and needs of beneficiaries.

The committee also was concerned that limiting the numbers of plans, beyond requiring them to meet benchmark[2] conditions of participation, would raise policy and political issues, given the size of the Medicare program and the proportion of total U.S. health care revenues that it represents. Setting limits would have a vast impact on competitors and the market as a whole.

Subrecommendations

The committee recommends that all *Medicare choices* that meet the benchmark conditions of participation be offered to beneficiaries. Conditions of participation should be carefully constructed to bear the burden of assuring informed choice by beneficiaries and accountability by health plans for access to

---

[2]Benchmark is defined as a floor, with the expectation that participating plans would exceed this level.

quality systems of care. All *Medicare choices* should have to meet common conditions of participation.

This policy may result in the marketing of plans with limited appeal and small numbers of Medicare beneficiary enrollees over time. The committee recommends that these kinds of plans be tracked over time and evaluated for their potential impacts on risk selection[3] and administrative costs and the extent to which they cause confusion among beneficiaries.

The Traditional Medicare Program

Findings

Given how little is known about ensuring informed choice and holding health plans accountable for providing quality care to Medicare beneficiaries and given the consequent risks for the beneficiaries, the committee believes that traditional Medicare must remain an option and a safe harbor for beneficiaries.[4] This option should be at least as good as the existing Medicare program in terms of benefits, beneficiary cost-sharing, choice of providers, geographic access, and other factors.

The committee believes that maintaining traditional Medicare as a choice is critical for allowing large numbers and a wide range of plans to be offered to Medicare beneficiaries. Without the ability to retain the traditional Medicare program as an option and safe harbor, particularly for beneficiaries who are physically and mentally frail, the committee would not recommend widening the Medicare marketplace to the extent that is advocated in this report.

The committee is aware that traditional indemnity plans are becoming a relic for the market under age 65; many fee-for-service plans have been discontinued because of their high pre-

---

[3]As in other sections of the report, the committee understands the inadequacy and limitations of current risk adjustment methods and recommends that further research be supported in this critical area. In the meantime, however, practical requirements necessitate that available techniques be used to make best-judgment decisions.

[4]The committee defines *safe harbor* as a program that is financially stable and that remains an option for the foreseeable future.

miums, their noncompetitive benefits, and adverse risk selection. Within this environment, special challenges exist for the future viability of the traditional Medicare program. Constraints on Medicare spending are adding new urgency to managing the costs of care delivered in the traditional Medicare program. Maintaining traditional Medicare as an option is likely to be difficult and could require additional costs to government.

The committee was not able, within the time frame and scope of its task, to make the difficult estimates of these potential costs to government or their wider social implications. The committee is mindful, however, of efforts by the National Academy of Social Insurance, the Prospective Payment Assessment Commission (ProPAC), PPRC, and others to explore ways in which Medicare's fee-for-service program can be shaped in the future to make it more efficient and to improve its management and delivery of care.

Subrecommendations

In the framework of the findings presented above, the committee recommends that HCFA, under its demonstration authorities, accelerate its efforts to identify private-sector purchasing and management techniques that can be adopted appropriately for use by the traditional Medicare program as an alternative to price reductions and, when possible, to offer additional benefits to maintain the program's value. HCFA's current development of "centers of excellence" for high-technology procedures seems an example of such an adaptation.

As indicated elsewhere, it is also critical that risk selection measurement and adjustment technologies be improved for use by traditional Medicare and health plans. As improved technology for measuring risk selection is developed, HCFA should study the traditional Medicare program's risk pool relative to those of other health plans and assess whether program funding fairly reflects Medicare's risk profile to enable it to offer a product of competitive value to beneficiaries. The federal government should also study and pilot test ways to pay health plans more fairly for chronically ill beneficiaries to encourage health plans to invest in and market to those beneficiaries.

Risk Selection

Findings

It was beyond the scope of the present study to address problems of risk selection among the multiple *Medicare choices* and to recommend steps to correct for those problems. During its deliberations, however, the committee found that mechanisms to prevent or correct for risk selection are critical to the ultimate success of any system offering multiple health plan choices and that the existing Medicare AAPCC cannot be relied on to achieve success in this area.

The number and range of health plan choices being proposed for Medicare beneficiaries and variations in benefits, premiums, and marketing are likely to greatly increase the potential for risk selection among those offering the various *Medicare choices*. Since risk selection can seriously undermine the viabilities of the traditional Medicare program and individual plans, it is important that this problem be addressed and controlled.

Ultimately, the committee is concerned about incentives and the capability of physicians with a direct financial interest in a plan to recruit (or avoid) subscribers on the basis of whether that individual is a high- or low-level user of health services.

RECOMMENDATION 2

Enrollment and disenrollment guidelines, appeals and grievance procedures, and marketing rules should reflect Medicare beneficiaries' vulnerability and lack of understanding of traditional Medicare and Medigap insurance and their current lack of trust in important aspects of alternative health plans.

Beneficiary Enrollment and Disenrollment

Findings

The committee found that numerous factors make it critical to facilitate the Medicare enrollment and disenrollment process in an environment of market competition and broader choice:

- Medicare beneficiaries are apprehensive about managed care, the concept of risk, the choice process, and lock-in provisions that would prevent beneficiaries from leaving a plan with which they become dissatisfied after enrollment.
- Many Medicare beneficiaries are poorly informed about traditional health insurance in general and are even more poorly informed about their *Medicare choices* and the choice process. A considerable amount of beneficiary dissatisfaction, especially among those beneficiaries who are new to managed care, appears to be related to misunderstandings of the basic structure, payment and care practices, and the choice process.
- Some beneficiaries unknowingly lose their Medigap insurance coverage or face a premium increase if they join a managed care plan and later return to Medicare.
- Managed care uses practice protocols and definitions of what constitutes medical necessity and appropriate care that vary from those used by the traditional Medicare program. These differences can result in various types and levels of service for specific illnesses and conditions. It is often difficult for beneficiaries to understand these protocols and their implications for the specific services offered by various plans before enrolling in a plan.
- Many Medicare beneficiaries are disadvantaged in the choice process by physical or mental frailty or by poor vision or hearing.
- Some Medicare beneficiaries who receive their care from HMOs now must enroll in and disenroll from plans as they move between summer and winter residences. The portability of a managed care plan may be further hindered by annual open enrollment policies and lock-in provisions.
- Beneficiaries can be negatively affected by health plan changes beyond their control, such as when their provider ceases to contract with the plan.
- Beneficiaries who make misinformed choices can be hurt financially or clinically, or both. The committee is most concerned with minimizing adverse clinical outcomes, but would err on the side of greater leniency in allowing beneficiaries to leave a plan with which they are dissatisfied.

Subrecommendations

Given the findings presented above, the committee recommends a transition period of 2 years from the time that legislation is implemented during which the federal government would continue the current option of permitting monthly changes of enrollment by Medicare beneficiaries. After this transition period, enrollees should be locked into the plan that they have selected for 1 year, with the following exceptions. All enrollees will have 90 days from the time of enrollment in a health plan to disenroll and enroll in traditional Medicare, and newly entitled beneficiaries and beneficiaries who have never before chosen a health plan (i.e., those who have been enrolled in the traditional Medicare program) should have the prerogative of changing plans or rejoining the traditional Medicare program within 90 days. Beneficiaries should be allowed to return to their previous Medigap policy with no additional premium costs and with no restrictions placed on preexisting conditions if they disenroll from a health plan within 90 days and return to the traditional Medicare program.

The committee would like to see the federal government encourage plans to offer adequate out-of-area coverage for their enrollees who reside out of the plan's service area for more than 3 months. This can be achieved through interplan reciprocity or point-of-service options.

Grievance and Appeals Procedures

Findings

The current Medicare appeals process has been shown to be slow and not adequately advertised by HCFA or health plans. Furthermore, the current appeals process is tailored more to reviewing whether a service should be reimbursed by Medicare or a health plan and less on the important issue of whether a needed service was denied.

In a competitive environment, to attain better risk selection, health plans have the incentive to encourage healthier people to enroll in the plan and to discourage from enrollment those who need more services. This could prompt plans to be less responsive to the grievances of sicker Medicare enrollees.

Subrecommendations

The committee recommends that the existing appeals process be strengthened, streamlined, and better publicized.

Furthermore, the committee recommends that the federal government make available an expedited review and resolution process for *Medicare choices* (by an agency independent of the health plan and the traditional Medicare program) to review emergency conditions, such as the following: (1) when a situation is life-threatening, (2) when the time involved to review the appeal under the usual process would result in a loss of function or a significant worsening of a condition or would render the treatment ineffective, or (3) when advanced directives or end-of-life preferences are involved.

The federal government should carry out this expedited review through an independent private nonprofit agency in each area of the country. The agency should review any negative findings with the health plan involved and report to the federal government any recommended changes to improve the plan's performance. The cost of this independent, expedited review process should be covered by the Informed Choice Fund (for a more detailed description of this fund, see below). The federal government should be able to assess the costs of these reviews on the health plans when the number of such reviews and negative findings becomes excessive.

Health Plan, Medigap Insurance, and Traditional Medicare Marketing Practices

Findings

Past experience with Medigap policy sales has demonstrated the potential for widespread abuse. Federal and state regulatory mechanisms have been put into place to deal with these abuses. However, greater incentives for abuse exist with the sale of alternative health plans. The commission on a single sale can be a significant portion of an agent's compensation.

Health insurance is also complex, and it is difficult for beneficiaries to compare the benefits offered by competing health plans. It will likely remain so for most Medicare consumers. Many Medicare beneficiaries are particularly vulnerable in their need and desire for adequate health care coverage and have been found to have low levels of understanding of *Medicare choices*.

All of these factors that make elderly beneficiaries especially susceptible to improper marketing practices are underscored by the fact that elderly people have a preference for and rely on one-to-one interactions as a way of learning about their health plan options.

Subrecommendations

To promote comparable levels of accountability, the committee recommends that serious consideration be given to having a new entity approve in advance the public information and marketing materials used by health plans and by the traditional Medicare program (see p. 107). Additionally, the federal government should work with state governments to oversee the marketing of Medigap policies to individuals in the framework of the new requirement for a single open season and conditions of participation.

The committee recommends that the agents and marketers of health plans and Medigap policies be required to inform Medicare beneficiaries up front of their commission for the sale of the policy. Unsolicited door-to-door marketing and outbound telephone marketing should be prohibited. Rigorous marketing rules of conduct should be required to protect beneficiaries. For example,

• retroactive disenrollment should be permitted if enrollment takes place as a result of misleading marketing,
• compensation to marketing agents should be tied to retention of the enrollee in the health plan, and
• retention rates should be reported to potential enrollees by the health plan and by agents.

The committee recommends that the federal government define the basic requirements of any marketing presentation by a health plan or Medigap insurance provider, including such items as providing a copy of a brochure or pamphlet that clearly compared standard health plans, a description of the lock-in provision and a discussion of the availability of the beneficiaries' providers under the plan, and marketing materials in the primary language of the buyer. The federal government should also collaborate with states to ensure consistency in these requirements and should be able to effectively sanction health plans and Medigap insurance providers that break the marketing rules.

RECOMMENDATION 3

The committee recommends that special and major efforts be directed to building the needed consumer-oriented information infrastructure for Medicare beneficiaries. This resource should be developed at the national, state, and local levels, with an emphasis on coordination and partnerships. Information and customer service techniques and protocols developed in the private sector should be used to guide this effort, and the best technologies currently available or projected to be available in the near term should be used.

Beneficiary Information Needs for Informed Choice

Findings

Many Medicare beneficiaries do not understand the *Medicare choices*. Many are fearful of any change in Medicare and distrust the new choices of health plans. A wide range of unbiased information about *Medicare choices* may increase the level of trust. The committee has found that Medicare beneficiaries want and need standardized, unbiased, clearly understandable information, including the following:

- how the different *Medicare choices* actually work;
- the out-of-pocket costs of the various plans;
- the experiences of people similar to themselves (e.g.,

people of the same age, health, sex, ethnicity, and cultural background) seeking care under the various *Medicare choices*;

• how patients have access to and are treated by their doctors (both primary care and specialist physicians) under the various options;

• the accessibility of the services that they are likely to need, especially hospital and ancillary services, as well as the accessibility to cutting-edge care and where it is provided;

• an indication that the information is accurate, timely, reliable, and trustworthy (beneficiaries are savvy in discerning the quality and inherent biases of the information); and

• how participating physicians are paid.

Some groups of beneficiaries, especially those with chronic conditions, desire more specific information, such as protocols for treatment or whether a particular prescription drug is provided in their *Medicare choice*.

Medicare beneficiaries appear to be active users of media of all types, older adults are particularly oriented toward one-to-one communications with another individual. Furthermore, the committee is pleased with the progress being made by private credentialing organizations like NCQA and the Joint Commission on Accreditation of Healthcare Organizations (JCAHO) to develop data sets that can be used to certify plans and inform consumers, such as HEDIS.

Subrecommendations

In efforts to communicate the information in Box 3-1, "Medicare Choices: Information for Beneficiaries," to Medicare beneficiaries, a broad range of mass media and other forms of communication should be used. Emphasis should be placed on providing beneficiaries with easy telephone access to individuals who can guide them on the use of the materials providing comparisons of health plans and who can provide additional clarification and information on plans and providers. To the degree possible, health plans will be asked to submit information in a format that will allow beneficiaries or their families to access the information via the Internet.

To establish trust, a private, nonprofit organization should validate and publish summaries of performance data and make more technical backup data available to beneficiaries and others who have a reasonable right to know. Beneficiary surveys should be standardized across plans, they should be audited, they should include a representative sample of those who are covered (including by ethnicity), and they should oversample beneficiaries with chronic or disabling conditions. Materials should be adapted for use by those with special physical limitations, such as poor vision and hearing.

To keep its information as complete and current as possible, this organization should obtain expert advice from national quality and service accreditation organizations in the continuing development of data needs, comparative reports, and surveys for the purposes described above.

Medicare Customer Service and Enrollment Center

Findings

There exists a critical need to increase understanding of and trust in the restructured Medicare program by the public. Medicare beneficiaries and the general public need to be provided with a broad and objective education about the coverages, costs, and purposes of Medicare and the new health plan choices.

Objective and responsive information on all aspects of *Medicare choices* is also needed to hold the health system and plans accountable. An increase in the amount of this type of information will augment Medicare beneficiaries' trust in the Medicare program and the choice process.

The committee finds that the private sector's information and communication technologies for assembling, cataloging, and making available information on various health plan features to consumers have advanced well beyond those currently being used to serve Medicare beneficiaries. An example cited frequently at the symposium and in the commissioned papers is the notion of customer service centers that allow telephone access to representatives with on-line support. The central availability of the federal government's access to standard data from participating health plans, the traditional Medicare program, and Medigap insurance offers an opportunity to use this tech-

BOX 3-1
Medicare Choices: Information for Beneficiaries

To provide the necessary information for informed purchasing, the committee recommends that the federal government make available to beneficiaries, directly or through health plans, the following types of information on *Medicare choices*:

1. The enrollment and disenrollment rules, the choice process, and the range of services available from the health plans.
2. How traditional Medicare and Medigap insurance, in comparison with alternative health plans, pay and contract with providers, for example, choice of providers and portability.
3. Comparative benefits, including
   - emergency and out-of-plan urgent care;
   - hospital services (including access to centers of excellence);
   - nursing home, home health, and hospice services;
   - prescription benefits;
   - physician services, including the availability of specialists;
   - foot care, dental care, and mental health care; and
   - services of alternative providers such as chiropractors.
4. Comparative costs, including premiums, cost-sharing, and balance billing, with examples of comparative costs for different classes of beneficiaries, for example, the well elderly; disabled, institutionalized, and chronically ill people; and individuals with major illness episodes while on Medicare. Medigap insurance premiums should be shown to be in addition to the Part B premium.
5. Comparative performance on clinical, structural, and satisfaction benchmarks:
   - scientifically valid process and outcome measures in a form salient and relevant to beneficiaries, including the
     —percentage of beneficiaries with diabetes who receive an annual eye examination,
     —percentage of female Medicare beneficiaries who receive an annual or biannual mammogram and Pap smear,
     —percentage of males who receive a prostate examination,
     —percentage of beneficiaries who receive preventive services, such as hypertension screening and influenza and pneumococcal vaccinations, and
     —recidivism rate for various diagnoses;

- access measures, including
  —the percentage of referrals denied or unavailable,
  —the average waiting time to obtain a referral,
  —average times to obtain an appointment once a referral has been made,
  —ease of phone access and average waiting times in a physician's office, and
  —physician turnover rates; and
- satisfaction measures (specifying those with chronic conditions or disabilities), including
  —disenrollment information, including the percentage of persons who disenroll within 3 months of enrollment,
  —appeals and grievance information, including the numbers, reasons, and resolutions of grievances and appeals per *Medicare choices* organization,
  —access and quality findings from HCFA monitoring surveys and relevant state regulatory reports, and
  —findings from surveys commissioned by the organization on satisfaction with physicians and hospital care, access to specialists, and other factors found to be important to beneficiaries.

6. A clear description of the details of each plan and the Medigap policy, including
- in- and out-of-network access and costs;
- how referrals are made (e.g., who makes the referral decisions and on what basis);
- appeals and grievance systems;
- up-to-date listings of all providers by type and specialty, credentials, and whether an individual provider is accepting new patients from the plan;
- financial and contractual arrangements between plans and providers that may influence their decisions regarding services in the judgment of the federal government;
- financial and solvency status; and
- use of out-of-area specialty centers.

On request, policies or protocols for covering or providing specific services (such as a prescription drug) or services for specific conditions (such as chronic obstructive pulmonary disease, congestive heart failure, diabetes, and joint replacement) should be provided.

nology to better ensure informed choice by beneficiaries and accountability by health plans.

Furthermore, regional and local variations in health plans and health care, coupled with the strong desire among beneficiaries for one-to-one communication, suggest that additional information and service activities be carried out by ombudspersons or agencies at the regional and area levels. Models for such activities exist in information, counseling, and assistance (ICA) programs, which are funded primarily by HCFA.

Subrecommendations

To further these objectives, the committee recommends that the federal government contract with and oversee a private, nonprofit agency to develop a state-of-the-art *Medicare Customer Service and Enrollment Center* that would (1) administer a Medicare customer services answer center; (2) develop, collect, and distribute open enrollment materials and enrollment data; (3) reconcile enrollment data and payments to plans, including monthly changes and related transactions; (4) provide an evaluation component for the purpose of continual improvement and plan feedback; and (5) contract for regular customer service satisfaction surveys.

The Center would strive to offer Medicare beneficiaries national and regional or local access to the types of services provided by the benefits departments of the nation's large employers, building on the regional-area work of organizations such as ICA programs.

The Center will provide education, counseling, and legal assistance and will process complaints, grievances, and appeals from plan members through regional and local agents such as ICA programs. It will install a tracking system to report all complaints, grievances, and appeals, and will report this information to beneficiaries annually and to health plan chief executive officers monthly.

In carrying out this effort, the Center will take advantage of the most effective and efficient methods of electronic communication, including toll-free telephone communication, on-line communications, town meetings, newsletters, and multimedia techniques, to provide information about plans and the process of choice that is as detailed as possible.

The Center's national, regional, and area activities would be funded by the federal government through the Informed Choice Fund (see below).

Choice Facilitating Organizations

Findings

The committee finds that many independent private organizations that already exist or that might well develop can assist beneficiaries with making informed choices among the options available through the Medicare program. These facilitating or mediating organizations offer services ranging from providing objective additional information on plans and choices beyond what the Center offers, to evaluating plans by additional objective criteria, to prescreening and selecting plans that the organization's customers or members might choose, to bargaining for better value from the plans. In fact, many employers are offering such services to their Medicare-eligible retirees, making Medicare HMOs or Medigap policies, or both, available to them during their annual open seasons.

These Choice Facilitating Organizations do raise some concerns. Insurance brokers or other parties with financial interests may misuse these opportunities to market products rather than provide objective advice. Also, even well-functioning organizations could divert feedback on the services offered by a plan from the Center and its regional agents and dilute the effectiveness of the Center's national reporting. The committee leans toward limiting the establishment of these organizations to groups that do not have a vested financial interest in the choices that consumers make or, at a minimum, requiring such organizations to adequately disclose their sources of funding and potential biases that might result from these financial interests.

Subrecommendations

The committee recommends that nothing in law or regulation should inhibit the development of private organizations whose major purpose is to facilitate choice for Medicare beneficiaries, including groups that offer preselected panels of health plans. Although the committee believes that such organizations should be limited to groups that do not have a vested financial interest in the choices that are made, at a minimum, these organizations should be required to fully disclose their sources of funding and potential biases that might result from these financial arrangements. One committee member raised some additional concerns about these organizations which are outlined in Appendix A.

To help make the Choice Facilitating Organizations as useful to beneficiaries as possible, the federal government should require health plans and the traditional Medicare program to make available appropriate information to such organizations that have a legitimate interest in that information, such as the data behind quality or accreditation scores.

The committee advocates that public and private entities experiment with such organizations, including providing funding from the Informed Choice Fund (see below) to those that meet the criteria of independence and objectivity to augment the work of the Medicare Customer Service and Enrollment Center. Choice Facilitating Organizations may be particularly useful during the early phase of Medicare choice development.

The Informed Choice Fund

Findings

The provision of information on *Medicare choices* to Medicare consumers is in its infancy stage. Most of the information about quality and performance that has been developed and collected has been for large purchasers, plan administrators, or clinicians, not as part of an effort to educate and inform individual consumers.

Subrecommendations

The committee recommends that an *Informed Choice Fund* be developed for use by the federal government for the purpose of strengthening the infrastructure used to inform Medicare beneficiaries of their health plan choices. The Informed Choice Fund would be used to fund the operations of the Medicare Customer Service and Enrollment Center. Demonstration grants to Choice Facilitating Organizations could be made from this Fund, as desired by the federal government, after the operations of the Medicare Customer Service and Enrollment Center are funded.

The Informed Choice Fund would derive its income from a predictable revenue source, such as a fixed amount from each Medicare beneficiary or a flat amount or a percentage of the monthly Medicare premiums.

RECOMMENDATION 4

The federal government should require all *Medicare choices* to be marketed during the same open season to promote comparability and to enable beneficiaries to adequately assess and compare the benefits and prices of the various options.

Coordination of Traditional Medicare, Medigap Insurance and Health Plans: *Medicare Choices*

Findings

Comparing the prices and benefits of the various *Medicare choices* is difficult at present because they are not marketed at the same time or under the same ground rules. For example, the beneficiary may not see the high cost (frequently $1,000 or more) of the traditional Medicare program with Medigap insurance relative to the cost of a managed care plan. In addition, beneficiaries who leave Medicare and their Medigap policy for a managed care plan may find that they cannot repurchase their Medigap policy because of a preexisting condition.

The committee finds that the division of responsibility for enforcing the rules of participation in and compliance with these programs between state and federal government complicates the process of informed choice, grievance and complaint resolution, and plan accountability and fragments the offering of health plans across state lines.

Subrecommendations

It is within this context that the committee recommends that the selection of *Medicare choices* be coordinated. All three types of plans should be offered during open enrollment periods and under the same conditions of participation (see page 104).[5]

The federal government should work with state governments to coordinate the federal requirements surrounding *Medicare choices* with existing state regulations for Medigap insurance and private insurance. The U.S. Congress should consider what policy-making and enforcement activities are most appropriately and effectively conducted by the federal government and which can be delegated to state governments to ensure consistency and economy.

Standardized Packaging, Pricing, and Marketing of Benefits

Findings

Through the course of its deliberations, the committee found that although standardized benefits might simplify the choice process for elderly individuals, standardization is likely to dampen innovation and responsiveness to a broader range of consumer desires and preferences. However, the committee also appreciates the advantage for the beneficiary of the current standard benefit categories under Medigap insurance, which facilitate comparisons of the benefits and costs of different benefit options and comparisons of different insurers providing the same option. The committee acknowledges that many employers and private organizations have developed formats that allow the benefits of competing health plans to be clearly displayed and compared. It would be relatively simple for Medicare to do the same.

Terminology relating to the benefits offered by health plans varies greatly and makes it difficult to make clear comparisons

---

[5]The Physician Payment Review Commission's 1996 Annual Report to Congress provides a worthwhile discussion of the pros and cons of annual versus continuous open enrollment seasons.

among health plans. More research is needed on the types of information that beneficiaries want and need to exercise informed choice and how best to present that information.

Subrecommendations

The committee wants to preserve the general approach taken by the law governing Medigap insurance without restricting choice to the same extent. It believes that health plans should be moved toward standardized packaging, pricing, and marketing of selected benefit packages to allow beneficiaries to more easily compare the benefits offered by different plans. The committee recommends all plans be required to offer and price a basic benefit package (current Medicare Part A and Part B services) and have the option of offering and pricing two other popular benefit packages defined by the federal government and included in basic comparisons promulgated by the federal government. These popular benefit packages should include added benefits shown by market sales and surveys to be of special interest to the elderly (services such as pharmacy, eye care, and foot care) and ones that are popular given the cost. Health plans would be free to offer and price benefit packages other than these two that add to the basic benefit, but these other packages must be clearly identified as nonstandard, must offer substantial differences from the basic benefit package, and would not be included in the Medicare Customer Service and Enrollment Center's standard published comparisons. The federal government should commission the Medicare Customer Service and Enrollment Center to develop and use formats that allow beneficiaries to make easy and clear comparisons of benefits and other information on *Medicare choices*, drawing on the best practices used by employers and private and public organizations. The federal government should also suggest questions that Medicare beneficiaries should ask about nonstandard packages.

To make this process even easier, the federal government should promulgate common terminology related to benefits. All *Medicare choices* should use this terminology to describe the benefits of each of their offerings.

The federal government should coordinate its activities with those of state governments to ensure consistency between these benefit packages and those of Medigap insurance.

RECOMMENDATION 5

The committee is concerned about the increasing restrictions on physicians (and the potential conflict of interest of physicians) when they act in their professional role as advocates for their patients and carry out their contractual responsibilities and receive economic incentives as health plan providers. The committee favors the abolition of payment incentives or other practices that may motivate providers to evade their ethical responsibility to provide complete information to their patients about their illness, treatment options, and plan coverages. So-called anticriticism clauses or gag rules should be prohibited as a condition of plan participation.

Physicians and Professionalism

Findings

The committee recognizes that physicians' advice to beneficiaries is a quintessential part of ensuring informed choice. Because of the inherently personal nature of the physician-patient relationship and its special importance to elderly patients, the committee is concerned about the increasing restrictions on physicians (and the potential conflict of interest of physicians) when they act in their professional role as advocates for their patients and carry out their contractual responsibilities and receive economic incentives as health plan providers. The committee is particularly concerned about reported contractual restrictions (such as anticriticism clauses) on physicians acting in their professional role as a source of advice to their patients. Physicians must maintain their freedom to talk to their patients with full honesty about the clinical aspects of their care and treatment options.

Subrecommendations

The committee recommends that neither the *Medicare choices'* payment incentives nor their coverage and treatment protocol policies motivate providers to evade their ethical responsibility to provide patients with complete information about their illness and treatment options (such as referrals to a specialist), what to the best of the provider's knowledge the patient's plan covers, and which health plans in the provider's experience provide the broadest range of services to the patient in question.

Competition among *Medicare choices* is likely to restrict the definitions of *inappropriate services* by refining the definitions of *medical necessity* and *appropriate services* to contain costs and ensure quality. The committee finds that it is important for beneficiaries to have access to the unbiased judgments of their practicing physicians regarding their health needs in the context of plan procedures and protocols so that they, as patients, can make informed choices and thereby shape this new understanding of "appropriate."

Within the scope of its responsibilities, the federal government should identify practices that inhibit open communication between a provider and a patient in any setting and either prohibit them as conditions of participation of plans or require the plan to disclose such practices to potential enrollees. The committee recommends that the federal government require plans to disclose to plan enrollees how physicians get paid, whether they are rewarded for withholding referrals, and any other restrictions affecting how physicians can inform or treat plan enrollees. Similarly, educational materials should make clear the incentives in traditional Medicare and Medigap insurance to provide unnecessary care and the risks of these incentives.

RECOMMENDATION 6

The federal government should hold *Medicare choices* accountable by requiring them to meet comparable conditions of participation as a Medicare option and by monitoring and reporting on their compliance with these conditions.

Conditions of Participation for *Medicare Choices*

Findings

Some private and public employers have administered choice programs for many years and have developed and are continuing to improve the conditions of participation of health plans for ensuring that beneficiaries can make informed choices and for ensuring accountability on the part of the health plans. The very nature of accountability for Medicare health plans suggests that minimum standards should be established for health plans in areas where beneficiaries cannot reasonably be expected to make informed choices or where they might be easily confused or misled. This process of informed choice should be facilitated so that plans compete to exceed those minimum standards.

The committee finds that managed care plans not only pay for the services of providers but that they also use contractual arrangements to establish incentives for and place controls on providers' services. Thus, a beneficiary's choice of health plan can affect not only whether services are covered but also how they are provided. To further the responsiveness of plan management and providers to the special needs and demands of Medicare beneficiaries, the committee suggests that plans actively and meaningfully include beneficiaries in their governance and board activities and otherwise integrate the consumer voice into the plan's management and decision-making structure.

This said, the committee acknowledges that performance and disclosure requirements cannot compensate for limits on monetary resources for coverage. No amount or type of oversight and regulation can offset the intrinsic limitations on quality and access that necessarily follow from low levels of funding by the political process or the inability or unwillingness of beneficiaries to pay additional fees for health services.

Subrecommendations

The committee recommends that the federal government be given the flexibility to adjust the conditions of participation to take into account the evolution of higher standards and new systems and structures for ensuring informed choice and public accountability of *Medicare choices*. (See Box 3-2.)

Quality Assurance and Outcomes

Findings

The availability of *Medicare choices* introduces a potential for competition among plans on the basis of improvements in quality of care. To capitalize on this potential, the quality of service provided by health plans must be measurable and must be communicated to beneficiaries in a way that is relevant to them so that quality can be taken into account and so that a beneficiary can make an informed choice. Choice in health care, as in any environment, also introduces incentives to restrict the provision of or payment for services to remain competitive. This can produce effective and needed economies by reducing inappropriate or noncovered services. It may also, however, reduce the amount of appropriate care provided. Quality measures, monitoring, and meaningful ways of disclosing and communicating findings are needed so that the federal government and beneficiaries can hold plans accountable for reaching an appropriate balance between restricting inappropriate care and providing appropriate care.

The committee finds that quality measurement and communication are still in the early stages of development, especially quality measurements based on outcomes. Important initial efforts are under way by private credentialing agencies, such as NCQA's HEDIS, JCAHO, the Foundation for Accountability, and others, to develop reporting systems and measures of health plan quality. These efforts, however, reduce but do not eliminate the risk of poor quality.

Subrecommendations

To best ensure quality, all *Medicare choices* should be subjected to comparable state-of-the-art standards and monitoring for quality. The federal government should use the best of the currently available technology to set standards and monitor the

BOX 3-2
Conditions of Participation

The committee recommends that all *Medicare choices* meet the following minimum standards:

• participate in the annual open season and sell policies to Medicare beneficiaries during that open season or on certain other occasions, such as when a beneficiary first becomes eligible;

• offer open enrollment, guaranteed renewal, and no clauses precluding enrollment because of a preexisting condition for newly eligible beneficiaries and for beneficiaries changing plans;

• offer Part A and B benefits (except for Medigap policies) and meet other Medicare benefits requirements;

• provide information specified by the federal government to ensure informed choice by beneficiaries;

• meet quality certification requirements comparable to those already in use and in development by recognized national private accrediting entities and require appropriate progress and improvement against such standards over time;

• have resources, including appropriate mixes of specialists and referral resources, to provide benefits throughout service areas to a reasonable degree defined by the federal government so as not to divide metropolitan areas or counties except when natural barriers or other conditions divide service areas;

• provide a user-friendly, well-communicated, and responsive appeals and grievance process and allow retroactive disenrollment of beneficiaries who are determined by a fair and appropriate process to have misunderstood the implications of their choice and who have suffered serious financial or other consequences;

• meet fair marketing standards;

• meet specified fiscal solvency and financial disclosure requirements, allow compliance audits of financial and quality assurance operations, agree to use federal government-promulgated terms for describing coverages, and agree to accept enrollees without prejudice in all circumstances and particularly when the beneficiary has been enrolled in a plan that has gone out of business or become insolvent within the prior 60 days;

• not discourage providers from advising patients regarding their treatment options and plan coverages;

• provide such data to the federal government as required for it to test the plan's performance and compliance; and

• provide such information as it may require to the Medicare Customer Service and Enrollment Center.

quality of health plans. When the standards and processes of private credentialing agencies meet or exceed those of the federal government, private organizations should be used to reduce duplication in the market. The federal government might well foster competition and innovation among private credentialing agencies for different aspects of this function.

Communication with beneficiaries about the quality of a health plan and traditional Medicare plans should be done by the Medicare Customer Service and Enrollment Center by using the latest information available from credentialing processes and the latest techniques for communicating plan performance. In this vein the federal government should give priority to research and demonstrations on communicating quality performance information to beneficiaries.

The committee recommends the development of common definitions for reporting quality for use by individual plans and for auditing plans against their own published reports to the federal government.

Managed Care and Underserved Populations

Findings

The committee is concerned about ensuring access to health plans and their services for all beneficiaries, including those in vulnerable populations and underserved areas. Although the average Medicare beneficiary has been shown to have good access to care, certain groups who have been identified as vulnerable in traditional Medicare may be at risk for access problems in Medicare managed care. These groups have been identified by PPRC to include African-American beneficiaries and those who live in Health Professional Shortage Areas or urban and rural poverty areas. Evidence indicates that managed care arrangements have been slow to include underserved populations, especially those in rural areas (Institute of Medicine, 1996).

At the workshop and through the commissioned papers the committee was made aware of the special value that elderly individuals place on having easy access to their physicians, and the importance that they place on being treated by their providers in a respectful and a socially and culturally sensitive way.

The committee heard again and again that elderly individuals place key importance on their ability to have access to "their" traditional providers with whom they have developed a personal relationship.

The importance of considering the effect of personal and cultural factors on access is heightened by the changing demographics of the U.S. population. The committee heard that certain Medicare beneficiaries (particularly low-income and minority groups) may be at significantly higher risk of not being able to continue to be seen by their traditional network of providers in an environment of managed care. Because of the lower socioeconomic status of many individuals who are members of minority groups, a managed care plan may be the only delivery option that is affordable.

As managed care plans continue to develop they will have an increased responsibility to improve access for underserved populations. The committee believes that health plans should be held responsible for serving their entire service area without compromising access or quality of care. The committee found that some providers who have served their communities for many years or who are part of essential community provider networks, have not obtained the credentials required by some managed care organizations either because of institutional racism or common practice within their specialty to forego board certification. It is important that health plans develop several measures of clinical competence that are sensitive, valid, and reliable in their ability to assess clinical competence through both outcome and process indicators. The committee heard testimony that managed care plans often do not disclose their credentialing standards and policies. At the very least, such disclosure should be required. The committee lauds the efforts under way in HCFA, PPRC, a number of health foundations and other groups to track and address key issues that could arise in monitoring access to care under a restructured Medicare program.

Subrecommendations

Broad access for Medicare beneficiaries is key. The committee recommends that the federal government ensure that there is adequate access and choice of plans for individuals in all socioeconomic, cultural, and language groups and for under-served areas and populations. Elderly beneficiaries particularly value care that is respectful, personalized, and culturally sensitive. When warranted and documented (i.e., when access is demonstrably inadequate), the federal government should require the plans in an area to improve their contracting with community-based providers who meet quality-of-care standards as a condition of participation.

RECOMMENDATION 7

Serious consideration should be given and a study should be commissioned for establishing a new function along the lines of a Medicare Market Board, Commission, or Council to administer the *Medicare choices* process and hold all *Medicare choices* accountable. The proposed entity would include an advisory committee composed of key stakeholders, including purchasers, providers, and consumers.

Medicare Market Board and HCFA

Findings

Bearing in mind the recommendations that the committee has made regarding ensuring public accountability and informed purchasing for beneficiaries in an environment of choice, the committee had a number of concerns as it relates to the choice management capabilities of HCFA, as it is currently structured, to effectively manage *Medicare choices*. The committee spent considerable time discussing the challenges and complexities of effectively managing two very different and potentially competing programs. For example:

• The administration of the multiple choice program and the management of the traditional Medicare programs involve very different missions and orientations.
• The two functions require different types of management, staff expertise, backgrounds, and knowledge. The committee is concerned that staff and senior managers with extensive experience in managing various aspects of multiple choice in the private sector be recruited and employed for this effort.

• The functions call for different organizational and corporate cultures, one operating a stable traditional public indemnity insurance program and the other a purchaser- and customer-oriented program that is required to be responsive to a diverse group of private programs in a rapidly changing and dynamic marketplace.

• A faster response to changing market conditions and opportunities is required for the effective management of competing plans to provide the best options for beneficiaries. Such responsiveness may be hard to achieve with the regulatory constraints of HCFA.

• The committee believes that these strengthened and new responsibilities for managing the choice of plans must be supported by adequate organizational, financial, and staffing resources, which are needed to effectively and efficiently accomplish the mission described here.

Subrecommendations

The committee believes that these growing choice management functions would benefit from an organizational identity with the stature to facilitate recruitment of the needed leadership and staff and to build public trust. For that reason the committee recommends that serious consideration be given to establishing a new function along the lines of a Medicare Market Board, Commission, or Council that would include an advisory committee with key stakeholders (i.e., purchasers, providers, and consumers).

The committee was not able to research adequately the question of where this function should be located in government. The committee is aware of current initiatives to simplify and streamline government regulations as well as the efforts being made by HCFA to address some of the committee's concerns. The committee's discussions included the option of incorporating the new Medicare Market Board entity within HCFA, but with dedicated management and resources; establishing a Federal Reserve Board type of agency that has greater flexibility in rule making; establishing a PPRC- or ProPAC-type entity reporting to the Congress; as well as other possibilities.

With that in mind and given the potential impact of the

proposed new entity on the health care economy and the well-being of 37 million beneficiaries, the committee recommends that the U.S. Congress commission a study on what functions should be included in any new entity and what functions should stay with the present organizational structure, the roles and experience of federal agencies with a comparable mix of functions, the rationale for their structure, their organizational placement (including their relationship to the U.S. Congress and the executive branch) to better assess the advantages and potential shortcomings of moving in this direction.

In recommending the consideration of a new function such as a Medicare Market Board, the committee was cognizant of the fact that even a new entity will be limited or circumscribed by the realities of the political and fiscal environments in which it must operate and be accountable.

The committee envisions any proposed entity to have general responsibilities in the following areas:

- *Data collection, data publication, consumer education, and support*
—Contract with a Customer Service and Enrollment Center for these functions and augment the Center's services by using Choice Facilitating Organizations.
- *Health plan standards*
—Consult experts and conduct research and demonstrations to refine the conditions of participation by health plans on an ongoing basis to reflect the service and quality that the government expects for Medicare beneficiaries, regardless of the plan that they choose. The conditions would be set on a national basis and would be measurable and subject to an annual evaluation of compliance. To the greatest extent possible they would be consistent with standards used by the private sector to minimize duplication.
—Invoke specific sanctions in the event that the standards of a plan fall below the set standards.
- *Benefits, quality, and fair payment to health plans*
—Continually review clinical developments and services pertaining to what constitutes quality or appropriate care and refine the definitions of benefits under Medicare Part A and Part B.

—Review developments in the health insurance marketplace and refine the standard benefit description, pricing, and marketing requirements.

—Review risk selection in the traditional Medicare program and health plans and develop procedures or recommendations to the U.S. Congress for controlling or adjusting for adverse and favorable selection.

- *Evaluation and improvement of multiple choice in Medicare*

—Review the workings of the multiple choice market for Medicare beneficiaries and report to the U.S. Congress on the extent to which beneficiaries are able to make informed choices, the extent to which government and beneficiaries are succeeding in holding plans accountable for ensuring quality of care and containing costs, and ways to improve the system's performance.

—Review traditional Medicare and health plan costs and performance to determine whether the amount and form of the federal government's contribution to costs (e.g., premium payment) yields the government and its beneficiaries both containment of costs and assurance of quality.

—Report and recommend changes to the U.S. Congress to better hold plans accountable to these ends.

In conducting each of its responsibilities, it would adhere to rigorous conflict-of-interest standards.

References

Aaron, H. A., and R. D. Reischauer. 1995. The Medicare reform debate: What is the next step? Health Affairs 14(4):8–30.

Adler, G. S. 1995. Medicare beneficiaries rate their medical care: New data from the MCBS. Health Care Financing Rev. 16(4):175–187.

Board of Trustees, Federal Hospital Insurance Trust Fund. 1995. 1995 Annual Report of the Board of Trustees of the Federal Hospital Insurance Fund. Washington, D.C.

Board of Trustees, Federal Hospital Insurance Trust Fund. 1996. 1996 Annual Report of the Board of Trustees of the Federal Hospital Insurance Fund. Washington, D.C.

Brown, R. S., J. Bergeron, D. G. Clement, T. W. Hill, and S. Retchin. 1993a. The Medicare risk program for HMOs: Final summary report on findings from the evaluation. Princeton, N.J.: Mathematica Policy Research.

Brown, R. S., D. G. Clement, J. W. Hill, S. M. Retchin, and J. W. Bergeron. 1993b. Do health maintenance organizations work for Medicare? Health Care Financing Rev. 15(1):7–23.

Bureau of the Census, U.S. Department of Commerce. 1995. 1995 Statistical Abstract. Washington, D.C.: Government Printing Office.

Butler, S. M., and R. E. Moffitt. 1995. The FEHBP as a model for a new Medicare program. Health Affairs 14(4):47–61.

Clement, D. G., S. M. Retchin, R. S. Brown, and M. H. Stegall. 1994. Access and outcomes of elderly patients enrolled in managed care. JAMA 271:1487–1492.

Congressional Budget Office. 1995a. The Economic and Budget Outlook: Update. Washington, D.C.: Government Printing Office.

Congressional Budget Office. 1995b. The Effects of Managed Care and Managed Competition. Memorandum. Washington, D.C.

Congressional Budget Office. 1995c. Medicare Baseline, March 1995. Washington, D.C.: Government Printing Office.

Congressional Research Service. 1989. Federal Employees Health Benefits Program. Washington, D.C.: Congressional Research Service, Library of Congress.

Cronin, C. 1996. Reaching and Educating Beneficiaries about Choice. A paper prepared for the Institute of Medicine Committee on Choice and Managed Care: Assuring Public Accountability and Information for Informed Purchasing by and on Behalf of Medicare Beneficiaries.

Cunningham, R., ed. 1996. HCFA retooling to keep pace with booming Medicare HMOs. Perspectives. Medicine and Health, March 25, 1996. Washington, D.C.: Faulkner & Gray.

Davidson, B. N. 1988. Designing health insurance information for the Medicare beneficiary: A policy synthesis. Health Services Res. 23(5):685–720.

Donaldson, M., K. Yordy, and N. Vanselow, eds. 1994. Defining Primary Care: An Interim Report. Washington, D.C.: National Academy Press.

Edgman-Levitan, S., and P. D. Cleary. 1996. What Information Do Consumers Want and Need: What Do We Know About How They Judge Quality and Accountability? Paper prepared for the Institute of Medicine Committee on Choice and Managed Care: Assuring Public Accountability and Information for Informed Purchasing by and on Behalf of Medicare Beneficiaries.

Emanuel E. J., and L. L. Emanuel. 1996. What is accountability in health care? Ann. Internal Med. 124(2):229–239.

Enthoven, A. 1995. Medicare reform based on successful experience in the private sector. Washington, D.C. on July 24, 1995.

Etheredge, L. 1995. Reengineering Medicare: From Bill-Paying Insurer to Accountable Purchaser. Prepared for the Health Insurance Reform Project, George Washington University. Washington, D.C.

Fortune. 1995. The Fortune 500 largest U.S. corporations. Fortune, May 15:F-1.

Foster Higgins. 1996. The Foster Higgins Health Care Benefits Survey: Tenth annual edition. New York: Foster Higgins.

Frederick/Schneiders, Inc. 1995. Analysis of Focus Groups Concerning Managed Care and Medicare. Prepared for the Henry J. Kaiser Family Foundation. Washington, D.C.

Health Care Financing Administration, U.S. Department of Health and Human Services. 1995. Design Overview and Participation Guidelines: Medicare Choices Demonstration. Washington, D.C.

Health Policy Alternatives, Inc. 1996. Overview of Medicare Provisions: A Side-by-Side Comparison of Medicare Provisions of the House, Senate, and Conference Agreements and the Clinton Administration's Balanced Budget Proposal. Prepared for the Henry J. Kaiser Family Foundation. Washington, D.C.

Iglehart, J. 1992. The American health care system. Medicare. N. Engl. J. Med. 327:1467–1472.

Institute of Medicine. 1996. Primary Care: America's Health in a New Era, Donaldson, M. S., K. D. Yordy, K. N. Lohr, and N. A. Vanselow, eds. Washington, D.C.: National Academy Press

Interstudy. 1995. The Competition Edge Industry Report, 5.2. Interstudy Publications.

Jost, T. S. 1994. Health system reform: Forward or backward with quality oversight? JAMA 271(19):1508–1511.

Kaiser Family Foundation, H. J. 1995. Medicare Program, June. Washington, D.C.

Kaiser Family Foundation, H. J., and Institute for Health Care Research and Policy, Georgetown University. 1995. Medicare Chart Book. Washington, D.C.

Keith, S. N., R. M. Bell, A. G. Swanson, and A. P. Williams. 1985. Effects of affirmative action in medical schools: A study of the class of 1975. N. Engl. J. Med. 313:1519–1525.

KPMG Peat Marwick. 1995. Health Benefits in 1995. KPMG Peat Marwick.

Kramer, A. M., P. D. Fox, and N. Morgenstern. 1992. Geriatric care approaches in health maintenance organizations. J. Amer. Geriatrics Society 40(10):1055–1067.

Mastry, O. 1995. Medicare and Managed Care. Presentation to the National Health Policy Forum site visit to St. Paul, Minnesota, November 15, 1995.

McCall, N., T. Rice, and J. Sangl. 1986. Consumer knowledge of Medicare and supplemental health insurance benefits. Health Services Res. 20:633–657.

Mechanic, D. 1989. Consumer choice among health insurance options. Health Affairs 8(1):18–48.

Mellman, Lazarus & Lake. 1994. Medicare: Holes in the Safety Net, An Analysis and Report of Focus Group Findings. Prepared for the Kaiser Family Foundation. Washington, D.C.: Mellman, Lazaus & Lake.

Miller, R. H., and H. S. Luft. 1994. Managed care plan performance since 1980: A literature analysis. JAMA 271:1512–1519.

Moon, M., and J. Mulvey. 1996. Entitlements and the Elderly: Protecting Promises, Recognizing Realities. Washington, D.C.: The Urban Institute Press.

National Academy on Aging. 1995. Facts on the Older Americans Act. Washington, D.C.: National Academy on Aging.

Network Design Group. 1995. Special report of HMO/CMP Reconsideration Results. Prepared for the Health Care Financing Administration, U.S. Department of Health and Human Services, Baltimore, Md.

Neumann, P. J., M. D. Bernardin, W. N. Evans, and E. J. Bayer. 1995. Participation in the qualified Medicare beneficiary program. Health Care Financing Rev. 17(2):169–178.

Office of the Inspector General. 1995a. Medicare: Beneficiary Satisfaction. No. OEI-06-91-0073. U.S. Department of Health and Human Services: Washington, D.C.

Office of the Inspector General. 1995b. Beneficiary Perspectives of Medicare Risk HMOs. No. OEI-06-91-00731. U.S. Department of Health and Human Services: Washington, D.C.

Office of Managed Care, Health Care Financing Administration, U.S. Department of Health and Human Services. 1996. Medicare and prepaid enrollment distribution by state. Washington, D.C.

Pemberton, J. H. 1990. The elderly consumer: A critical review of information source use and advertising recommendations. Health Services Management Res. 3(2):127–136.

Physician Payment Review Commission. 1995. Annual Report to Congress. Washington, D.C.: PPRC.

Physician Payment Review Commission. 1996. Annual Report to Congress. Washington, D.C.: PPRC.

Price Waterhouse LLP. 1996. Is there biased selection in HMOs? Prepared for the American Association of Health Plans. Washington, D.C.

Prospective Payment Assessment Commission. 1995. Medicare and the American Health Care System. Report to the Congress, June 1995. Washington, D.C.: ProPAC.

— —. 1983. The Random House Dictionary of the English Language, second edition. Unabridged. New York: Random House.

Research Triangle Institute. 1995. Information Needs for Consumer Choice: Final Focus Group Report. Research Triangle Park, N.C.: Research Triangle Institute.

Rice, T. 1987. Economic assessment of health care for the elderly. Milbank Memorial Fund Quarterly 65:488–520.

The Robert Wood Johnson Foundation. 1995. Sick people in managed care have difficulty getting services and treatment, new survey reports, June 28, 1995. Robert Wood Johnson Foundation: Princeton, N.J.

Rodwin, M. A. 1996. Consumer protection and managed care: Issues, reform proposals and trade-offs. Houston Law Review 32:1319–1381.

Rossiter, L.F., K. Langwell, T. T. H. Wan, and M. Rivnyak. 1989. Patient satisfaction among elderly enrollees and disenrollees in Medicare health maintenance organizations. JAMA 262:57-63.

Shaughnessy, P. W., R. E. Schlenker, and D. F. Hittle. 1994. Home health care outcomes under capitated and fee-for-service payment. Health Care Financing Rev. 16:187–222.

Sofaer, S. 1993. Informing and protecting consumers under managed competition. Health Affairs 12(Suppl.):76–86.

U.S. General Accounting Office. 1995a. Medicare: Adapting Private Sector Techniques Could Curb Losses to Fraud and Abuse. Testimony before the Subcommittee on Oversight and Investigations and the Subcommittee on Health and Environment, Committee on Commerce, U.S. House of Representatives. GAO/T-HEHS-95-211. Washington, D.C.

U.S. General Accounting Office. 1995b. Medicare: Increased HMO Oversight Could Improve Quality and Access to Care. Report to the Special Committee on Aging, U.S. Senate. GAO/HEHS-95-155. Washington, D.C.

U.S. General Accounting Office. 1995c. Medicare: Modern Management Strategies Needed to Curb Program Exploitation. Testimony before the Subcommittee on Human Resources and Intergovernmental Relations, Committee on Government Reform and Oversight, U.S. House of Representatives. GAO/T-HEHS-95-183. Washington, D.C.

U.S. General Accounting Office. 1995d. Medicare: Rapid Spending Growth Calls for More Prudent Purchasing. Testimony before the Subcommittee on Health and Environment, Committee on Commerce, House of Representatives. GAO/T-HEHS-95-193. Washington, D.C.

U.S. General Accounting Office. 1995e. Medicare Managed Care: Enrollment Growth Underscores Need to Revamp HMO Payment Methods. Testimony before the Subcommittee on Health and Environment, Committee on Commerce, U.S. House of Representatives. GAO/T-HEHS-95-207. Washington, D.C.

U.S. General Accounting Office. 1995f. Medicare Managed Care: Growing Enrollment Adds Urgency to Fixing HMO Payment Problem. Report to the Chairman, Subcommittee on Health, Committee on Ways and Means, House of Representatives. GAO/HEHS-96-21. Washington, D.C.

U.S. General Accounting Office. 1996. Medicare HMOs: Rapid Enrollment Growth Concentrated in Selected States. Report to the Honorable John F. Kerry, U.S. Senate. GAO/HEHS-96-63. Washington, D.C.

U.S. Senate Special Committee on Aging. 1995. Federal oversight of Medicare HMOs: assuring beneficiary protection. Hearing Before the Special Committee on Aging, U.S. Senate, Serial No. 104–6, Washington, D.C., August 4, 1995.

U.S. Senate Special Committee on Aging, American Association of Retired Persons, Federal Council on the Aging, U.S. Administration on Aging. 1991. Aging in America: Trends and Projections. Washington, D.C.

Vladeck, B. C. 1995. Managed care and quality: From the Health Care Financing Administration. JAMA 273:1483.

Vladeck, B. C. 1996. Speech before the Group Health Association of America/American Managed Care and Review Association, Washington, D.C., February 26, 1996.

Washington Post. January 28–February 1, 1996. Reality check: The politics of mistrust, A five-part series. A1.

Williams, M. V., R. M. Parker, D. W. Baker, N. S. Parikh, K. Pitkin, W. C. Coates, and J. R. Nurss. 1995. Inadequate functional health literacy among patients at two public hospitals. JAMA 274(21):1677–1682.

References Consulted*

American Enterprise Institute for Public Policy Research. 1995. Medicare Reform: What Can the Private Sector Teach Us? Conference Report. Washington, D.C.: Health Policy Studies, American Enterprise Institute.

Armstead, R. C., P. Elstein, and J. Gorman. 1995. Toward a 21st century quality-measurement system for managed care organizations. Health Care Financing Rev. 16(4):25–37.

Christensen, S. 1995. Managed Care and the Medicare Program. Memorandum to Health Staff. Washington, D.C.: Congressional Budget Office.

Congressional Budget Office. 1995. Cost Estimate for H.R. 2485, the Medicare Preservation Act of 1995, as introduced on October 17, 1995. Washington, D.C.

Dallek, G., C. Jimenez, and M. Schwartz. 1995. Consumer Protections in State HMO Laws, Volume I: Analysis and Recommendations. Los Angeles, Calif.: Center for Health Care Rights.

Davidson, B. N., S. Sofaer, and P. Gertler. 1992. Consumer information and biased selection in the demand for coverage supplementing Medicare. Soc. Sci. Med. 34(9):1023–1034.

Davis, K. 1995. Managing care in the public interest: Protecting access, quality and patients in a new era of managed care. Keynote address before the Eleventh annual Rosalynn Carter symposium on mental health policy, Atlanta, November 15, 1995.

---

*These references, although not directly cited in the body of the report, provided key background information.

Davis, M. H., and S. T. Burner. 1995. Data Watch. Three decades of Medicare: What the numbers tell us. Health Affairs 14(4):231–243.

Freudenheim, M. May 31, 1995. Medicare, jot this down: employers offer valuable lessons on saving money with managed care. The New York Times. D1, D4.

Friedman, M. A. 1995. Issues in measuring and improving health care quality. Health Care Financing Rev. 16(4):1–13.

Gagel, B. J. 1995. Health care quality improvement program: A new approach. Health Care Financing Rev. 16(4):15–23.

Gold, M. R., R. Hurley, T. Lake, T. Ensor, and R. Berenson. 1995. A national survey of the arrangements managed-care plans make with physicians. N. Engl. J. Med. 333(25):1678–1683.

Gottlieb, M. January 14, 1996. Picking a health plan: A shot in the dark, Who's best? It can be hard to tell. The New York Times.

Greenlick, M., P. Hanes, and D. Jones. 1995. Oregon Consumer Scorecard Project Information Review and Synthesis. Prepared for the Agency for Health Care Policy and Research, University of Washington, and the Oregon Consumer Scorecard Consortium Steering Committee. Portland, Ore.: Oregon Consumer Scorecard Consortium.

Group Health Association of America. 1995. Medicare at 30: An Opportunity for all Americans. Washington, D.C.: Group Health Association of America.

Health Economics Research, Inc. and Research Triangle Institute. 1994. Information, Counseling and Assistance Programs. Prepared for the Office of Beneficiary Services, Health Care Financing Administration, U.S. Department of Health and Human Services. Washington, D.C.

Health Systems Research, Inc. 1994. Consumer Survey Information in a Reformed Health Care System. Conference Materials, Vienna, Virginia, September 28–29, 1994.

Institute of Medicine. 1995. Real People Real Problems: An Evaluation of the Long-Term Care Ombudsman Programs of the Older Americans Act. Washington, D.C.: National Academy Press.

Jeffrey, N. A. November 30, 1995. HMOs say 'Hola' to potential customers. Wall Street Journal. B1, B3.

Kaiser Family Foundation, H. J. 1995. Medicare and Managed Care. Washington, D.C.

Kaiser Family Foundation, H. J. 1994. Seniors have mixed emotions about Medicare. Press Release, October 4, 1994. Menlo Park, Calif.

Kilborn, P. T. March 26, 1996. Tucson HMOs may offer model for Medicare's future. The New York Times. A1, B11.

Levinsky, N. G. 1996. Social, institutional, and economic barriers to the exercise of patients' rights. N. Engl. J. Med. 334(8):532–534.

Meyer, J. A., S. Silow-Carroll, and M. Regenstein. 1995. Managed Care and Medicare. Prepared for the American Association of Retired Persons. Washington, D.C.: New Directions for Policy.

Minnesota Health Data Institute. 1995. You and Your Health Plan: 1995 Statewide Survey of Minnesota Consumers. St. Paul, Minn.: Minnesota Health Data Institute.

National Committee for Quality Assurance. 1994. Consumer Information Project: Phase I Final Report. Washington, D.C.: NCQA.

National Committee for Quality Assurance. 1995. Consumer Information Project Focus Group Report. Washington, D.C.: NCQA.

National Health Policy Forum. 1995. Medicare Reform: Balancing Beneficiary Needs and Trust Fund Solvency. Issue Brief No. 677. Washington, D.C.: National Health Policy Forum.

National Health Policy Forum. 1996. Site Visit Report: November 1995, Minneapolis/St. Paul and New Ulm. Washington, D.C.: National Health Policy Forum.

Physician Payment Review Commission and Prospective Payment Assessment Commission. 1995. Joint Report to the Congress on Medicare Managed Care. Washington, D.C.: PPRC and ProPAC.

Prospective Payment Assessment Commission. 1996. Report and Recommendations to the Congress, March 1, 1996. Washington, D.C.: ProPAC.

Research Triangle Institute. 1995a. Design of a Survey to Monitor Consumers' Access to Care, Use of Health Services, Health Outcomes, and Patient Satisfaction: Final Report. Prepared for the Office of Program Development, Agency for Health Care Policy and Research, U.S. Department of Health and Human Services. Research Triangle Park, N.C.: Research Triangle Institute.

Research Triangle Institute. 1995b. Information Needs for Consumer Choice: Final Focus Group Report. Prepared for the Office of Research and Demonstrations, Health Care Financing Administration, U.S. Department of Health and Human Services. Research Triangle Park, N.C.: Research Triangle Institute.

Richardson, D. A., J. Phillips, and D. Conley Jr. 1993. A Study of Coverage Denial Disputes between Medicare Beneficiaries and HMOs. Prepared for the Health Care Financing Administration, U.S. Department of Health and Human Services. Washington, D.C.: Network Design Group, Inc.

Robinson, J. C., and L. P. Casalino. 1995. The growth of medical groups paid through capitation in California. N. Engl. J. Med. 333(25):1684–1687.

Saucier, P., and T. Riley. 1994. Managing Care for Older Beneficiaries of Medicaid and Medicare: Prospects and Pitfalls. Portland, Maine: Center for Health Policy Development/National Academy for State Health Policy.

Segal, D. January 19, 1996. HMOs: how much, not how well. The Washington Post. F1, F3.

State of Minnesota Department of Employee Relations. 1995. 1995 State of Minnesota Survey of Employees, Health Plans and Medical Care: What Employees Think. St. Paul, Minn.: Department of Employee Relations.

Tompkins, C. P., S. S. Wallack, J. A. Chilingerian, S. Bhalotra, M. P. V. Glavin, G. A. Ritter, and D. Hodgkin. 1995. Bringing Managed Care Incentives to Qualified Physician Organizations. Prepared for Office of Research and Demonstrations, Health Care Financing Administration, U.S. Department of Health and Human Services. Waltham, Mass.: Brandeis University.

U.S. Congress, House of Representatives. 1995. Medicare Preservation Act of 1995. Report of the Committee on Ways and Means, House of Representatives on H.R. 2425 together with Dissenting Views. 104th Cong., 1st sess., Rept. 104-276, part 1. Washington, D.C.

U.S. General Accounting Office. 1994a. Health Care Reform: Potential Difficulties in Determining Eligibility for Low-Income People. Report to the Chairman, Subcommittee on Regulation, Business Opportunities, and Technology, Committee on Small Business, House of Representatives. GAO/HEHS-94-176. Washington, D.C.

U.S. General Accounting Office. 1994b. Health Care Reform: "Report Cards" are Useful but Significant Issues Need to be Addressed. Report to the Chairman, Committee on Labor and Human Resources, U.S. Senate. GAO-HEHS-94-219. Washington, D.C.

U.S. General Accounting Office. 1995. Medicare: Reducing Fraud and Abuse Can Save Billions. Testimony before the Subcommittee on Oversight and Investigations and the Subcommittee on Health and Environment, Committee on Commerce, U.S. House of Representatives. GAO/T-HEHS-95-157. Washington, D.C.

U.S. General Accounting Office. 1996. Fraud and Abuse: Medicare Continues to be Vulnerable to Exploitation by Unscrupulous Providers. Testimony before the Special Committee on Aging, U.S. Senate. GAO/T-HEHS-96-7. Washington, D.C.

Vibbert, S., J. Reichard, and B. Rosenthal, eds. 1996. The 1996 Health Network and Alliance Sourcebook. New York: Faulkner & Gray.

Woolhandler, S., and D. U. Himmelstein. 1995. Extreme Risk: The New Corporate Proposition for Physicians. N. Engl. J. Med. 333 (25): 1706–1707.

Appendixes

A

Additional Commentary Regarding Choice Facilitating Organizations

One committee member raised some additional concerns about the committee's recommendations on Choice Facilitating Organizations and wanted the following comments to be included in this report.

I can see many advantages to organizations that will assist beneficiaries with making informed choices by evaluating, pre-screening, and selecting plans that the organization's members might choose.

However, I am concerned about a number of potential problems with these organizations. First these organizations could segment the Medicare market by including in their membership younger and healthier Medicare beneficiaries and steering those members to selected plans.

Second, no standards exist for these organizations. What are they and who will they represent? How will they be funded: by their membership? by the managed care plans (who will provide them an enrollment fee for all members signed up through the organization)? Without some standards for the types of entities that can become Choice Facilitating Organizations, we could see a new type of fraud perpetrated on Medicare beneficiaries.

Third, what standards will these organizations use to select plans. What is to stop a Choice Facilitating Organization from selecting the poorest quality plans because they provide the highest payment for enrollment of members?

Fourth, these plans may well add a new layer of marketing on top of the massive marketing of plans to Medicare beneficiaries occurring in a number of communities. Medicare beneficiaries may be tempted to join a Choice Facilitating Organization because of sophisticated marketing techniques, not because they have carefully selected plans.

For these reasons, I think extra caution is in order. Perhaps HCFA could establish a demonstration project to assess the effectiveness of Choice Facilitating Organizations. At a minimum, some standards should be established for these organizations.

B

Invitational Symposium Agenda

Thursday, February 1, 1996

8:30 a.m.–9:00 a.m. *Welcome and Summary of*
Committee Charge
Karen Hein
Executive Officer
Institute of Medicine
and
Stanley B. Jones, Committee Chair
Director
George Washington University
 Health Insurance Reform Project
Washington, D.C.

9:00 a.m.–10:15 a.m.
  Morning Moderator: Stanley B. Jones, Committee Chair
Director
George Washington University
 Health Insurance Reform Project
Washington, D.C.

	Developing a Structure for Consumer Choice: Looking at the Continuum of Options for Assuring Public Accountability
Paper Author:	Lynn Etheredge Private Consultant Washington, D.C.

10:15 a.m.–10:30 a.m.	*Break*

10:30 a.m.–12:00 p.m.	*The Content and Process of Informed Choice: Reviewing the State-of-the-Art from the Corporate Community and Other Purchasing Alliances*
Paper Author:	Elizabeth Hoy Director, Health Systems Management Issues Institute for Health Policy Solutions Washington, D.C.

Responding Perspectives:	Kathleen P. Burek Manager, Employee Insurance Division Minnesota Department of Employee Relations St. Paul, Minnesota
	Richard E. Curtis President Institute for Health Policy Solutions Washington, D.C.
	Barbara Decker Division Manager, Health Policy and Planning Edison International Rosemead, California

12:15 p.m.–1:30 p.m.   *Assuring Informed Choice and*
                        Public Accountability: A Report on
                        Activities at HCFA
                        Kathleen M. King
                        Special Assistant to the
                            Administrator
                        Health Care Financing
                            Administration
                        Washington, D.C.

1:45 p.m.–3:15 p.m.
    Afternoon Moderator: Shoshanna Sofaer
                            Associate Professor and
                            Associate Chair for Research
                            Department of Health Care Sciences
                            The George Washington University
                                Medical Center
                            Washington, D.C.

                            Who Is the Medicare Consumer:
                            One Size Does Not Fit All, Special
                            Issues for Vulnerable Populations
    Paper Author: Joyce Dubow
                            Senior Analyst
                            Public Policy Institute
                            American Association of Retired
                                Persons
                            Washington, D.C.

    Responding   L. Gregory Pawlson .
    Perspectives: Professor and Chair
                            Department of Health Care Sciences
                            The George Washington University
                            Washington, D.C.

                            Peter Fox
                            PDF, Incorporated
                            Chevy Chase, Maryland

3:15 p.m.–3:30 p.m.   *Break*

3:30 p.m.–5:15 p.m.   *What Information Do Consumers*
                          Want and Need?
Paper Author: Susan Edgman-Levitan
                         Executive Director
                         Picker Institute for Patient-Centered
                           Care
                         Boston, Massachusetts

                         Communicating Information
                         Effectively
Paper Author: Carol Cronin
                         Senior Vice President
                         Health Pages
                         Annapolis, Maryland

Responding   Diane Archer
Perspectives: Executive Director
                         Medicare Beneficiary Defense Fund
                         New York, New York

                         Priscilla Itscoitz
                         Manager, Health Insurance
                           Counseling Program
                         United Seniors Health Cooperative
                         Washington, D.C.

                         Marcia A. Laleman
                         Director, Medicare Programs
                         Keystone Health Plan East
                         Philadelphia, Pennsylvania

Friday, February 2, 1996

8:15 a.m.–9:30 a.m.	*Choice and Managed Care: Enrollee Satisfaction and Consumer Protections / The States' Role in Holding Plans Accountable*
Moderator:	Lynn Shapiro Snyder Partner Epstein Becker & Green, P.C. Washington, D.C.
Paper Author:	Patricia A. Butler Health Care Consultant Boulder, Colorado
Responding Perspectives:	Dixon F. Larkin Deputy Insurance Commissioner State of Utah Salt Lake City, Utah
	Robert Berenson Associate Clinical Professor of Medicine Georgetown University School of Medicine Washington, D.C.
	Garry Carneal Vice President American Association of Health Plans Washington, D.C.
9:30 a.m.–10:45 a.m.	*Assuring Public Accountability and Informed Purchasing: Case Studies of Medicare and CalPERS*
Moderator:	Stanley B. Jones Director George Washington University Health Insurance Reform Project Washington, D.C.

Paper Author: Judy Moore
                             Independent Health Care Consultant
                             (former Senior Advisor to the
                                 Administrator, HCFA)
                             McLean, Virginia

Paper Author: Tom J. Elkin
                             Independent Health Care Consultant
                             (former Director of Operations,
                                 CalPERS Health Benefits Program)
                             Sacramento, California

11:00 a.m.–12:00 p.m.   *A Review of Relevant Provisions in*
                             Current Legislative Proposals
                             David B. Kendall
                             Senior Analyst, Health Policy
                             Progressive Policy Institute
                             Washington, D.C.

C

Symposium Participants

RESPONDING PERSPECTIVES

Diane Archer, JD
Executive Director
Medicare Beneficiaries
  Defense Fund
New York, New York

Robert Berenson, MD, FACP
Associate Clinical Professor of
  Medicine
Georgetown University School
  of Medicine
Washington, D.C.

Kathleen P. Burek
Manager, Employee
  Insurance Division
Minnesota Department of
  Employee Relations
St. Paul, Minnesota

Garry Carneal, JD
Vice President
Group Health Association of
  America/AMCRA
*(now American Association of
  Health Plans)*
Washington, D.C.

Richard E. Curtis
President
Institute for Health Policy
  Solutions
Washington, D.C.

Barbara L. Decker
Manager, Health Policy and
  Planning
Southern California Edison
(now Edison International)
Rosemead, California

Peter D. Fox
PDF, Incorporated
Chevy Chase, Maryland

Priscilla S. Itscoitz, MA
Manager, Health Insurance
  Counseling Program
United Seniors Health
  Cooperative
USHC Development
  Corporation, Inc.
Washington, D.C.

David B. Kendall
Senior Analyst for Health
  Policy
Progressive Policy Institute
Washington, D.C.

Kathleen M. King
Special Assistant to the
  Administrator
Health Care Financing
  Administration
Washington, D.C.

Marcia A. Laleman, MSW
Director, Medicare Programs
Keystone Health Plan East
Philadelphia, Pennsylvania

Dixon F. Larkin, MD, JD
Deputy Insurance
  Commissioner
State of Utah
Salt Lake City, Utah

L. Gregory Pawlson, MD,
  MPH
Professor and Chair
Department of Health Care
  Sciences
George Washington
  University Medical Center
Washington, D.C.

Lynn Shapiro Snyder, JD
Partner
Epstein Becker & Green, P.C.
Washington, D.C.

Shoshanna Sofaer, DrPH
Associate Professor of Health
  Care Sciences
Division of Research
  Programs
George Washington
  University Medical Center
Washington, D.C.

RESOURCE EXPERTS

Sue Anderson
Health Insurance Counseling
  Program
George Washington
  University Law School
Washington, D.C.

William F. Benson
Deputy Assistant Secretary
Administration on Aging
Department of Health and
  Human Services
Washington, D.C.

Judy Berek
Senior Advisor to the
  Administrator
Health Care Financing
  Administration
Washington, D.C.

Peter Bouxsein
Acting Director
Office of Managed Care
Health Care Financing
  Administration
Baltimore, Maryland

Craig Caplan
National Academy of Social
  Insurance
Washington, D.C.

Nancy Chockley, MBA
Executive Director
National Institute for Health
  Care Management
Washington, D.C.

Sophia R. Christie
Research Fellow—The
  Harkness Fellowships
Health Policy Analysis
  Program
University of Washington
Seattle, Washington

Kenneth R. Cohen, MHSA,
  MPP
Investigator, Minority Staff
U.S. Senate Special
  Committee on Aging
Washington, D.C.

Barbara Cooper
Acting Director
Office of Research and
  Demonstration
Health Care Financing
  Administration
Baltimore, Maryland

Linda K. Demlo, PhD
Acting Director
Center for Quality
  Measurement and
  Improvement
Agency for Health Care Policy
  and Research
Rockville, Maryland

Kathleen M. Eyre, JD
Senior Director of Policy and
  Research
National Institute for Health
  Care Management
Washington, D.C.

Theresa M. Forster
Minority Staff Director
U.S. Senate Special
  Committee on Aging
Washington, D.C.

Beth C. Fuchs, PhD
Specialist, Social Legislation
Education and Public Welfare
  Division
Congressional Research
  Service
Washington, D.C.

Michael E. Gluck, PhD, MPP
Health Policy Associate
National Academy of Social
  Insurance
Washington, D.C.

Marsha Gold, ScD
Senior Fellow
Mathematica Policy Research
Washington, D.C.

Sarah C. Gotbaum, PhD
Director, Managed Care
  Project
United Seniors Health
  Cooperative
USHC Development
  Corporation, Inc.
Washington, D.C.

Leslie Greenwald
Office of Research and
  Demonstration
Health Care Financing
  Administration
Baltimore, Maryland

John F. Hoadley, PhD
Principal Policy Analyst
Physician Payment Review
  Commission
Washington, D.C.

Lucy Johns, MPH
Health Care Planning and
  Policy
San Francisco, California

Judith Miller Jones
Director
National Health Policy Forum
Washington, D.C.

Janet Kline
Acting Coordinator of
  Research
Education and Public Welfare
  Division
Congressional Research
  Service
Library of Congress
Washington, D.C.

Kala Ladenheim, MSPH
Senior Research Scientist
Intergovernmental Health
  Policy Project
George Washington
  University
Washington, D.C.

Debra J. Lipson
Associate Director
Alpha Center
Washington, D.C.

Kathleen E. Means
Majority Staff Member
Subcommittee on Health
Committee on Ways and
  Means
U.S. House of
  Representatives
Washington, D.C.

Celeste Newcomb, MS
Analyst
Office of Managed Care
Health Care Financing
  Administration
Baltimore, Maryland

Trish Newman
Program Officer
Henry J. Kaiser Family
  Foundation
Washington, D.C.

Susana Perry
AARP/Andrus Foundation
  Intern
National Council on the
  Aging
Washington, D.C.

Richard Price, MA
Health Policy Analyst
Congressional Research
  Service
Library of Congress
Washington, D.C.

Sandra K. Robinson
Coordinator
Consumer Initiative
Agency for Health Care Policy
  and Research
Rockville, Maryland

Marc A. Rodwin, JD, PhD
Associate Professor of Law
  and Public Policy
School of Public and
  Environmental Affairs
Indiana University
Bloomington, Indiana

William J. Scanlon, PhD
Director, Health Systems
U.S. General Accounting
  Office
Washington, D.C.

Anne Schwartz, PhD
Senior Analyst
Physician Payment Review
  Commission
Washington, D.C.

Mary Beth Semkewicz, JD
Legislative Counsel for
  Health Policy
National Association of
  Insurance Commissioners
Washington, D.C.

Cary Sennett, MD, PhD
Vice President
National Committee for
  Quality Assurance
Washington, D.C.

Ellen R. Shaffer
Bethesda, Maryland

Janet L. Shikles, MSW
Assistant Comptroller
  General
U.S. General Accounting
  Office
Washington, D.C.

Walter A. Zelman, PhD
Health Care Analyst
McLean, Virginia

D

Commissioned Papers

E

The Structure and Accountability for Medicare Health Plans: Government, the Market, and Professionalism

*Lynn Etheredge**

The U.S. Congress and President are now considering major reforms in the Medicare program that would, among other major provisions, rapidly expand the opportunities for 37 million aged and disabled Medicare enrollees to join private sector health plans. This legislation follows the rapid movement of most of the insured population under age 65 from traditional health insurance plans into managed care plans.

The reconciliation bill's health plan provisions reflect many agendas for Medicare's future. The most widely discussed goal is to limit future Medicare spending. More enrollment of Medicare beneficiaries in health plans—with preset capitation payments—would help to achieve that end. Another important aim is to develop competition for excellence among health plans to provide better medical care than the fee-for-service Medicare program. Federal budget restraints will automatically be achieved through legislative spending formulas. Improved health care for Medicare enrollees, however, is not guaranteed. It will depend on how effectively health plans are held accountable for excellence. If the accountability measures work well,

*Private consultant, Washington, D.C.

the Medicare program's future may see unprecedented advances in improving the lives of its elderly and disabled enrollees, as well as a sound financial future.

The reconciliation bill structures a market that will allow Medicare enrollees to choose to join (or leave) private health plans that provide Medicare benefits. The proposed design is similar to the Federal Employees Health Benefits Plan (FEHBP), the nation's largest health insurance purchasing arrangement, which now covers some 9 million government employees, their families, and retirees. In this model, health plans are held accountable to the federal government for meeting basic statutory conditions of participation and, via consumers' ability to switch plans, to enrollees for excellence in meeting their needs.

This paper is intended to provide a framework for the Institute of Medicine (IOM) committee to discuss the key accountability issues in structuring this new Medicare health plan market. It is organized into three sections:

- an overview of how governments structure markets, including the traditional fee-for-service health care market;
- a consideration of how the new Medicare model would differ from the traditional health care market in terms of who is accountable, what they are accountable for, and how they are held accountable; and
- a discussion of three strategies for how federal legislation might structure the respective influences of government, consumers, and professionalism differently to achieve excellent performance from Medicare health plans.

ACCOUNTABILITY IN CONTEXT

In the modern world, a vast amount of day-to-day activity is organized around "the market." Individuals purchase (rather than produce) most of the goods and services that they use; most individuals work for organizations that exchange their products for money. Although the concept of the market can be a useful abstraction, there are many individual markets that differ greatly by the actors involved, how they interact, their industry, government policy, cultural norms, and in other ways (Fukuyama, 1995; Hamilton, 1994; Swedberg, 1994).

A generic model for how government and consumers are related in most U.S. markets would include two basic features:

- *Government* structures the basic market framework, such as the entry requirements and rules of the game; provides for incorporation, licensure, and enforceable contracts; and prohibits fraud, misleading advertising, and anticompetitive practices.
- *Consumers* exercise broad freedom of choice in how to spend their own money, including choices that some might regard as unwise or foolish.

A totally "free" market with no government involvement, although sometimes romanticized as an ideal, can hardly be found. Nevertheless, rhetoricians can spin beguiling tales about the "hidden hand" of the market. There is an economist's joke which goes, Question: "How many free-market economists does it take to change a light bulb?" Answer: "None. If the light bulb needed to be changed, the market would already have changed it."

Examples of instances of more extensive government involvement include the following:

- establishing health and safety standards for products and services, for example, food quality, prescription drugs, automobile seat belts, public health inspections, building codes, and Federal Aviation Administration airline standards;
- regulatory oversight of the banking and insurance industry to ensure financial solvency;
- standardizing information disclosure, for example, requirements for audited corporate financial statements, food labelling, and credit card insurance rates;
- standards and inspections, particularly where public funds are involved, to ensure service quality for vulnerable populations, for example nursing home inspections; and
- licensure of professions and trades.

Many of these interventions involve, to some degree, the

issue of how best to deal with the practicalities of a world with imperfect knowledge and competence among consumers, a world where some choices are not good ones for some consumers, where suppliers pursue their own interests, and where advertising and marketing aim to persuade more than inform. Government market interventions often involve strategies such as (1) making sure that better consumer information is available and/or (2) acting, on behalf of consumers, to remove choices from the market. With such correctives, consumers can buy with greater confidence that they will get what they think they are buying.

The research evidence on how best to structure markets is more equivocal than the idealized perfect competition theory—with easy market entry and many suppliers—taught in undergraduate economics courses. A leading economics text on markets and industrial structure summarizes the field this way:

> Readers seeking a precise, certain guide to public policy are bound to be disappointed by this survey, for we have found none. The competitive norm does seem to serve as a good first approximation, but it is difficult to state in advance how much competition is needed to achieve desirable economic performance, nor can we formulate hard and fast rules for identifying cases in which a departure from competition is desirable (Scherer and Ross, 1990, p. 55).

The imperfections of a market do not, however, mean that government interventions will prove a desirable remedy. There is a long history of regulatory capture by private interests, especially to block new entrants and stifle change. When government limits options it may also reduce the welfare of consumers who would have chosen an excluded possibility. As well, the recent savings and loan scandals should be an apt reminder that even layers of regulatory oversight may not protect the public's interests.

U.S. health care financing has departed from a competitive market system by sharply reducing the role of consumer purchasing decisions that are the ultimate adjudicatory force in most markets. Reliance has been placed, instead, on *professionalism* (supported by open-ended insurance financing) as the primary determinant of performance. In the traditional health system, individual physician decisionmaking was estimated to control 70 to 80 percent of health care spending. Government helped to erode the market and ensure professional dominance through large tax subsidies for insurance coverage, profession-dominated licensure and accreditation, and (until recently) sparse funding for consumer-oriented effectiveness and outcomes studies.

When Medicare was enacted 30 years ago, it adopted this private health insurance model. Medicare has seldom been a market-oriented purchaser of care, nor has it made much effort to inform Medicare enrollee choices about health care providers, treatment options, or competing private health plans. Several laudable exceptions have been disclosure of nursing home inspections, public listing of hospitals with high mortality rates, preventive care mailings, and some use of centers of excellence arrangements.

A NEW ERA OF ACCOUNTABILITY

The Era of Assessment and Accountability is dawning at last (Relman, 1988).

As winds of change have swept across the health care landscape, they have brought with them new ideas on how to improve the health care system's performance via market accountability to purchasers and consumers. The most important of these concepts, now becoming private sector practices, are reflected in the reconciliation bill's proposals for how to restructure the Medicare program (this paper does not discuss the bill's medical savings account option).

These new market-oriented concepts alter *who* is accountable, *what* they are accountable for, and *how* they will be held accountable.

Who Is Accountable?

The fundamental change in the new health care model is to introduce the health plan as a locus of accountability.

Reorganizing fragmented medical care suppliers into systems of care, managed within a capitated budget, has been a favored idea of health care reformers for most of this century. Nearly every major health system actor has been nominated, at one time or another, as the best theoretical manager for such a system: the federal government, state governments, health alliances, community hospitals, tertiary care hospitals, community health centers, multispecialty physician groups, physician-hospital organizations, insurance companies, health maintenance organizations (HMOs) and their kin, employers, and individuals. During the last few years, private sector managed care plans, with a variety of sponsors, have replaced most traditional health insurance plans.

The health plan's management role—overseeing physicians and holding them accountable to the health plan—conflicts with the traditional deference to individual physician decisionmaking. Yet it also creates opportunities for new professional influences through a health plan's medical director and groups of health professionals working collectively to improve quality of care, assess new medical research and treatment protocols, and devise team approaches to disease management.

The reconciliation bill creates the basic market rules for a new Medicare health plan market. Its requirements deal with subjects such as (1) who can offer such plans, such as expanding sponsorship to include provider-sponsored organizations and association-sponsored plans; (2) types of plans, such as expanding beyond HMOs to include preferred provider organization (PPO) and fee-for-service options; (3) benefits, such as providing at least the basic Medicare benefit package; (4) licensure and regulation, such as requiring that most plans be licensed under state or federal law; and (5) key marketing rules, such as guaranteed issue, renewal, and antidiscrimination provisions.

What Are They Accountable for?

The second systemic change is to conceive of a health plan as accountable for the health of its enrolled population.

Health care providers, in fee-for-service arrangements, have been accountable for technical competence in dealing with specific medical issues for individual patients, for example, diagnosis and treatment of individuals who show up in their offices or hospitals. This accountability has proved to be too narrow to deal with non-acute care issues, such as prevention (immunizations, prenatal care) and chronic care (mental health, substance abuse, AIDS). Many government programs have been started to fill in such gaps in services that a fragmented, fee-for-service system does not do well. The broadened accountability of an organized health plan makes possible the establishment of a single point of accountability for all aspects of medical care.

The notion that a health care system should be accountable for the health of its population has also been influenced by the best practices in private sector quality management. Quality management started more than a century ago with a workstation and individual procedure focus (standardizing equipment, training personnel) and then progressed to a focus on production processes and assembly lines through end-of-the-line measures (statistical quality control). It has since expanded to total (institution-wide) quality management and continuous quality improvement (TQM/CQI), comparisons of performance with benchmarks and best practices, and an emphasis that quality should ultimately be measured by value to the consumer.

Seen in light of these private sector advances, the health system's practices have been defective because they have been too narrowly concerned with the performance of individual workers and procedures. Only recently has the health sector started to adopt institutional TQM and benchmarking techniques; its ability to deal with the whole patient is seriously limited so long as hospitals, physicians, and other service providers are fragmented. In 1990, an IOM committee recommended that Medicare adopt modern quality management techniques (Lohr, 1990). What society should want from its health system—clear, powerful, and reliable accountability for improving health status— needs a health plan that is accountable for dealing with all aspects of care.

The reconciliation legislation addresses these aspects of a health plan's accountability primarily by requiring that health plans have internal quality assurance programs, in accordance with U.S. Department of Health and Human Services (DHHS) regulations, that include features such as (1) stressing health outcomes, (2) health professional review of the provision of services and written protocols for utilization review, and (3) external review or accreditation by a qualified independent organization.

How Is Accountability to Be Achieved?

The third major shift is to structure a market so that consumer choice among competing health plans rewards excellence in health care quality and outcomes, service, and economy.

In contrast to the traditional approach of viewing quality as conformity to professional norms (and reviews that mostly seek to identify bad practices and errors), the competitive Medicare market is intended to foster competition for improving state-of-the-art practices and to reward excellence in performance. This is consistent with the ideas of continuous quality improvement (the second half of the acronym TQM/CQI) that managers should be accountable for ensuring that quality is continuously improving.

To generate such competitive market forces, the federal government would provide consumers with comparative information on health plan performance (report cards). The income gain or loss from Medicare enrollees—collectively, the largest untapped market for managed care—deciding to join or leave a health plan on the basis of such information and their own experience could be a powerful lever on health plans to offer quality products and services that match or exceed those of their competitors.

In the private sector, the National Committee for Quality Assurance, through its Health Plan Employer Data and Information Set (HEDIS), has pioneered efforts to develop such reporting standards. To date, this effort has focused on HMOs for the nonelderly. The next version of HEDIS is being expanded to include Medicare health plans, and there is a joint private sector-Health Care Financing Administration (HCFA) effort through the new Foundation for Accountability (FAcct) to provide assessment measures common to both public and private payers. In the proposed Medicare model, the government would exert no preselection, screening, negotiating, or purchasing role; the consumer alone would choose, and government premium payments would be determined by a formula.

The grading of professional performance may have another competitive dynamic working for its success. At a meeting with medical society leaders, after describing the theory of consumer choice, I was approached by a psychiatrist who said (with a smile), "I'm always fascinated to hear economists talk about their theories about why people do things. . . . I do think these proposals are going to work, but not for the reasons you described. I know a lot of physicians—and they're the most competitive people in the world. They got to be physicians by being compulsive about getting top grades. The report cards are going to be what makes this proposal work; no physician is going to want to be known as second-rate."

The reconciliation bill structures this market by assigning to DHHS responsibility to (1) provide an annual open season in which Medicare enrollees may enroll or disenroll in health plans and (2) provide comparative information about health plans to assist individuals in making an informed choice. In turn, health plans would be required to provide DHHS with the information that it requested for this purpose and would need to have government approve their marketing materials.

ACCOUNTABILITY FOR MEDICARE HEALTH PLANS

How well will the reconciliation bill's health plan accountability structure, through government statutory requirements and consumer choice, work to produce competition for excellence?

Skeptics question how well Medicare enrollees, on their own, will be able to be sophisticated and demanding purchasers of health care. This is an extremely difficult task today, even for experts. The report cards with which Medicare enrollees are expected to make informed judgments have yet to be developed, and it is not clear just how many data will really be available, how soon they will be available, and whether they will be valid, reliable, and useful for beneficiaries. The utility of health plan-level data is also questioned; some researchers report that consumers do not understand the relevance of population-based plan statistics and are, instead, much more interested in information relevant to their choice of a physician. Others worry that Medicare enrollees can be misled by sophisticated marketing, particularly individuals who have reduced capacities to make wise choices.

Skeptics also question that motives of health plans, particularly the large numbers of for-profit organizations that are likely to seek Medicare enrollees aggressively. They note that, in the absence of appropriate premium risk adjustors, health plans have better business strategies than competing for excellence— notably profiteering from artful risk skimming (practices that the insurance industry has honed in the FEHBP program). With health plans seeing per capita premiums averaging $5,000+ per enrollee (and rising to multiples of that amount), the profit potentials for plans and commissioned sales forces for signing up profitable patients is quite large. (The distribution of health care expenses among Medicare enrollees follows that of the population under age 65; that is, about 10 percent of enrollees use 70 percent of the care in a year, and about 20 percent of enrollees do not file claims.) Health plans also have incentives to avoid being known as better than their competitors at services that would lead to enrollment by populations with greater needs (on whom they will predictably lose money). There is also a history of substandard health plans and fly-by-night operators in two previous national efforts to expand Medicare HMO enrollments, and many other health insurance scams can be found (Multiple Employer Welfare Associations [MEWAs], Medicaid) (Dallek et al., 1995). If the accountability system does not work, it is conceivable that the arrangements in the reconciliation bill will prove to be simply a budget-cutting exercise, and even that competition could lead to health plans' exploitation and underservice of elderly persons who trusted in government's oversight of health plans, resulting in worse medical care and outcomes.

Although there are grounds for seriously questioning the reconciliation bill's provisions, there are a number of ways in which it is a major advance for Medicare's elderly and disabled population. Today's enrollees may only choose between Medicare and HMOs and have no comparative information or organized open season; the reconciliation bill features an organized health plan market, with a common open season for all plans, comparative report card information, more types of plans (including the PPO and point-of-service [POS] options that are most popular among those under age 65), and many more plans from which to choose. The FEHBP consumer-choice model is not untried—it is the nations's largest employer-sponsored plan and includes many retirees. The Medicare plans will offer enrollees more benefits, lower costs, and less paperwork than the basic Medicare program. Medicare consumers' satisfaction with HMO enrollment is generally high, and there are several areas, for example, in California and Florida, where 50 percent of Medicare enrollees have switched to HMOs. The reconciliation bill leaves the decision up to the Medicare beneficiary whether to remain with the traditional Medicare program or to switch to a private plan that he or she decides will better meet his or her needs.

Public policy can opt for a consumer-choice, competitive health plan model for Medicare reform and still strengthen health plan accountability compared with that in the reconciliation bill's provisions. Three broad strategies could make Medicare health plans more effectively accountable and could promote competition for excellence. They would involve a stronger role of government for enhancing consumer use of consumer purchasing power and for strengthening professional influences on health plan policies and practices. These strategies are described below, along with some specific options.

A Stronger Role for Government

The reconciliation bill provides Medicare beneficiaries, in important respects, with far less assistance than employers normally provide their employees in the health care market. Most private and public employers, for example, take an active "purchasing" role in the competitive selection of the health plans to be offered to their workers. This strong employer role allows for the use of group purchasing power to obtain better premium rates and performance guarantees, to lessen the potential for risk skimming, to obtain large amounts of data, and to engage professional expertise (benefit consultants, actuaries) in evaluating available plans.

The FEHBP model, by contrast, involves little preselection of plans. FEHBP makes available some 400 plans nationally, with approximately 20 to 40 plans being offered to enrollees in many metropolitan areas. In general, the federal government sponsors HMOs that meet basic conditions (but limits the number of fee-for-service plans) and provides some comparative plan

TABLE E-1 Number of Health Plan Choices for Private
Sector Employees, 1993

Number of Health Plans Offered per Establishment	Weighted by Number of Establishments (%)	Weighted by Number of Employees (%)
1	76	48
2	16	23
3	5	12
4	2	6
5 or more health plans	1	11

SOURCE: Preliminary tabulations from the 1993 Robert Wood Johnson
Foundation Employer Health Insurance Survey (courtesy of Steve
Long).

information and an annual open season. The federal government does not normally negotiate on behalf of federal employees to achieve better cost or improve quality.

Table E-1 from recent RAND research by Steve Long and colleagues, provides national estimates for the number of health plan choices available to private sector employees.

As shown in the right column, the most usual arrangement for employees (nearly half [48 percent]) is to be offered only a single plan [no choice], and an additional 23 percent of workers can choose among only two health plans. Some 83 percent of workers can choose among three or fewer health plans, and only 17 percent can choose among four or more offerings. When the number of offerings is tabulated by establishment, which reflects the large number of smaller firms, the range of choice is even more limited; 76 percent of firms offering health insurance offer only a single plan, and an additional 16 percent offer only a single option (i.e., two plans). Some 97 percent of private establishments offer three or fewer health plans, and only 3 percent offer four or more health plans.

Employer purchasing alliances expand the very limited choices typically available to workers at small firms and also typically play a strong role in selecting the plans to be offered, in negotiating premiums, and other issues. Table E-2, developed

TABLE E-2   Number of Health Plan Choices by Purchasing
Alliances

Purchasing Alliance	Number of Health Plans and Options
Health Insurance Plan of California	20 insurance companies, 18 HMOs, and 3 PPOs
Connecticut Business Industry Association	4 insurance companies, each offering an HMO and a POS plan
Cooperative for Health Insurance Purchasing (Colorado)	4 insurance companies, each offering an HMO and a POS plan
Employers Health Purchasing Cooperative (Washington, mostly Seattle)	3 POS plans with 3 plan designs, a choice of 9 plan options
Florida Community Health Purchasing Alliances (11 alliances)	Statewide: 46 Accountable Health Partnerships offering 75 plan options
Illinois Employer Benefits Alliance	Plans to offer a POS, PPO, and 2 or 3 HMO plans
PlanSource (Kentucky)	13 health plans
LIA Health Alliance (Long Island)	3 insurance companies, each offering an HMO and POS plan
Minnesota Employees Insurance Program	4 HMOs and 3 indemnity plans (where HMOs are not available)
Texas Insurance Purchasing Association	13 insurance companies offer 20 plans with multiple options in Gulf region; across 6 other regions, 11 carriers offer 15 plans

SOURCE: Institute for Health Policy Solutions, 1995.

by the Institute for Health Care Solutions, summarizes the number of plans available for 10 of these alliances.

All of the purchasing alliances (except for those in Florida) have the ability to selectively contract with health plans. In Washington State, employers choose the health plan for their workers, and Florida and Illinois employers choose the plans from which their workers may select. Other purchasing alliances offer open employee choice.

A recent Lewin-VHI study of the nation's nonfederal public employer plans—which are large group purchasers covering 3.7

million workers—shows that they also usually select a number of health plans, on a competitive basis, from which workers can choose. Nearly all report that they actively negotiate with plans to restrain costs and on other provisions; in general, their practices mirror those of the large private sector employers. Some states go much farther than others in the number of plans made available. The California Public Employees' Retirement System (CalPERS) offers enrollees a choice of six PPOs and 21 HMOs; CalPERS is an active negotiator with these health plans. In the Lewin-VHI study, about two-thirds of the states (30 of 47 states responding) reported offering at least a choice of three types of plans (indemnity, PPO or POS, and HMO); 12 states (27 percent) limited choice to two types of plans; only 3 states offered only a single plan (Lewin-VHI, 1995). An active government-run bidding process is also used by the federal government for the U.S. Department of Defense's (DOD) Civilian Health and Medical Program of the Uniformed Services health insurance program.

Structuring a competitive market so that it will have an active group-purchasing agent has clear analogies to wholesale markets in other sectors. Often, it is this wholesale level, where professional, expert purchasers can buy in quantity, that features the toughest competition for technical quality and price, for example, Sears purchasing for its Kenmore appliance line or the Giant grocery chain procuring the products that it will put on its shelves. Consumers can then choose, in the retail market, from among products and product features with better assurance of receiving good value merchandise.

The proposed FEHBP-Medicare model thus forgoes whatever preselection, negotiating for better features and performance, improved risk adjustment mechanisms, and consumer protection potential an active group purchaser would bring to the market. Medicare's 37 million enrollees would certainly get more choice than is available to most Americans but would also face a greater possibility of making a bad choice.

The following are among the options for a more active government role in helping Medicare enrollees.

Option #1. *Raise the standards for entry into the Medicare health plan market.* Tightening the rules on market entry is one of the options most often used by government to intervene in markets. Applied to the Medicare health plan market, a higher entry threshold could be used to help ensure that the plans offered to Medicare beneficiaries had already proven themselves to be viable, well-run companies that offer high-quality health care. The concerns about anti-managed care bias in DHHS administrative decisions could be lessened by using objective criteria.

Of the reconciliation bill's provisions that are more lenient than current law, the ones that are most open to question are the minimum plan enrollment provisions (5,000 individuals in current law would be lowered to 1,500 individuals generally and to 500 individuals in rural areas) and 50/50 requirements (health plans could be more than 50 percent Medicare enrollment). Both of these rules have helped to ensure that the health plans offered to Medicare enrollees were well-established operations that had already proved that they could grow and prosper in the competitive employer-choice market and that they were not started solely to profiteer off skimming the Medicare market. The current law's provisions might be continued and strengthened in several ways, such as (1) requiring that a health plan would need to be in existence for at least 3 years to demonstrate financial and operational competence and lessen the market's attractiveness to quick-buck operators; (2) providing that none of the plan's executives or marketing personnel could have prior convictions for violating state insurance or HMO laws, to lessen the prevalence of sharp operators, after being shut down in one state, simply moving to another state; and (3) setting benchmark scores on report card ratings, above minimal accreditation thresholds, that would need to be met for Medicare market entry.

Option #2. *Strengthen the federal government's role as a purchaser of health plans on behalf of Medicare enrollees.* The federal government could go beyond setting higher minimum entry requirements to actively using Medicare's purchasing power, $160 billion of outlays, to promote competition for excellence in the Medicare health plan market.

This option would involve the federal government making use of the best practices of large employer and purchasing alliances as wholesale or group purchasers. Plan selection could be done through an extensive request-for-proposal (RFP) competitive bidding process in which the government requires that proposers address a number of quality, service, and other measures that are important to Medicare's elderly and disabled populations. Only a selected menu of plans would be offered. Contract provisions could be negotiated to get quality and service performance guarantees for Medicare enrollees. Contract terms could also include financial incentives and penalties related to performance; for example, the St. Louis business coalition will put 4 percent of plan premiums aside for its plans to earn depending on their scores on objective, audited performance criteria.

An expertly run RFP process would allow for the use of more, and more sophisticated, criteria for selection than consumer report cards and could be designed to strengthen competition for excellence in serving Medicare's higher-need populations. A stronger purchasing or negotiating role would also allow the federal government to take much more effective measures to deal with risk adjustment problems on a market-by-market basis, ranging from banning plans that skim the Medicare market or that "demarket" higher-expense populations to closed-door bargaining with plans' representatives to develop appropriate risk adjustors, high-cost capitation arrangements, and other approaches to fair pricing. Over time, this negotiating capability would allow the federal government to move beyond the Average Adjusted Per Capita Cost (AAPCC) payment formula to implement competitive premium bidding.

The implementation barriers to this approach are challenging because of the potential need for the federal government to take on this new, sophisticated role in a large number of market areas. Fortunately, the Medicare health plan market is now so concentrated that this expanded role could be initiated selectively on a demonstration or research and development basis. The most promising areas would likely include Florida and California, which have 60 percent of Medicare HMO enrollees and a highly competitive Medicare market.

This type of purchasing strategy could also be fostered by the federal government by chartering competing consumer purchasing cooperatives (as described in the next section) to perform the same functions. If the consumer cooperative approach is followed, the federal government could assume this purchasing role in areas underserved by private cooperatives such as rural areas. The federal government could also contract out its purchaser function to state-chartered health plan cooperatives or state employees plans, for example, CalPERs or the Health Insurance Plan of California. Contracting issues for government programs have been discussed by Donahue (1989).

Enhance Consumers' Information and Influence

A second strategy for competitive excellence is to seek ways to make consumers even better shoppers on the basis of health plan performance and to increase health plan responsiveness to them.

Option #1. *Expand information about health plans for consumers.* The information provided to consumers is a critical link for the actuality of accountability. It is clear, however, that a lot more work still needs to be done in this area, for example, the National Committee on Quality Assurance's (NCQA) Medicare HEDIS is still under development; these technical efforts need to be complemented by market research on consumers' choice criteria. Other papers address these issues in depth.

The information needed may go beyond the report card performance measures on health care quality and outcomes. A few more critical elements—now not provided even to FEHBP participants—might simply be called full disclosure so that the consumer has a better idea of what he or she is getting and how a plan operates. In a recent *New York Times* piece, Michael Stocker (1995) (Chief Executive Officer of Empire Blue Cross/Blue Shield) recommended that HMO enrollees be given much more information about health plans. Among the items of information that he suggested HMOs be required to advise their Medicare and other enrollees of are

• guidelines that they want their doctors to follow when treating patients,
• treatments not covered, including limitations on drugs that physicians may prescribe, and

- payments to physicians, including bonuses related to cost containment and quality of care.

Other types of information that should help to make sure that health plans know that they are being carefully watched for misbehavior include enrollee complaints. The Minnesota HMO law, for example, requires each health plan to list its four highest administrative (e.g., scheduling) and four highest clinical (e.g., poor service) complaints and describe what is being done to deal with them. This information needs to be part of each plan's marketing material.

Option #2. *Create Medicare ombudsman offices.* A network of Medicare ombudsman offices, operating in areas with significant Medicare health plan enrollments, could be provided to assist Medicare enrollees who are considering health plan enrollments and those who have complaints about their health plans. The Medicare program now has an underdeveloped consumer assistance function; its placement of personnel in local Social Security offices ceased when HCFA was created. Assistance in addition to enrollment would be useful because of the many potential problems that consumers can encounter. The Medicare data on health plan performance show complaint rates that vary by a factor of 25:1, from 0.18 complaints per 1,000 enrollees for Group Health of Puget Sound to 4.58 complaints per 1,000 enrollees at Humana (Florida). The ombudsman office would assume some of the functions normally undertaken by an employer benefits office on behalf of employees in trying to deal with health plan issues that arise in day-to-day operations. The ombudsman could have the right to investigate patient complaints; to make unannounced inspections of facilities and records; to make public reports on findings; and to seek actions from DHHS such as "cease and desist" orders, suspension of new enrollments, and fines and U.S. Justice Department and state attorney general referrals for instances of criminal negligence, recurrent malpractice, and other egregious misbehavior. Various ombudsman functions could also be carried out by state and local governments and by private sector groups.

Option #3. *Create voluntary consumer purchasing cooperatives.* An idea recently proposed by David Kendall of the Progressive Policy Institute is that Medicare beneficiaries be given an option to join voluntary consumer cooperatives. James Firman and the National Council on the Aging have also proposed consumer cooperatives for Medicare beneficiaries. These cooperatives would have the power to negotiate on behalf of their Medicare enrollees with health plans on cost, quality, and other issues. They would be federally chartered, would offer a menu of options, and would be financed by a fixed percentage of the premiums that they handle. Multiple, competing cooperatives would be allowed, and beneficiaries would be able to decide whether to select their plans from the federal government's FEHBP-type arrangement or from one of the consumer cooperatives. In this approach, the voluntary consumer cooperatives, selected by beneficiaries, would assume the purchasing functions that government would take on in a previously described option. Compared with federally run purchasing arrangements, private sector cooperatives may have more flexibility and freedom from political pressures (Kendall, 1995).

Strengthen Professional Influences

Strengthening the influence of health care professionals who are committed to advancing clinical practice is a third strategy that could be used to promote health plan excellence. The following options are among the measures that could be considered.

Option #1. *Provide a better clinical basis for medical care of the Medicare elderly and disabled population.* At the American Association of Retired Persons' (AARP) 30th anniversary conference on Medicare, Robert Brook suggested a major national effort on clinical effectiveness and outcomes studies for the elderly. He noted that although many such studies are still needed for the population under age 65, the research literature is far more sparse for the population over age 65. Given the advances in research methods, his view was that this clinical knowledge could now advance rapidly. If health plan medical directors, accrediting agencies, health care professionals, report card designers, and Medicare enrollees are to perform their roles better, they need a far better scientific basis for their judgments.

IOM might be well suited for sponsoring a study by a com-

mittee of clinicians, health services researchers, medical directors of health plans, and others that would consider how to
organize and conduct a major national effort on clinical effectiveness and outcomes for Medicare's elderly and disabled populations. This effort would build on the Agency for Health Care
Policy and Research's work and other efforts in these areas.

Option #2. *Assure effective public accountability and high
professional standards for the accrediting organizations for
Medicare health plans.* The reconciliation bill's requirement
that health plans pass muster with an accrediting organization
is potentially a critical element of their accountability for meeting high professional standards. The accrediting organizations'
identities, structure, and accountability are not spelled out. Too
often, health care licensing and accrediting organizations have
settled for (or eroded to) standards that can easily be met and
become rubber stamps for second-rate performers. There are
also examples of professional standard setting, under government oversight, that seem to work well, for example, the Financial Accounting Standards Board (which is sponsored by all of
the major professions involved)–Securities and Exchange Commission relationship. NCQA, FAcct, and the Joint Commission
on Acreditation of Healthcare Organizations are among those
already vying for an accreditation role. The nature, sponsorship, funding, and accountability of the accrediting organiza-
tion(s) for Medicare health plans are worthy of careful consideration by public policy makers if they are to require high
standards rather than minimally acceptable performance.

Option #3. *Develop best practice benchmarks and centers of
excellence as competitive Medicare options.* The competitive
market can be used to influence health plan performance by
making sure that the fee-for-service Medicare program offers
the toughest possible competition with health plans for excellent health care. If the Medicare program identifies best practices and outstanding providers—and selectively contracts with
such providers, possibly using a centers of excellence and preferred provider model—it can ensure that there are high competitive standards, on a procedure-by-procedure and disease-by-
disease basis, that health plans will need to meet if they want to
attract patients. If health plans do not measure up to these

competitive benchmarks, they would risk losing enrollees and being seen as second rate. Medicare's selective contracting can extend to organized programs of care that specialize in the treatment of various chronic or high-cost conditions and to negotiated payment arrangements combining fee-for-service, capitation, risk sharing, and performance incentives.

COMPETITION FOR EXCELLENCE

There are as yet many unanswered questions about how well a consumer-choice health plan market, based on the FEHBP model, will work in fostering competition for excellence. This paper has focused on strategies for strengthening the roles of government, the consumer, and high professional standards while still retaining the basic reconciliation bill market reforms. The Medicare program could better assure competition for excellence by adopting elements from among these strategies.

REFERENCES

Dallek, G., C. Jimenez and M. Schwartz. 1995. *Consumer Protection in State HMO Laws.* Los Angeles: Center for Health Care Rights.
Donahue, J. 1989. *The Privatization Decision.* New York: Basic Books.
Fukuyama, F. 1995. *Trust.* New York: Free Press.
Hamilton, G. 1994. Civilizations and the Organizations of Economies. In N. Smelser and R. Swedberg, eds. *The Handbook of Economic Sociology.* Princeton, N.J.: Princeton University Press.
Institute for Health Policy Solutions. 1995. A Comparison of Small Employer Purchasing Alliances. Washington, D.C.: Institute for Health Policy Solutions.
Kendall, D. 1995. *A New Deal for Medicare and Medicaid: Building a Buyer's Market for Health Care (Report 25).* Washington, D.C.: Progressive Policy Institute.
Lewin-VHI. 1995. States as Purchasers: Innovations in State Employee Health Benefit Programs. Washington, D.C.: National Institute for Health Care Management.
Lohr, K. 1990. Medicare: A Strategy for Quality Assurance. Washington, D.C.: National Academy Press.
Relman, A. 1988. Assessment and accountability: The third revolution in health care. *N. Engl. J. Med.* 319:1221–1222.
Scherer, F. M., and D. Ross. 1990. *Industrial Market Structure and Economic Performance*, p. 55. Boston: Houghton Mifflin.

Stocker, M. 1995. The ticket to better managed care. New York Times, October 28.

Swedberg, R. 1994. Markets as social structures. In N. Smelser and R. Swedberg, eds. *The Handbook of Economic Sociology.* Princeton, N.J.: Princeton University Press.

F

Best Practices for Structuring and Facilitating Consumer Choice of Health Plans

*Elizabeth W. Hoy, Elliot K. Wicks, and
Rolfe A. Forland*[*]

INTRODUCTION

As Medicare contemplates a system in which Medicare recipients would be encouraged to enroll in managed care plans, questions arise about the extent to which enrollees should be given a choice among different plans and how such choice should be structured to meet the needs of enrollees and to achieve objectives related to health care efficiencies. This paper reviews the experiences of private employer purchasing organizations in particular, and those of some public employee organizations as well, that have experience with consumer choice. The purpose is to see what lessons that may be applicable to Medicare can be learned.

Giving consumers a choice of health plans has two objectives: (1) to allow people to choose a plan and associated providers that best match their needs and preferences given the constraint of what they are able and willing to pay and (2) to create incentives for health plans to compete for customers both by becoming more efficient, and thus, less costly, and by improving

[*]All authors are affiliated with the Institute for Health Policy Solutions, Washington, D.C.

quality and levels of service. The underlying assumption is that
if the first objective is achieved, the second one will follow: If
people can choose among plans on a rational basis, they will
choose plans that perform well; thus, plans must strive to improve performance to survive. People get what they want and
need, and the system performs better.

Achievement of these objectives requires that consumers
have both the economic incentives and the kind of information
that leads them to rationally weigh the marginal benefits and
the marginal costs of various health plans and to choose the one
that best matches their preferences. With respect to economic
incentives, the key is to have people bear the full marginal cost
of choosing a more expensive plan. With respect to information,
the challenge is to give consumers sufficient information of the
right kind, in a form that is understandable and simple enough
to be manageable, so that they can validly compare plans.

In structuring a system that allows consumer choice, the
"organizers of choice"—whether they are large corporations,
health purchasing groups of small private employers, or administrators of state employee benefit programs—must make decisions about a number of fundamental issues, bearing in mind
how those decisions affect the probability that the system will
achieve the objectives described above. Key issues include the
following:

- *How will health plans be selected?*

There are two basic approaches. The first is to establish
criteria and then accept any plan that meets the threshold criteria. This approach would maximize the number of qualified
plans and would have the organizers of choice play a more passive role. The second is to issue something like a request for
proposals from potential health plans, asking for information
that allows comparison of plans against specified criteria, and
then to select only the best plans. This approach involves a
more active role for the organizer of choice. That role can be
expanded even further by having the organizer actively negotiate with health plans, bargaining for a better price or changes to
improve efficiency, quality, service, and so forth. Because this
approach of limiting the number of health plans can deliver a

higher volume of business to the plans that are selected, they can more realistically anticipate economies of scale if they participate. This may give the organizers of choice more ability to achieve lower costs.

• *To what extent will benefits be standardized to simplify plan-to-plan comparisons?*

Even with the best kind of information on price and performance differences among plans, it is difficult for consumers to weigh the relative costs and benefits of a large number of plans. If this comparison also involves many service coverage and cost-sharing differences from plan to plan, the likelihood that consumers will make rational choices is significantly reduced. The number of variables to compare and weigh against one another can simply be too great to be manageable (the task may be somewhat more manageable if the benefit differences are confined to differences in consumer cost-sharing liabilities).[1] For reasons such as these, the organizations described herein have adopted standardized benefit plan designs to one degree or another as a way of facilitating choice. Offering some differences in benefit levels may be desirable to accommodate different preferences and abilities to pay.

• *How many and which types of benefit plan designs will be offered?*

Ideally, it would be desirable to offer a sufficient number of plans of different kinds (health maintenance organizations [HMOs], point-of-service [POS] plans, and indemnity plans) to provide genuine choice and diversity but not so many as to make the process of comparison overwhelmingly complex. In some regions, the number or type of available qualified plans that are willing to participate may be so small that choice is necessarily limited. On the other hand, offering more than the optimum

---

[1]For example, most consumers have a difficult time predicting whether or not they will need a given service. The choices of those consumers who do know they have a high probability of needing a service creates adverse selection for the plans they select. Although risk adjustment tools such as those developed in California can mitigate such problems, they are far less feasible without standardized benefits.

number of plans may fragment the covered population and reduce the market clout of the purchaser. Furthermore, there is
potential for major risk selection problems if there are too many
health plans of different types.

- *How will the employer's premium contribution be structured?*

To an employee, the price of a health plan is the difference
between the premium and the amount that the employer contributes. So the employer's contribution policy can be expected
to have a strong influence on employees' choice of plans. At one
extreme, if the employer pays 100 percent of the premium for
any plan, employees will have no incentive to consider price and
will often choose whichever plan they believe to be the most
generous. On the other hand, if the employer contributes a flat
dollar amount that is no more than the cost of the least expensive plan, employees pay the full additional cost of any more
expensive plan and thus have strong incentives to economize. If
the employer pays a fixed percentage of any plan, the employer
is subsidizing some, but not all, of the marginal cost of more
expensive plans, so the incentives to economize are weaker than
in the second approach but stronger than in the first one. Of
course, the higher the percentage of premium paid by the employer, the weaker the financial incentives for consumers.

- *How much and what kind of information will be given to
employees to help them choose among plans? Who will convey
the information and be accountable to answer consumers' questions?*

Ideally, before choosing a health plan, consumers would
know and understand how plans differ with respect to price,
covered benefits, organization, availability and range of medical
providers and services, philosophy, flexibility in choice of providers, quality (in terms of structure, process, and outcomes),
consumer satisfaction, and perhaps a number of other characteristics. The challenge for the organizers of choice is that not
all of this information will be available for all (or perhaps any)
health plans, consumers may not want all of this information,
and they may have difficulty understanding much of it. Deciding what information to collect and make available and how to

present it in a form that consumers will use and understand is a major task. Furthermore, consumers often want and need objective assistance in understanding health plan differences that relate to their particular needs and circumstances. How and through whom to provide such assistance is also an important consideration for facilitators of health plan choices.

CASE STUDIES

Each of the following purchasers has deliberately adopted a consumer-choice model as a means of achieving their purchasing objectives. These objectives may include reducing the cost of health coverage, improving access to health care services for the population served, and improving the quality of health care services and delivery. Each example offers a unique interplay of purchaser objectives, market characteristics, and philosophy.

Xerox

Xerox purchases benefits on behalf of approximately 48,000 U.S. employees, plus retirees and eligible dependents, spread geographically throughout the United States. Corporate health costs grew 51 percent between 1987 and 1990, leading Xerox to seek new alternatives for managing these rapidly escalating business expenses (Darling, 1991). Strategically, shifting more costs to employees was not an acceptable option and cutting benefits was not a desirable option. Thus, Xerox chose to apply the same "total quality management" business strategy used in all other aspects of their business to the purchase of health benefits (Darling, 1992).

Xerox's objectives were to structure a system that creates incentives for employees to move into more efficient HMOs, to increase the accountability of the HMOs contracting with Xerox, and to improve the health status of Xerox employees. To accomplish these objectives, Xerox chose a strategy to structure competition among plans based on value. This strategy includes similar health benefits across health plans, benchmark pricing, commitment to continuous quality management, information gathering and dissemination strategies to support continuous quality improvement (CQI), and consumer choice.

HealthLink HMO Managers

Prior to implementation of the HealthLink network in 1990, 40 percent of Xerox employees were enrolled in more than 200 HMOs nationwide. In an effort to create a national network of well-managed, high-quality HMOs, Xerox launched a competitive process to contract with HMO organizations that would help Xerox manage what would eventually become the nationwide HMO network. They asked those HMOs not only to provide health care services but to help manage other HMOs as well. Six national HealthLink managers (Kaiser, Blue Cross and Blue Shield of Rochester, UltraLink [created by FHP, Inc.], Prudential HealthCare System, The HMO Group, and U.S. Healthcare) were chosen to coordinate the contracting of HMOs. A seventh was added in 1994.

HealthLink managers are responsible for conducting on-site surveys and other evaluations of HMOs to be offered through the network. Xerox selects the system managers, reviews and approves local plans for inclusion in the networks, establishes and refines the benefit levels and programs for individual plans, and manages and evaluates the performance of the network coordinators using reports and operational reviews. Once accepted into the HealthLink program, all billing and reporting for individual HMOs is consolidated through the network managers.

The HealthLink program became operational in 1990. In 1990, Xerox employees were still allowed to select previously offered HMOs that were not yet selected for the HealthLink program. Beginning in 1991, new Xerox employees were only offered coverage through HealthLink HMOs or the self-insured fee-for-service (FFS) plan. Employees hired prior to 1991 are allowed to remain in non-HealthLink HMOs if they are currently enrolled in those plans; however, the cost-sharing requirements are structured to encourage enrollment in HealthLink HMOs (see below). Non-HealthLink HMOs are encouraged to qualify as members of the HealthLink network.

Benefit Plan Design

Xerox has not specified an exact detailed standard benefit

plan design. All HMOs serving Xerox enrollees are required to cover *all* medically necessary and appropriate services, including reasonable coverage for organ transplants and for mental health and substance abuse treatment. In general, the range of services provided must meet those specified for federally qualified HMOs and must include more coverage for substance abuse treatment, rehabilitation services, and mental health and substance abuse services at a level between inpatient and outpatient (e.g., day/night care or a residential treatment option). Health plans are allowed to offer their richest standard plan design, but may vary benefits on items that are easy for consumers to understand and would not promote risk segmentation, such as modest copayments.

For the first 4 years of the program, Xerox produced identical benefit summaries for every HMO to ease comparisons. For 1996, however, Xerox stopped producing the reports. There were several reasons for this change, including the following: The costs of collecting and verifying the information were very high; the general "lay" language of the reports sometimes created problems because of a lack of exact detail on covered and uncovered items; Xerox believed that plans should be responsible for producing the information and enrollees should be responsible for reading the plans' summaries and marketing materials; and often, the plan's marketing materials contained key information that was not easily incorporated into the plan summaries, yet was useful for making choices among health plans (such as the opening of a new health center or the addition of new services).

Xerox reports that they have not experienced any significant problems with this approach to benefit plan design. Xerox health benefits management staff work closely with health plans to resolve any questions that arise if enrollees encounter a service that is perceived to be medically necessary but that was not disclosed by the health plan as a noncovered service.

Retirees have been included in the program since its inception. Early retirees participate in the same manner as active employees. Xerox encourages the health plans to offer Medicare risk programs for retirees over age 65. Medicare-eligible retirees are eligible to select a Medicare risk program upon turning age 65, not just at open enrollment time. Xerox has experienced some administrative difficulties related to this program. Medicare requires that enrollees be allowed to disenroll from health plans at will; this is at odds with Xerox program rules, which allow one health plan change per year for cause. In addition, Medicare requires that enrollees be disenrolled from a health plan if the enrollee leaves the plan service area for more than 90 days. A number of Xerox retirees move seasonally, and thus cannot remain in the Medicare risk programs throughout the year.

Benchmark Pricing

A key component of the Xerox program is "benchmark pricing" to create financial incentives for consumers to realize the savings associated with choosing efficient HMOs. Xerox's contribution for health premiums is tagged to the "benchmark" plan in any given area. The benchmark plan is chosen on the basis of submitted premiums for a given year compared with the premiums of other HMOs in that geographic area. Consideration is also given to quality and performance measures; Xerox provides a $10 per month additional benefit—or "performance credit"—to health plans that are fully accredited by the National Committee for Quality Assurance (NCQA). If the employee chooses the benchmark plan, then Xerox pays 100 percent of the premium. If the employee chooses any of the other plans offered, then the employee pays the full difference between the premium for the plan chosen and that for the low-cost plan.

Cost sharing in the FFS plan is structured to appropriately reflect the real differences in efficiency between FFS and managed care.[2] If the enrollee picks the FFS plan, then the employee pays the difference in premium, and he or she is subject

---

[2]In 1992, Xerox per capita HMO costs were $1,700 lower than those of the FFS plan, even with the richer benefits of the HMO. Xerox conservatively estimated that approximately one third of that difference could be attributed to differences in the characteristics of the enrolled populations. The rest was attributed to the greater efficiencies of the HMOs.

to heavy coinsurance and deductibles with high out-of-pocket maximums as well. (For example, the annual deductible for the FFS plan is 1 percent of the employee's salary for the previous year, and the maximum out-of-pocket payment is 4 percent of salary or $4,000, whichever is lower [Darling, 1991]).

Performance Reporting and Consumer Information

Consistent with Xerox's commitment to total quality management, the company works closely with the HealthLink network managers and participating HMOs to measure and improve health plan performance. Xerox has been an active supporter of NCQA and a leader in the development of the NCQA Health Plan Employer Data and Information Set (HEDIS) for measuring health plan performance. Xerox has indicated that it expects all HealthLink HMOs to obtain NCQA accreditation as one measure of health plan quality.

To assist Xerox employees in evaluating and choosing among health plans, Xerox provides each employee with an HMO performance report. This report includes comparison tables representing the characteristics and performances of all health plans in the employee's geographic area across a number of dimensions, including structure, network characteristics, access to services, member satisfaction and wait times, and HEDIS quality-of-care measures. Unlike many other examples of consumer choice information, the Xerox report card explicitly states the goals for each measure. In this way, consumers can judge how well plans are performing compared with a set of absolute benchmarks, not just plan performance relative to other plans.

Another characteristic that makes the Xerox performance report stand out is the inclusion of an explanation (in language that is understandable to typical consumers) of why each measure has been included in the report card. This builds upon the understanding that providing information to support consumer choice has an educational component. Although issues such as employee cost and whether the employee's doctor is available through the network will probably continue to be of primary salience to most consumers, performance measures and the supporting education to use those measures are expected to expand the foundation on which Xerox employees choose plans and focus competition more clearly on quality.

Southern California Edison

The Southern California Edison health program provides coverage for approximately 17,000 active workers (plus dependents) and 7,000 retirees (including some early retirees not yet eligible for Medicare)—a total of 55,000 covered lives. Prior to 1995, the company itself administered a self-insured preferred provider organization (PPO), but the company decided that it should not be in the insurance business and that it needed to find an approach that would produce cost savings and improve quality as well. The company chose to substitute a program that would give employees (located primarily in Southern California but also in Nevada and Arizona) a choice of up to eight plans offering standardized benefits. The changes had to be bargained with employee unions—which cover about 45 percent of the work force—and this constrained the degree to which the company could change the program. The health plans that are offered include several HMOs (including individual practice association [IPAs] and Kaiser) and POS plans but no indemnity plan. Most employees can choose from approximately six plans. Medicare-eligible retirees can also choose risk-based HMOs (although relatively few do because the standard company plan is so rich that the HMO benefits are not significantly more comprehensive, and those who choose the POS plans have the option of selecting any provider).[3]

The company's process for choosing plans started with a preliminary review of characteristics of plans—cost, quality, design, and so forth—and development of criteria. Selected

---

[3]The typical plan has an HMO benefit structure as the core, an in-network PPO benefit structure layer, and then a POS option on top of that. The person who uses only the HMO providers pays nothing in cost sharing and nothing for gatekeeper-approved referrals to network physicians. If the patient self-refers to a network physician, the patient pays a portion of the fee. If the patient uses the POS option and self-refers to a non-network physician, the patient's share of the fee is greater still.

plans were invited to respond to a request for proposals. The plans that were ultimately selected signed a three-year contract, which included a commitment to maximum yearly premium increases over that period.

Selecting Health Plans

To be eligible for continued participation, plans must have or be seeking NCQA accreditation. They must also provide HEDIS data. The company establishes performance standards against which to judge plans. The standards address the plan's organization and financial status, service integration, clinical care, use of protocols, and customer service, among other things. The company's evaluation process includes site visits. Plans that fail to meet a standard are not automatically ineligible for further participation; the company is looking for continuous improvement in meeting the performance goals. It monitors plans' strategies for addressing problems as well as their success in solving those problems.

Enrollment

Open enrollment is offered once a year, in the fall for coverage that begins in January. The company pays 90 percent of the premium for any plan chosen. Almost 60 percent of employees have chosen a POS option. It appears that employees give the highest priority to having a plan that offers choice of providers and includes "their" doctor. Price—in the form of employee contribution to premium—does not appear to be very important in influencing choice, in part because the contribution structure requires employees to pay only 10 percent of the additional cost of more expensive plans and in part because the plans' premiums do not differ much. However, copayments for out-of-network use (another measure of "price" to enrollees) does appear to influence choice of plans.

Educating Employees

The company made a major commitment to educating and equipping employees and retirees to make an informed choice among plan options. Now in the second year of enrollment, the company has found that the effort was justified and will need to be continued, particularly for retirees. Much attention was given to communicating with employees—through mailings and several sets of meetings. The company publishes a consumer guide and maintains two toll-free telephone help lines, one for active employees and one for retirees. (In a 9-month period, these lines received 38,000 calls, with perhaps one half to three fourths being from retirees and with an average call length of 10 to 20 minutes.) The consumer guide emphasizes shared responsibility among the consumer, the health plan/provider, and the company. To obtain feedback on how the plan is working, the company created several consumer advocacy groups and has funded surveys and consumer focus groups to determine employee needs and concerns.

Educating retirees is especially challenging and requires substantial resources. Retirees are often very hesitant to give up what they see as traditional Medicare coverage. They need assistance in understanding choices and benefits and seem to be easily confused by the range of choices—especially the more complicated structure of the POS option. The company recruited retiree volunteers to provide peer support and found this approach to be quite effective.

Company administrators conclude that in a situation in which employees have a choice of a number of plans, it is important that part of the employee education be done not by the health plans but by an objective party. Such an approach gives employees greater confidence that plan comparisons are unbiased. Providing such assurance is particularly important because of the extensive negative media coverage of managed care plans, as well as general resistance to change.

Although company-specific data on the performance of participating health plans is not yet available, the company sponsored publication of a Los Angeles edition of *Health Pages* and made available plan-specific consumer satisfaction data based on the experience of other enrollees in participating plans.

Anticipated Improvements

In assessing the program to this point, company administrators note several areas where further work is warranted. They hope to make plan performance goals more quantifiable so that they can more accurately assess progress. They will be working to use in-house resources more effectively in monitoring the performance areas where plans need to improve. They seek to better integrate mental health services, which are now offered through a "carve-out" arrangement. They also see a need to continue to work on educating both consumers and physicians. Better communication is needed with physicians because some have not "bought into" the program and seem too ready to tell patients that their hands are tied by the program rules rather than trying to explain to patients how the system works and what their options are. The company hopes to address these problems by more communication with physicians in cooperation with health plans.

In assessing the company's efforts to provide consumer education and monitor health plan performance, company officials suggested that ultimately these activities should probably be done not by individual purchasers but by some entity that represents a number of purchasers. That approach would be more manageable for health plans and would reduce administrative costs.

Health Insurance Plan of California

The Managed Risk Medical Insurance Board (MRMIB) was given authorization under California's state reform legislation of 1992 to create and administer a small-group health plan purchasing cooperative, which is known as the Health Insurance Plan of California (HIPC). The legislation required HIPC to make coverage available to groups of 3 to 50 employees statewide and to establish rating and group participation requirements in accordance with state law.[4]

As of December 1995, HIPC offered 24 HMOs and PPOs to small employers throughout the state of California (although

---

[4]The authorizing statute requires HIPC to regionalize by July 1996 in accordance with the geographic rating areas established by the statute/insurance department. This provision of the statute could be amended in the 1996 California legislative session.

not all enrollees have access to all health plans). HIPC has enrolled more than 5,000 employers, providing coverage to more than 100,000 individuals.

Although HIPC's authorizing statute was silent as to whether it should allow for employer or employee choice of health plans, the Board decided to implement employee choice because it felt that choice was critical to controlling costs in the long run. In addition, because opportunities for choice are usually very limited in the small-employer market, MRMIB thought that choice would be one of HIPC's biggest selling points.

Purchasing Role

HIPC was granted authority to negotiate and select health plans, and the managers believe that HIPC has been able to use its negotiating and health plan selection authority to generate sizable savings. In the first year of HIPC's operation, it was able to negotiate rates that were approximately 15 percent below the market average, and in the past 2 years it has been able to reduce rates by 5 percent per annum. Over the past 3 years, HIPC has seen a convergence in premiums toward the low price.

Plans Offered

HIPC's authorizing statute required that it offer health plans with more than one delivery structure but did not specify what those structures had to be. Because of the preponderance of managed care in the California market, HIPC decided that it would offer only HMO and PPO plans.

Initially, staff at HIPC wanted to pursue an "exclusive" strategy and contract with at most six or seven health plans. However, because of the response that HIPC received to its request for proposals, as well as other political considerations, it decided to adopt an "inclusive" strategy and contract with a larger number of health plans.

In the first year of operation, HIPC offered a choice of 18 health plans—15 HMOs and 3 PPOs. Now in its third year of operation, HIPC currently offers a choice of 22 HMOs and 2 PPOs. However, because of the size and diversity of California, not all 24 plans are available to every small employer in the state. In fact, in some rural areas only one plan is available.

Benefits Structure

The Board of MRMIB decided to develop a benefits structure that, in terms of covered services, is essentially identical for the PPO and HMO offerings. The Board's reasoning was that it wanted to facilitate consumer choice on the basis of the price, network, and quality of care of the competing plans rather than on the basis of the benefits offered. HIPC also established two cost-sharing options—standard and preferred—for the PPO and HMO products. In this way, employees can decide whether they want to pay more for a plan in which they will have lower out-of-pocket costs for services received.

Participation Rules

HIPC requires participating employers and the health plans to have an open enrollment period during May of every year. In this way, HIPC facilitates consumer choice of health plans and providers by granting existing enrollees an opportunity to change health plans. During HIPC's second open enrollment, 9,614 members opted to change carriers, which was 10.9 percent of the 87,700 members who were eligible to switch. The management of MRMIB believes that this small number of changes indicates the value of the employee-choice model: Employees are more satisfied with their health insurance because they have made the right choice for themselves.

Enrollee Information

Prospective enrollees are provided a written brochure that describes HIPC and the health plans offered. HIPC staff refer to this brochure as "first generation" information materials. The brochure

- lists HIPC's eligibility requirements for employees and dependents,
- describes how HIPC operates,

- lists the benefit structure and cost-sharing levels for the four different plan offerings (HMO and PPO standard and preferred plans),
- discusses the steps that an employee should follow to select a health plan, including listing the health plans that are available in an employee's geographic region and specific county of residence,
- provides rate tables for each geographic region that show the premium rates for each available health plan by family status and employee age, and
- provides descriptive information on each health plan.

After conducting intensive focus groups with consumers, HIPC is now making available "second generation" enrollment materials. This information provides prospective enrollees answers to questions that HIPC members frequently have asked, cross-referenced by the participating health plans. For example, using this information, a prospective enrollee can determine which health plans require an enrollee's dependents to have the same primary care physician as the enrollee.

Program Assessment

HIPC staff believe that the employee-choice model is working; that is, employers or agents are not, in essence, channeling all employees into one plan; employees really are making individual choices. Their reasoning is based in part on how HIPC is marketed to small employers. Small employers either can contact HIPC directly to get enrollment information or can go through an agent or broker. Because agents are paid a flat commission rather than on a percentage of premium basis, HIPC staff are not concerned that agents may be steering enrollees into higher-cost plans and thus working counter to the purpose of employee choice.

Further evidence that employees really do have choice is shown by the fact that the average group enrolled in the HIPC consists of 10 employees who enroll in three health plans. Moreover, HIPC staff point to the statistic that 45 percent of employers enrolled in HIPC have employees who have switched health plans during open enrollment.

Connecticut Business and Industry Association

The Connecticut Business and Industry Association (CBIA) is a state-wide organization with more than 9,000 employer members. CBIA provides a range of business and consulting services to its members and represents the interests of its members on different legislative initiatives. For more than 30 years, CBIA had offered its members an indemnity insurance plan at a premium level competitive with those of large corporations. In 1993, the management of CBIA decided that it would also develop a health plan purchasing arrangement for small employers that would offer employees a choice of several competing managed care plans.

Purchasing Role

CBIA views itself as an active purchaser in the health care marketplace but would not characterize itself as a "hard" negotiator because it was most interested in forming partnerships with health plans. However, CBIA did develop a request for proposals that laid out its requirements for participation by health plans. These criteria, which fall into a multitude of areas, reflect many of the objectives of CBIA. For example, several key objectives of CBIA were that its health plans have broad geographic coverage, that they include most of the hospitals in the state in their combined networks, that they employ continuous quality initiatives to monitor and improve internal processes, and that they provide sufficient data for consumers to adequately assess the quality of care provided by the health plans.

CBIA also had to evaluate other less tangible criteria when deciding with which plans to contract. For instance, for marketing purposes, CBIA had to consider the reputation of the health plans and their appeal to the small-employer market. Because CBIA relies solely on the agent and broker community to distribute its health plans, it also had to take into account whether the health plans were familiar with that community.

Plans Offered

Beginning January 1, 1995, CBIA has made available four HMOs—CIGNA, Aetna, Kaiser, and Physicians Health Services, Inc.—to small employers through its purchasing cooperative.[5] CBIA requires that these four health plans offer services statewide. Three of them have complied with this requirement, and the fourth, which is available in three of the four geographic rating regions in Connecticut, will soon be in compliance as well.

CBIA consciously decided that it would offer only managed care plans to its members. They concluded that any traditional indemnity plan (PPO or FFS plans) offered alongside the managed care plans would likely be subject to adverse risk selection, and in any case, the combination of several managed care networks would allow most consumers to have access to the providers of their choice.

Benefits Structure

To enhance consumer choice of a health plan on the basis of price, network, and quality rather than on the basis of the benefits offered, CBIA has developed a single benefit plan that all its health plans offer. Because managed care is not too prevalent in Connecticut, CBIA also requires each participating health plan to provide a POS delivery structure in addition to the HMO coverage. The intent behind the POS option is to ease those employees who are used to indemnity coverage into managed care. For each delivery structure, each health plan must offer two different cost-sharing levels—a preferred and a standard option—so that an employee can buy into better coverage if he or she desires. Thus, each employee has a choice of four plan offerings (two delivery structures and two cost-sharing levels) that are offered by each of the four health plans.

Although CBIA developed a single benefit plan that all of its

---

[5]Employees who work for a Connecticut employer but reside outside of Connecticut are eligible for an indemnity plan, or they may choose a Kaiser Permanente medical office.

health plans must offer, it is having some difficulty ensuring real benefits consistency among the four health plans. The reason for the problem is that the benefit structure that each health plan is offering through CBIA is one that each health plan had already filed with the state's Department of Insurance. That benefit structure is similar to but not identical to the one developed by CBIA. CBIA's benefit plan has, in essence, become a floor. CBIA is negotiating with its health plans to bring their benefit offerings into compliance. To ensure that no health plan has a competitive advantage in attracting healthier persons during enrollment, CBIA does not allow its health plans to advertise the benefits that they offer that are richer than those contained in CBIA's package. For example, CIGNA has a fitness benefit contained in its benefit plan, but a prospective enrollee will not become aware of that benefit until he or she enrolls in the health plan.

Participation Rules

CBIA requires participating employers to conduct an open enrollment period for 1 month each year, from November 1 to December 1. In this way, all employees, both those newly enrolling and those renewing, can compare the different plans available and choose the coverage that meets their needs and financial resources.

Enrollee Information

Prospective enrollees are provided only written materials about CBIA's multiple-choice health plan product. Prospective enrollees are given a brochure that walks them through the employee choice process. The brochure

- lists the benefit levels and cost-sharing provisions for the four different plan offerings (HMO and POS preferred and standard plans) and recommends that an employee choose the one that "looks right" for him or her,
- briefly describes the four participating health plans and lists toll-free customer service numbers that enrollees can call

for more information about plan networks or specific benefit offerings,

- refers employees to the provider network directory given to employers to see with which health plans their doctors are affiliated,
- assists employees in determining in which of one of four geographic regions their employer is located,
- provides rate tables for each geographic region that, for each benefit plan, shows the premiums for the four health plans by family status and employee age (for each age and family status cell for each benefit plan—for example, under age 30, employee only, HMO Standard—the premium of the lowest cost plan is in bold text), and
- lists the eligibility requirements and cooperative procedural information (open enrollment, waiver of coverage, etc.).

Enrollment Process

The administrative structure used by CBIA that supports the enrollment process also facilitates choice of health plan by consumers. Each employee selects his or her choice of health plan, benefits option, and primary care physician and indicates these choices on a standardized enrollment form. All enrollment forms are then processed by CBIA, and the results of the enrollment process are transmitted electronically by CBIA to the participating health plans. CBIA also uses a "passive" reenrollment system, such that during the open enrollment period, an enrollee is automatically reenrolled in the same health plan (with the same delivery structure and cost sharing) unless he or she indicates otherwise by submitting an enrollment change form.

Program Assessment

In assessing the consumer-choice element of their product offering, CBIA management has several concerns. First, because CBIA relies solely on the agent and broker community to distribute its product, the organization believes that it may need to engage in more training and education of its brokers to facilitate consumer choice. In some instances, all of an employer's employees are enrolled in just one plan. Agents may be influencing the decisions that lead to this result; that is, at the very least, they may not be explaining and promoting the individual-choice concept, and they may be channeling patients into a single plan. That approach may be easier for agents, simply because employers are used to having everyone enrolled in a single plan. To remedy this situation, CBIA plans to provide practical examples to agents and brokers so that they will become comfortable with the many options available in the CBIA model and will learn how best to present those options to an employer. Agents have been receptive to this approach. The compensation arrangement for agents could also be influencing agents to promote some plans over others, since their commission is a percentage of the premium. To further promote a level playing field, CBIA is interested in moving to uniform commissions, regardless of the plan chosen by individual enrollees.

Another area of concern for CBIA is that they are uncertain what information each employee sees about its multiple-choice product. This uncertainty arises because CBIA has strong ties to employers and agents but limited exposure to individual employees. To address this issue, CBIA is considering revising its communications materials to ensure that individual employees are knowledgeable about the consumer-choice element of its health plan offering.

Cooperative for Health Insurance Purchasing

The Alliance in Denver, Colorado, has been providing health benefit-related services on behalf of self-insured employers of all sizes since 1988. In its traditional program, The Alliance contracts directly with providers in the community to develop a provider network that can be accessed by self-insured employers to individually design PPO and exclusive provider organization plans for their employees. The Alliance also provides utilization management services, data analysis and reporting services, a consumer information line staffed by nurses, and written health promotion materials tailored to individual employers.

In late 1994, The Alliance determined that it should expand its offerings to include fully insured managed care plans in order to better meet its goals of assisting the entire employer community to purchase health care services. Serving the entire employer community is a central objective of The Alliance for two reasons. First, it believes that high costs and cost shifting in one segment of the market adversely affects purchasers in other segments of the market. Second, it believes that data and information from all purchasers in the market concerning all providers in the market are necessary to bring about systemic improvements in the health care market.

After an intensive product development process, The Alliance began enrolling employers and their employees in the Cooperative for Health Insurance Purchasing (CHIP) in October 1995. CHIP has contracted with four HMOs, each of which offers CHIP's three standardized benefit plan designs: a basic HMO plan, a standard HMO plan, and a POS option on the standard HMO plan. Employers purchasing through CHIP select the benefit plan design, and the employees choose from among the four health plans. CHIP produces the price quote on the group, processes the enrollment and informs the health plans of enrollment changes, collects premiums from employers, and distributes the premiums among the participating health plans. Employers are required to contribute at least 50 percent of the premium for the lowest-cost HMO or an equivalent flat dollar contribution.

In its contracting process, The Alliance deliberately sought to balance the characteristics of the health plans offered through the cooperative. The plan offerings include a group model HMO (Kaiser), IPA model HMOs (HMO Colorado and FHP, Inc.) and a physician hospital organization-based HMO (Frontier Community Health Plans). The health plans have complementary networks—although there is substantial overlap—so that 93 percent of the physicians in the state are available through at least one of the four HMOs.

CHIP is marketed through agents and brokers. Agents must attend a 2-hour training session taught by The Alliance staff in order to be certified to sell CHIP. They must also be "appointed" by all four HMOs (a state regulatory requirement). Agents are paid a single commission by CHIP, and the commission is the same percentage of the premium for any plans chosen by the employees.

Blending Multiple Market Segments

One distinguishing characteristic of CHIP is that employer groups of all sizes are eligible to purchase through the Cooperative. The Alliance specifically wanted to leverage the market clout of large employers on behalf of small employers. However, merging the different segments of the market into a purchasing structure that appears seamless to employers and employees has proven to be very complicated. The characteristics of the large-employer market and the small-employer market for health insurance differ substantially along some key variables, such as employee eligibility standards, waiting periods prior to commencing coverage, the use of medical underwriting, rating structures and practices, self-insurance options, premium contribution policies, and so forth. Failure to accommodate for these differences could leave CHIP open to adverse risk selection, which could destroy the viability of CHIP overall.

CHIP's approach was to standardize those characteristics that could be standardized across market segments—benefit plan design, health plan offerings, enrollment, and other administrative services—while separating employers into three different risk pools for rating purposes. Health plans bid a single base premium rate for employers with fewer than 50 employees and another base rate for employers with more than 50 employees. The base rates for employers are then adjusted according to rating rules agreed to by all of the plans. Rate adjustment procedures vary somewhat for each market segment. Rating practices for employers with fewer than 50 employees are regulated under Colorado small employer market reform rules; rating practices for midsize employers (51 to 200 employees) are designed to allow CHIP to remain competitive in the market yet minimize risk segmentation; and rate variations for large employers (200+ employees) based on experience can be used by participating health plans, but are limited to ±10 percent of the base rate.

CHIP does all of the underwriting and price quoting on behalf of the four health plans. Therefore, although the risk management practices vary for each employee size category, a given firm's employees of any age (except for the very smallest firms) can have a single composite rate[6] for each health plan. Employers and employees in all employee size categories have the same choice of benefit plan designs and use the same information about health plan structure, access, customer service, and quality to choose a health plan through CHIP.

Performance Standards and Common Measurement Tools

Information for choosing among the HMOs is provided to enrollees in a single trifold brochure that contains comparison charts highlighting plans' network characteristics (for example, number of primary care physicians and the percentage of board certified physicians), access to wellness and preventive services (for example, ability to self-refer for obstetric/gynecologic services), customer service capabilities (for example, languages spoken), and key quality indicators. On the back of the brochure are maps of each plan's service area and a comparison chart of the plans' participating hospitals. Enrollees also receive a provider directory for each health plan and a price comparison sheet. Enrollees who want more detailed information about the health plans and their participating providers, or who have questions about CHIP itself, are encouraged to call CHIP's toll-free customer service line.

Health plans participating in CHIP have agreed to withhold up to 2 percent of premiums. In the event that the perfomance standards have not been met at the end of the year, half of the withheld funds will be distributed to the best-performing plans. The seven indicators of performance measures include member service standards, clinical quality standards (from HEDIS), and consumer satisfaction standards. Participating plans have agreed to use common data definitions and common measurement tools to assess plan performance.

---

[6]As in most states, Colorado's small employer insurance rules allow differences in premium on the basis of the age of the employees. Thus, it is typical in this segment of the market for employers to receive a bill that lists a separate premium for each employee that reflects these variations.

State of Wisconsin Employee Trust Fund

The state of Wisconsin purchases health benefits on behalf of active state employees and their dependents, retired state employees and their dependents, and employees of local governments in Wisconsin. This program is managed by the Wisconsin Employee Trust Fund (ETF). Beginning in 1984, ETF decided to retain only the two state-sponsored, self-insured FFS plans and to contract exclusively with HMOs for other health plan options for state employees and their dependents. The system operates much like a purchasing cooperative in that individual enrollees choose from among a variety of health plans offering standardized benefits and many of the administrative functions for the system are centralized for efficiency.

In 1987, ETF opened the program to local government participation. There was concern that since local government participation was voluntary, the pool would attract the higher-risk groups. Therefore, ETF opted to maintain separate risk pools for local governments and state employees, while still offering the same benefit plan designs and health plan choices to both groups.

ETF has made a deliberate decision not to micromanage the system, but to focus on facilitating consumer choice and allowing market competition to drive plan performance. Prior to 1993, ETF contracted with any plan that could meet the guidelines for participation and did not select health plans or negotiate the price benefits. Over time, the Group Insurance Board (which oversees the insurance plans on behalf of ETF) has concluded that, to have a greater impact on the cost and quality of health plans, ETF should negotiate more aggressively on price and health plan service.

Beginning in 1993, ETF introduced some negotiation of the price of health plans using a two-step process. Prior to negotiations, ETF uses actuarial consultants to price the benefit plan design. Using each plan's utilization data and demographic mix, a target premium is developed for the individual health plans. If a plan's proposed price is significantly higher than the actuarial target, ETF meets with the plan and discusses the discrepancy. Plans are then allowed to generate a "best and final" offer. Most such health plans have offered second bids that are substantially lower than their original bids.

Benefit Plans Standardardized to Reduce Biased Selection

ETF currently defines the standard benefit plan design for all participating HMOs. There may be differences in how plans implement that coverage to encourage efficiencies; however, copayments and covered services are uniform across plans. This was not always the case. Prior to 1993, HMOs had to only offer "substantially equivalent" benefits package. However, that still allowed plans some latitude to modify basic benefits and offer additional benefits. As a result, plans were adjusting their benefits to deter higher-risk enrollees, and consumers found it increasingly difficult to compare plans. In 1993, HMOs were required to offer identical benefit structures, so plans can no longer design for risk selection, employees can better understand coverage and compare value, and ETF can better evaluate plans' efficiencies.

ETF has a fixed employer contribution policy for all participating enrollees. Currently, the employer share of the premium equals the lower of 90 percent of the premium for the standard FFS or 105 percent of premium for the low-cost HMO. However, the employer contribution never actually exceeds 100 percent of the premium of any chosen plan. Thus, although the premium for the low-cost HMO would be covered in full, there is less incentive for enrollees to choose the low-cost plan—particularly if the higher-cost plans fall within 5 percent of the low-cost plan—because the financial consequences of choosing a higher-cost plan are mitigated.

State Agencies Facilitate Consumer Education

ETF itself operates with a relatively small administrative budget. ETF collects an add-on administrative fee to the premium of approximately $1.16 per contract per month (roughly equivalent to one third of 1 percent of the premium) to cover the administrative services that are performed centrally. These include policy development, selecting and negotiating with health plans, tracking funds flow, consumer information development, consumer ombudsman activities, and data development and reporting. ETF relies heavily on the 26 state agencies and 150 local government participants, each with their own benefit staffs, to perform enrollment, premium collection through payroll deductions, and consumer education functions.

The agencies use common consumer materials developed by the state (such as summary benefit plan descriptions) and host an annual health fair that employees can attend to obtain more information. Benefit staffs in the agencies coordinate most questions about how the system works; however, ETF acts as the final arbiter of any questions that health plans and benefit staffs in the agencies cannot answer. These typically include eligibility questions, coverage questions, and (rarely) exceptions to benefits.

Health plans are allowed to market directly to enrollees within defined parameters. ETF provides mailing labels for all enrollees to each participating health plan. However, ETF must review and approve all promotional materials sent to enrollees by the health plans.

Consolidated Consumer Choice Materials

Enrollees covered through the ETF make their choice of health plans on the basis of a consolidated booklet of information about the program and all of its participating plans. This single document contains all of the different kinds of information that a consumer needs to understand the program, review the covered benefits, and choose among the health plans offered. A copy of this booklet, titled "It's Your Choice," is mailed to each employee during the annual open enrollment period.

The booklet contains information about eligibility and administrative procedures for the ETF program in a question-and-answer format. Summary plan descriptions, comparative price tables by geographic area, comparative tables containing the results of a consumer satisfaction survey, and information about consumer assistance services available through the agencies and ETF are also included. Employees can complete a plan comparison worksheet from the booklet. This worksheet walks consumers through the process of comparing plans as they fill in the blanks with information concerning plan structure, network

characteristics, referral requirements, differences between HMO
coverage and FFS coverage, and appeals processes for dispute
resolution. The booklet contains telephone numbers for consumers to call if more information is needed.

The summary plan descriptions for each health plan offered
are standardized and are two pages long. Each plan submits
one page of text (subject to ETF approval) which answers the
following questions: What type of plan is this? What geographic
areas are covered by the plan? What does the plan think are its
distinguishing characteristics? What are the plan's exclusions
and limitations? The second page is a table detailing covered
services, cost-sharing provisions, and service-specific limitations
for both the required standard benefits and any additional features offered by the plans. (Plans may choose to provide dental
and orthodontic coverage.) Again, each plan provides a phone
number to contact for more information about the plan, such as
participating providers and exclusions and limitations to coverage. Any changes from the previous year's coverages are highlighted in a dark background with white text to make them easy
to identify.

In 1995, ETF began administering and reporting the results
from a consumer satisfaction survey. ETF uses a modified version of the Group Health Association of America (GHAA) survey
questionnaire. The results of this survey are used to develop
plan report cards, which were included in 1996 open enrollment
materials. Survey results are reported by geographic area and
cover topics such as health plan and provider endorsement, satisfaction with health plan services, access to care, effectiveness
of care, the consideration with which providers treat their patients, provision of information to consumers about their care,
and prevention and wellness services. Although the survey is
more detailed, only key indicators in each subject area are published in the booklet. Most of the results are presented in the
form of bar graphs, although some are tabular percentages.

CONCLUSIONS

Each of the purchasers reviewed in this paper has chosen a
consumer-choice model as a means of reducing the cost of health
coverage, improving choice of providers and plans, improving

access to health care services for the enrolled population, and improving the quality of health care services and delivery. In examining their experiences, a few key characteristics stand out as contributing to the success of these endeavors. All of these characteristics enhance the ability of consumers to make valid comparisons across multiple health plans that are competing within a common system of rules and accountability. These examples also suggest a few key issues that should be addressed if a consumer-choice model is to be applied to Medicare.

Characteristics of Systems That Facilitate Choice

In general, all of the organizations studied do four things to facilitate consumer choice. First, they create a level field for comparison among health plans by requiring plans to provide comparable, comprehensive health benefits, providing objective and reliable information, and hosting a structured open enrollment period during which consumers make choices. Second, these organizations provide comprehensive information to support the choice process. This includes information about benefit plan features, health plan structures and network access characteristics, health plan quality information, information about participating providers, and the price to the consumer of the health plan choices. Third, they support the choice process with consumer education. Topics typically covered by consumer education include an introduction to the concepts of managed care, the value of the consumer information provided, support for making trade-offs among plan features and choosing among plans, and administrative information necessary to complete the enrollment process. Finally, these organizations hold the participating health plans accountable for meeting performance standards through the use of common reporting requirements, standard definitions of performance, and standard objective measurement tools and processes.

Consumer Information

Consumer information is the linchpin of consumer choice. It is beyond the scope of this paper to perform a comprehensive analysis of the issues involved in collecting, analyzing, and presenting information to assist consumers choosing among health plans. However, these examples highlight some key operational considerations about the content and mode of delivery of consumer information.

- Consumers require several different kinds of information about the available options, including program and administrative information (e.g., enrollment forms and procedures) as well as individual plan characteristics, price, providers, and performance measures.
- When consumer information about health plans is combined in a single document and in side-by-side comparison tables, it encourages enrollees to make an active choice. In some cases, purchasing groups have put information about each health plan into a separate document (e.g., separate sheets in a pocket folder). This may make it easier for carriers or their agents to limit which health plans are presented to enrollees, thus subverting the choice process.
- Consumers should have easy access to more detailed information about their health plan choices if they desire it. For example, consumers with specific health problems usually want more detailed information about specialists and how health plans treat others with that condition. Most of the organizations described here have toll-free numbers for enrollees. Even if they do not have the information that the consumer wants right at their fingertips, personnel are trained to help the consumer figure out how to get what they want.
- They make the information as simple and as understandable as possible. Consumer choice documents are written in language that typical consumers can understand, without legalistic benefits language or technical statistical terminology. Important information about program characteristics and requirements for enrollees is repeated more than once in multiple forums. The Southern California Edison program illustrates the fact that the more complicated the benefits structure, the more effort is required to ensure that consumers truly understand their benefits, rights, and responsibilities under the system.

Numerous studies have shown that whether an individual's physician is in the health plan is an important determinant of choice. At least two of the sites included in these case studies (the California HIPC and CBIA) are in the process of developing a single provider directory—or superdirectory—for all health plans offered. The purpose of this is to identify all of the participating plans that a given provider participates with, so that enrollees can begin to make comparisons of those plans where they can access their current physician. Although this sounds like a relatively simple undertaking, it is in fact very difficult to ensure that the information in the superdirectory is current and accurate, especially in highly fluid markets like California. It is interesting to note that although Kaiser in California has exclusive relationships with physicians, it is enthusiastic about supporting the superdirectory. Kaiser believes that the greater percentage of women physicians in its panel provides a marketing edge.

Many purchasers have chosen to require health plans to submit the information for consumer choice materials by using common definitions and methodologies, such as HEDIS. In the case of consumer satisfaction surveys, there is a great deal of skepticism by consumers of health plan-generated consumer satisfaction data. Therefore, most purchasers cited here have opted to use a common consumer satisfaction survey instrument and to either administer the survey themselves or have these surveys administered by a qualified survey organization other than the health plans. This is relatively simple to do when the purchaser has direct access to the enrollment files.

The way that the comparative information is presented to seniors is also critical. Comparisons among plans, especially on issues related to quality and performance, can be technical, yet the differences must be easily grasped. Understanding such information is often difficult even for people who are faced with making such decisions regularly, such as federal employees. The experience of Southern California Edison strongly suggests that it is likely to be doubly difficult for seniors. Therefore, great attention should be given to the form of presentation. For example, use of graphics rather than dense text in type that is too small for some seniors to read may be necessary. (Considerable work in developing such easily understand comparative presentations has been done already.)

Consumer Education

Educating Medicare recipients will be a key factor in making recipient choice work for the benefit of the elderly. Education will be important at two stages in the decision-making process: when they are faced with the choice of moving out of traditional fee-for-service Medicare plans to a managed care plan and when they choose among managed care plans.

First, enrollees need education about what managed care is and how managed care plans work. Experience of the Southern California Edison program indicates that people already enrolled in Medicare will be reluctant to move to a managed care plan for a variety of reasons. Thus, it will be important to show Medicare recipients what they gain and what they give up by switching to managed care.[7]

The second point where education is crucial is when recipients are choosing among plans. Again, the information that people have available to use in making decisions should be both unbiased and perceived as unbiased. Furthermore, it must be sufficiently detailed and complete so that people really know what they are doing in choosing one plan over another, but yet not so complicated as to be beyond the understanding of typical Medicare recipients. The experience of all of the purchasing arrangements reviewed in this paper leads to the conclusion that the health plans should not be the only source of information about plan characteristics and performance. Some independent third party—either a government agency or some independent private organization—should have responsibility for providing unbiased information that compares plans in terms of characteristics and performance.

Whether they use benefits managers, benefits counselors,

---

[7]This problem is likely to be reduced in magnitude in the future because many people who become eligible for Medicare will already be in managed care plans. They will be familiar with that form of delivery, and in many cases their plan will also participate in Medicare, so they will not even need to change health plans.

enrollment staff, agents, or peer counselors, most purchasers have individuals who are available to educate enrollees about their health plan options. Of the examples presented here, Southern California Edison probably has the most formalized consumer education process, with newsletters, trained peer counselors, and educational meetings. Whoever performs this education function, it is important that the information enrollees receive both be objective and be perceived as objective. This suggests that health plans cannot be the only source of information, that Medicare recipients have some additional source to turn to for help in making health plan choices.

Number of Health Plans

The number of health plans from which to choose should be manageable. Obviously, the more health plan offerings, the more information each consumer must process in order to select out the information most salient to their decision. With a large number of health plans, written consumer choice materials become thicker, denser, and more difficult to decipher. A number of interactive computer programs are under development; these can offer an alternative to written materials that will present individual consumers with only the information most pertinent to them. When thinking about consumer choice for an elderly population, confusion resulting from the number of health plan options can become a critical issue.

A second reason to limit the number of participating health plans is to maintain a reasonable span of control for the purchaser. In most local markets, there are not so many health plans as to make this infeasible. In markets such as California, where there are numerous health plans, or for purchasers that cover large geographic areas, it begins to get complicated. The greater the number of health plans, the more time-consuming and complex the activities related to monitoring health plan performance become. Xerox has effectively reduced the span of control by using network managers as the liaison between corporate headquarters and the health plans. Each network manager can manage accountability for a limited number of plans and then report up to Xerox corporate headquarters.

Standard Benefit Plan Designs

Sites chosen for this review offer individual consumers a choice of multiple health plans offering standard benefit plan designs. Xerox represents, in essence, the most generous of standardized benefits; as long as care is medically necessary and appropriate, it is covered. At least three of the sites reviewed here incorporated standard benefit plan designs from their inception (CBIA, the California HIPC, and CHIP). They reasoned that consumers should be able to compare plans on the basis of value—the relationship of quality and cost. Few consumers are knowledgeable enough to know the true difference in the actuarial values of different benefits. Thus, when benefits vary between health plans, consumers are often not capable of evaluating relative value when choosing among plans. To accommodate consumer preferences, these purchasers offer different levels of benefits (e.g., a standard option and a high option) reflecting different levels of cost sharing and/or a POS option providing some coverage for out-of-network benefits.

It is important to note that when individual health plans are able to define the benefits offered, they have an incentive to offer a set of benefits that will attract healthy enrollees and deter enrollees with ongoing or expensive medical needs. Wisconsin ETF moved to a standard benefit plan design for its HMOs because it wanted to eliminate this kind of risk segmentation by health plans, as well as facilitate choice.

Open Enrollment

All of the example plans include an open enrollment period, during which each enrollee can opt to change plans. The methods of managing these open enrollment periods vary. All of the plans cited use passive reenrollment rather than active reenrollment during open season. Under a passive enrollment system, enrollees choosing to stay in the same plan from year to year are not required to complete an enrollment form; they are automatically reenrolled. Only those employees choosing to change plans must complete an enrollment form. Under an active open enrollment system, each enrollee must fill out an enrollment form whether or not they change plans. From an administrative standpoint, a passive enrollment system is simpler and less costly because there are fewer forms to process. Also, a smaller percentage of enrollees change plans in any given year under passive enrollment than change plans under active reenrollment. On the other hand, active reenrollment can provide a ready-made vehicle for collecting information from all enrollees in a system by tagging a few consumer-related questions onto the enrollment form.

Another administrative issue related to open enrollment is whether to have a single open enrollment period at the same time every year or to have an open enrollment period based on the enrollees' anniversary date. With a single open enrollment period, all enrollees are choosing plans at the same time for the same contract period. This makes it relatively simple for the administrator to coordinate data collection and reporting to ensure that current information is available for comparing and choosing among plans. However, it also results in a large spike in administrative activity to process enrollment forms once per year. Under continuous reenrollment, administrative resources are used more evenly throughout the year, but some enrollees are then choosing a plan on the basis of information about health plans and their providers that may be outdated.

Key Issues

In addition to the above characteristics of structures and processes for facilitating consumer choice, several key policy issues will need to be addressed when designing a consumer choice model for Medicare enrollees.

• How will the enrollee cost-sharing requirements (if any) be structured? If one objective is to reduce the cost of the Medicare program through consumer choice, then cost sharing should be structured to encourage enrollment in cost-effective plans rather than encourage risk selection.

• How will health plans be held accountable for performance? Although the ability of enrollees to "vote with their feet" creates a marketplace system of accountability, all of the purchasers examined here also use negotiated performance guarantees, common measures of plan performance, and an objective process for measuring performance (e.g., centralized, standardized consumer surveys). Such a system of accountability is not currently in place for Medicare enrollees.

• Should consumer information only compare plans with each other or should plans also be compared against benchmarks or standards? Relative plan comparisons provide useful information for selecting among alternatives; however, several purchasers (notably Xerox and Southern California Edison) are setting objective standards, based on regional and national norms, and reporting plan performance against these norms directly to consumers.

• How will plans be marketed and presented to enrollees? Those purchasers described here who serve the small group and individual markets use agents as brokers to some degree. Among the concerns related to using agents to market to Medicare enrollees are standard agent training or certification, equitable compensation regardless of the plan selected by the enrollee, and systems of monitoring and accountability for agents.

REFERENCES

Darling, H. 1991. Employers and managed care: What are the early returns? Health Affairs 10(Winter):147–160.

Darling, H. 1992. HealthLink–Xerox innovative healthcare strategy. Xerox Corporation Report. April 1992. Photocopy.

G

Medicare Managed Care: Issues for Vulnerable Populations

Joyce Dubow[*]

INTRODUCTION

Recent interest in managed care, a system of care that accepts responsibility for the delivery of health services and the financing of coverage, stems largely from its purported ability to save money.[1] In the private sector, employers have turned to managed care to contain steadily rising outlays for employee health insurance premiums. Now, the U.S. Congress also seeks to curb Medicare's rate of growth by restructuring the Medicare program through the introduction of a broader range of health care options that feature managed care arrangements (Balanced Budget Act of 1995). However, the plan to shift the Medicare

---

[*]Public Policy Institute, American Association of Retired Persons, Washington, D.C.

[1]A definitive conclusion on whether managed care generates true savings must rest on whether the rate of growth of health expenditures is reduced over time. In the Medicare program, there is evidence that HMOs can produce savings, but these have not been passed along to the federal government. To generate savings to Medicare from expanded enrollment in HMOs, changes in Medicare's enrollment conditions and payment system for HMOs would have to be made (Congressional Budget Office, 1995).

195

program so rapidly to managed care raises key questions about this approach, in part because the intended shift is so rapid and also because many are not persuaded that managed care plans are ready for a large influx of vulnerable new members (Braveman and Bennett, 1995). Others caution that the expectations of managed care are unrealistic (Ginzberg, 1995; Mashaw and Marmor, 1995; Meyer et al., forthcoming).

Unlike their younger counterparts, Medicare beneficiaries have had relatively little exposure to diverse managed care models. As of January 1996, only slightly more than 10 percent, or approximately 4 million individuals, have been enrolled in any form of managed care, mainly risk-based health maintenance organizations (HMOs). Enrollment is concentrated in just a few areas. In January 1996, about 50 percent of the Medicare beneficiaries enrolled in risk-based HMOs lived in just four states, California, Florida, Arizona, and New York (Health Care Financing Administration, Office of Managed Care, 1995a). Furthermore, those beneficiaries who have been enrolled in Medicare HMOs have tended to be healthier and younger than those enrolled in the traditional Medicare program (Brown et al., 1993). In January 1994, only 4.8 percent of Medicare risk enrollees were disabled (compared with approximately 11 percent in the traditional Medicare program) (Health Care Financing Administration, Office of Managed Care Operations and Oversight Team, 1995b). Finally, a recently released survey of Medicare beneficiaries (U.S. Department of Health and Human Services, 1995a) indicates that many beneficiaries (64 percent) do not even know if they live in areas where they could currently enroll in a managed care plan—this, in spite of the fact that three fourths of beneficiaries do have such an option. Thus, managed care is unknown or unfamiliar to many beneficiaries.

The purpose of this paper is to consider the prospect of managed care enrollment for Medicare beneficiaries, particularly those who are vulnerable. How can such individuals be expected to fare in a health delivery environment that is vastly different from the one that most of them have known and understood? The paper first defines "vulnerable" and presents selected demographic characteristics of such individuals. The experiences of vulnerable individuals in managed care programs is then considered by examining some of the research literature with regard to medical outcomes, patient satisfaction, and disenrollment. Ways that managed care plans currently organize to treat their vulnerable enrollees are presented, and promising innovations and practices that appear to have potential for the successful treatment of vulnerable or high-risk persons are highlighted. Finally, the unique responsibility of public (versus private) purchasers to safeguard the interests of Medicare and Medicaid beneficiaries is identified and the protections that are needed by vulnerable populations enrolled in managed care plans are described.

DEFINITION OF VULNERABLE

The changing demographic characteristics of the Medicare population will have a profound effect on the future of the program, particularly with respect to expenditures and the provision of services to beneficiaries. As policy makers develop strategies for restructuring Medicare, it is imperative that they take into account the individuals who use and rely on program benefits. Medicare beneficiaries are vulnerable because of age-related physiologic changes, multiple chronic physical and mental conditions, limited social resources, and a limited ability to manage change (Bates and Brown, 1988). Those segments of the Medicare population that are growing will have the greatest needs: the "old old," people of color, those with disabilities such as end-stage renal disease (ESRD), and cognitive impairments. Therefore, delivery systems must adjust to address the unique needs of an older, frailer population.

To one degree or another, virtually the entire Medicare population can be considered vulnerable because of its greater need for health care services and the higher health care costs that beneficiaries incur on account of their age, health status, economic status, or disability. To be sure, many of the "young old" are vibrant and healthy. Nevertheless, as a group, Medicare beneficiaries need more health care services, develop more chronic conditions as they age, and on average, have relatively low incomes and who, but for Social Security and Medicare, would be poor. Therefore, in this paper, "vulnerable populations" are considered Medicare beneficiaries, both aged and dis-

abled, including those dually eligible for Medicaid and Medicare.

As of 1994, there were 36.7 million Medicare beneficiaries of
whom 32.6 million were aged (age 65 and over) and 4.1 million
were disabled (Health Care Financing Administration, Bureau
of Data Management and Strategy, 1995). This estimate includes 229,000 persons with ESRD.

In 1994, 14 percent of all Medicare beneficiaries were minorities: 8 percent were African Americans, 2 percent were Asian
or Pacific Islanders, less than 1 percent were American Indian
or Native Alaskan, and 4 percent were of Hispanic origin (who
may be of any race) (American Association of Retired Persons/
U.S. Department of Health and Human Services, Administration on Aging, 1995). Seventy-four percent of beneficiaries lived
in urban areas, whereas 26 percent were from rural areas. The
racial compositions of those living in urban and rural areas
were similar, with whites making up about 84 percent of the
beneficiary population in urban areas and 87 percent in rural
areas (Health Care Financing Administration, 1995). Elderly
populations of color, as a percentage of the total U.S. population, are projected to increase; by 2020, 21 percent of elderly
persons are projected to be persons of color; by 2050, 30 percent
(American Society on Aging, 1992).

Disabled beneficiaries account for a growing proportion of
total Medicare enrollees. In 1994, disabled enrollees accounted
for 11 percent of all beneficiaries, a proportion that is projected
to increase to 17 percent by the year 2010; the ESRD population
is projected to double by this date, largely because of improved
technology and a greater availability of dialysis machines
(Health Care Financing Administration, Office of Research and
Demonstration, 1995; U.S. General Accounting Office, 1995a).
With respect to their racial composition, 18 percent of disabled
Medicare beneficiaries are African Americans. Ten percent of
beneficiaries are of Hispanic origin (Adler and Phil, 1995).

Age

In 1992, 12.7 percent of the U.S. population or 33.2 million
people, were 65 years of age or over (American Association of
Retired Persons, U.S. Department of Health and Human Ser-

TABLE G-1 Actual and Projected
Growth of those 65 and over, 1990, 2030
(percent of total population)

Year	≥65	65-74	75-84	≥85
1990	12.6	7.3	4.0	1.3
2030	21.8	12.0	7.1	2.7

SOURCE: U.S. Congress, Senate, et al., 1991.

vices, Administration on Aging, 1995). The older population, as a proportion of the total population, has tripled in this century. By 2030, the number of persons over age 65 is expected to grow to 65.6 million, representing 22 percent of the total population (Table G-1). There is an upward trend in life expectancy. The increase in life expectancy since 1970 has resulted from declines in mortality among middle-aged and elderly persons U.S. Congress, Senate, et al., 1991) (Figure G-1).

Like the general population, the elderly population is growing older. By 2000, of the 35 million persons who will be 65 years of age or older, half will be between the ages of 65 and 74 and almost half will be age 75 or over (U.S. Congress, Senate, et al., 1991). The population over age 85 is the fastest-growing portion of the population.

In 1994, among Medicare beneficiaries, 46 percent were between 65 and 74 years of age; as a percentage of total Medicare enrollees, the number of people in this age group has been steadily declining (Health Care Financing Administration, Bureau of Data Management and Strategy, 1995; Health Care Financing Administration, Office of Research and Demonstration, 1995). Thirty-one percent were between the ages of 75 and 84, and almost 12 percent were age 85 and over, a group whose numbers have steadily been increasing as a percentage of the total Medicare population (Health Care Financing Administration, Bureau of Data Management and Strategy, 1995; Health Care Financing Administration, Office of Research and Demonstration, 1995). In 1994, Medicare expenditures were greatest for the cohort over age 85; Medicare expenditures for this group are projected to increase sixfold from 1987 to 2040 (Schneider

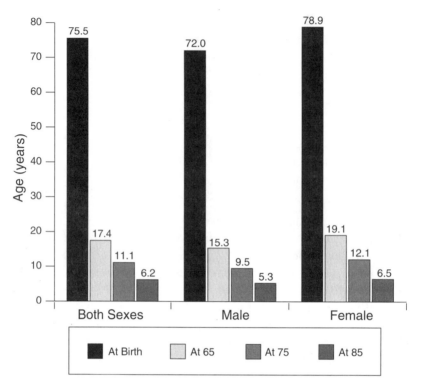

FIGURE G-1 Life expectancy at birth and at age 65, 75, and 85, 1991.
SOURCE: U.S. Department of Health and Human Services, 1995d, Table 1,
pp. 136-137.

and Guralnik, 1990). Of the disabled population on Medicare,
almost 35 percent were under 45 years of age, 27 percent were
between the ages of 45 and 54, and 38 percent were between the
ages of 55 and 64.

Health Status

Data from the Medicare Current Beneficiary Survey indicate that when asked how each would rate his or her own health
compared with the health of others the same age, almost 46
percent of aged Medicare beneficiaries rated their health as
excellent or very good, a proportion that is considered "remarkably stable" across all age groups (Adler and Phil, 1995). However, other survey results (Figure G-2) suggest that individual

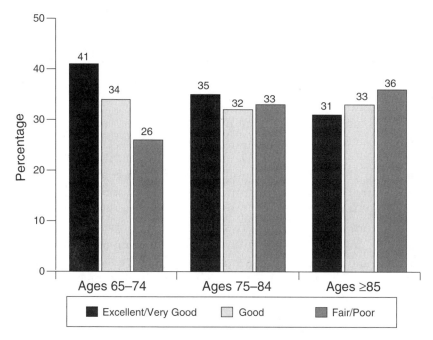

FIGURE G-2 Self-reported health status, percent distribution of persons by age according to respondent-assessed health status, 1992. SOURCE: U.S. Department of Health and Human Services, 1995d, Table 1, p. 36.

perceptions of health may decline with age. Self-assessed health status also differs markedly by disability status and race. Only 17 percent of disabled beneficiaries and approximately 25 percent of African Americans reported their health as excellent or very good (Adler and Phil, 1995; Health Care Financing Adminstration, 1995).

Data from a 1994 National Research Corporation survey indicate that those Medicare beneficiaries enrolled in HMOs report health status similar to those receiving care in the traditional Medicare program. Forty-seven percent of HMO members considered their health status to be excellent or very good, whereas 46 percent in the fee-for-service program considered their health status to be excellent or very good (Group Health Association of America, 1995d).

Disability and Chronic Health Care Problems

Medicare beneficiaries have diverse needs and service preferences that range from medical care for those with acute chronic conditions to services that help individuals compensate for chronic health problems or disability.

With advancing age, the incidence of acute conditions diminishes as chronic conditions become more frequent (U.S. Congress, Senate, et al., 1991). In 1991, the Institute of Medicine reported that among those age 60 and over, 8 of 10 had one or more chronic diseases or impairments (Pope and Tarlov, 1991). The top 10 chronic conditions for people over 65 years of age in 1989 were arthritis, hypertension, hearing impairment, heart disease, cataracts, deformity or orthopedic impairment, chronic sinusitis, diabetes, visual impairment, and varicose veins (U.S. Congress, Senate, et al., 1991). Chronic conditions are the main cause of disability among elderly persons (Bates and Brown, 1988).

Researchers use different measures to assess varying degrees of impairment, in part, on the basis of how well individuals function in the community. The following data illustrate variations in the prevalence of disability in the population over age 65 reflecting three different ways of evaluating impairment from less to more severe. (1) In 1991-1992, almost half of those over 65 years of age had difficulty with or were unable to perform everyday activities such as seeing words and letters, hearing normal conversations, having their speech understood, and climbing stairs without resting. (2) A more limited number, about 22 percent, had difficulty with or needed personal assistance with specific tasks (i.e., instrumental activities of daily living that help them remain in the community), such as keeping track of money, preparing meals, or getting around outside the home. (3) Finally, about 15 percent had difficulty with an activity of daily living (ADL) such as getting in and out of bed, bathing, eating, or dressing (McNeil, 1993).

In addition to functional impairments, many older persons also have mental or cognitive impairments. The various forms of dementia that affect behavioral, emotional, and social functioning are the primary mental disorders of elders. Other causes of cognitive impairment in elderly persons include delirium, the toxic effects of medications, trauma, and psychiatric illness. The prevalence of dementia among those over 65 years of age living in the community is approximately 3 to 6 percent, with the prevalence increasing with advancing age (Callahan et al., 1995). Nationally, in 1991, the total cost for those with senile dementia was estimated at $67 billion (Callahan et al., 1995). Nearly 5 million individuals over 65 years of age experience serious symptoms of depression. However, this estimate may undercount the prevalence of this condition because depression is probably underdiagnosed (Rolnick et al., 1994). There is research indicating that rates of depression are high among chronically ill, older adults (Williams et al., 1995). Approximately 5 percent of older adults have an anxiety disorder, with perhaps 10 to 20 percent displaying anxiety symptoms (Smyer, 1993).

Utilization of Services

Those over 65 years of age use more health services than younger persons. On average, in 1993, those over age 65 had almost 10 physician contacts compared with approximately 6 visits for those under age 65 (U.S. Department of Health and Human Services, Public Health Service, 1995). Likewise, in 1992, those over age 65 averaged 2,711 hospital days per 1,000 persons compared with about 456 days per 1,000, for persons 0 to 64 years of age (Gabel et al., 1994; Health Care Financing Administration, Bureau of Data Management and Strategy, 1995). Differences in the utilization of health services between younger and older populations appear to hold true in managed care as well. In 1992, HMO members who were group enrollees averaged 3.9 ambulatory physician encounters per year, compared with 7 ambulatory physician encounters per Medicare risk enrollee (Gabel et al., 1994). In 1992, HMO enrollees over 65 years of age averaged 1,295 hospital days per 1,000 persons, compared with 270 days per 1,000 members for HMO enrollees 64 and under (Gabel et al., 1994).

Income and Poverty Status

In 1994, 83 percent of Medicare spending was on behalf of

those with annual incomes under $25,000, suggesting that Medi-
care (as well as Medicaid) primarily serves the needs of lower-
income individuals (Armstead et al., 1995). In fact, as a group,
Medicare beneficiaries are people who have relatively low incomes. In 1993, 30 percent of all Medicare beneficiaries had
annual incomes under $20,000; more than 20 percent had an-
nual incomes under $10,000 (The Public Policy Institute/Ameri-
can Association of Retired Persons, 1995, using Current Population Survey data) (Table G-2).

In 1994, the poverty rate for persons over age 65 was 11.7
percent. The threshold used by the Census Bureau to establish
poverty status for the elderly is lower than that for other age
groups (The Public Policy Institute/American Association of
Retired Persons, 1995) (Table G-3). As a result, older persons
must have lower incomes than younger persons to be considered
"poor" by the federal government.

In 1994, 2.5 percent of elderly persons had incomes under
50 percent of the federal poverty level, 11.7 percent had incomes
below 100 percent of the federal poverty level, and almost 18.7
percent had incomes below 125 percent of the federal poverty

TABLE G-2 Income of Persons Covered
by Medicare in 1993

Family Income in Thousands ($)	Age 0-64, %	Age ≥65, %	Total, %
0-10	30.4	20.2	21.3
10-20	25.2	30.1	29.5
20-30	17.4	19.2	19.0
30-50	15.9	17.9	17.7
50-75	7.5	7.6	7.6
75-100	2.3	2.5	2.5
>100	1.3	2.5	2.4
Total	100.0	100.0	100.0

SOURCE: The Public Policy Institute/AARP. Compiled from Current Population Surveys, March
Supplement, 1994, Bureau of the Census.

TABLE G-3 Threshold Income for Federal Poverty Level, 1994

	Elderly	Nonelderly
Single	$7,108	$7,718
Couple	$9,976	$8,967

SOURCE: The Public Policy Institute/ American Association of Retired Persons, 1995, Current Population Survey Data.

level (The Public Policy Institute/American Association of Retired Persons, 1995).

Social Security accounts for half or more of annual income for approximately 60 percent of elderly persons. Thirty-two percent of older persons rely on Social Security for 80 percent of their incomes (Health Care Financing Administration, 1995).

Medicaid

The Medicaid program assists low-income Medicare beneficiaries with premiums, deductibles, and Medicare cost-sharing requirements under the Qualified Medicare Beneficiary program. For those who are eligible, it also covers benefits not covered by Medicare, such as prescription drugs and long-term care. Less than one-third of poor elderly persons are Medicaid beneficiaries, and less than 10 percent of elderly people with incomes between 100 and 200 percent of the federal poverty level are covered under Medicaid. In 1995, nearly 5 million Medicare beneficiaries received some assistance from Medicaid (Health Care Financing Administration, 1995). Although only 12 percent of Medicaid beneficiaries are elderly, 28 percent of Medicaid program expenditures are made on behalf of this population; three quarters of this spending goes for long-term care services (The Kaiser Commission on the Future of Medicaid, 1995).

Out-of-Pocket Expenditures

Out-of-pocket health costs represent a substantial burden for older Americans. This is especially true for those with lower incomes. Low-income beneficiaries pay a larger share of their incomes for out-of-pocket costs than those with higher incomes. Furthermore, the oldest old pay even larger out-of-pocket costs than their younger elderly counterparts. Compared with younger persons, the elderly spend nearly four times more out-of-pocket for health costs than those under 65 years of age ($2,519 versus $668) (American Association of Retired Persons, The Urban Institute, 1995).

EXPERIENCES OF VULNERABLE INDIVIDUALS IN MANAGED CARE

In its report, *Access to Health Care in America*, the Institute of Medicine asserted that regular care is necessary for those with chronic conditions to improve functioning and minimize discomfort. Although regular care does not always prevent adverse consequences of chronic conditions, the absence of such care is associated with more negative outcomes for individuals (Millman, 1993). For those who are sick, poor, or disabled, special attention must be paid to ensure that such vulnerable persons actually have access to and receive regular care.

The different incentives that exist in managed care and fee-for-service care have important implications for beneficiaries in terms of access, use of services, and health outcomes. Clement and colleagues (1994, p. 1492) have written that "whether . . . reductions in services (that managed care plans achieve) are due to a more judicious use of services, rather than limiting beneficial care, remains uncertain." Schlesinger and Mechanic (1993, p. 129) note that "because norms of appropriate treatment are ill-defined for many chronic conditions, it is difficult to determine if reduced spending or shifts in the nature of service have led to poorer outcomes."

Most managed care plans have had little experience treating older, sicker, or disabled patients (Armstead et al., 1995; Tanenbaum and Hurley, 1995). Although some analysts believe that managed care can well serve the majority of the population, such plans may not be suitable for those who make heavier use of the health care system. There is also evidence that elderly persons and those who are disabled are apprehensive about changes that will "force" them into managed care plans. In focus groups conducted in 1995, the greatest concerns expressed by seniors who were not enrollees in managed care plans were the restrictions on physician choice and the perceived lower quality of care in HMOs (Frederick/Schneiders, Inc., 1995).

Advocates for those with chronic illnesses are concerned as well about managed care. "The fear among . . . patients, their families, and advocates is that managed care organizations— prepaid health plans that share the risk of losing money on services—are too inexperienced, too inflexible, and too profit-oriented to meet their special needs" (Families USA Foundation, 1995, p. 1). Others express concerns about the financial incentives in managed care. "Many mental health advocates, who believe that the financial incentives inherent in HMOs, as well as HMOs' lack of experience in providing services to seriously mentally ill individuals, could lead to ineffective or inappropriate care, and a deterioration in the mental health status of these persons" (Christianson and Osher, 1994, p. 899). Still others recognize that although "managed care itself is not the enemy," . . . there are plans that "cut costs by recruiting the healthiest patients, rationing care by making it inconvenient to obtain, and denying care by a variety of mechanisms" (Kassirer, 1995, p. 50). Patients with chronic illness have "ongoing, often complex and expensive health care needs [that] make them unattractive in a capitated environment" (Safran et al., 1994, p. 1579). These kinds of concerns are raised often and must be taken seriously. The research evidence is limited because managed care has not been the major health delivery system for vulnerable populations. Furthermore, the industry is changing rapidly. Thus, what is known about one particular model may not necessarily apply to the newer managed care entrants. Nevertheless, some of the research evidence may be helpful in predicting how vulnerable populations will experience managed care.

Health Outcomes

In general, HMOs save money by reducing the use and intensity of services. A comprehensive examination of the Medicare HMO risk program conducted by Mathematica Policy Research, Inc., found that Medicare risk plans may spend about 10.5 percent less than the Health Care Financing Administration (HCFA) would have spent for the provision of all medical services in the fee-for-service sector.[2] These savings result from the reduction of the number of hospital days and the average length of stay, but not hospital admissions. Furthermore, enrollment in HMOs increased the likelihood that beneficiaries will receive some services (e.g., physical examinations and skilled nursing facility care), but reduced their intensity or frequency (e.g., skilled nursing facility stays rather than rehabilitation hospital stays and fewer home health visits). Finally, HMOs increased the use of some services for members who were in the poorest health but reduced the intensity of services more for this group than for other enrollees. The Mathematica study found that, compared with fee-for-service plans, HMOs produced similar outcomes for inpatient and ambulatory care (Brown et al., 1993).

Other researchers have studied whether the conclusions from the Medicare Competition Demonstrations apply to the ongoing Medicare Managed Risk Program. Clement and colleagues (1994) compared Medicare beneficiaries in risk HMOs with two symptoms, chest pain and joint pain, with their fee-for-service plan counterparts to determine differences in access to care and medical outcomes. The authors reported three consistent findings: (1) For both conditions, HMO enrollees were less likely to report that they had seen a specialist than those in fee-for-service plans. (2) HMO enrollees were less likely to have reported that follow-up care had been recommended. (3) Despite these differences, outcomes were similar for HMO and fee-for-

---

[2]Nevertheless, the Mathematica study also reported that Medicare risk HMOs have increased estimated costs to HCFA by 5.7 percent more than it would have spent had the HMO enrollees remained in the traditional Medicare program (Brown et al., 1993).

service enrollees in three of four outcomes measures. Only among HMO patients was there less symptomatic improvement of joint pain. The authors observe that "less intensive HMO care may have led to less satisfactory outcomes for some patients" (Clement et al., 1994, p. 1491). The fact that HMO enrollees experienced less relief from joint pain is a concern, because arthritis is a chronic condition commonly found among elderly persons and, in the view of Clement et al., "should have been better ameliorated." Clement has suggested that failure of HMO patients to have experienced improvement similar to those in fee-for-service plans could reflect an overall lack of knowledge about the management of chronic illnesses in the elderly (Winslow, 1994).

Additionally, Clement and colleagues (1994) observe that the reduced likelihood of referral to specialists "warrants consideration." This is an important issue for individuals with chronic conditions, many of whom rely on the care of specialists for treatment. However, Clement and colleagues acknowledge that "for most symptoms and illnesses the appropriate rate of specialty referrals, as with other resource-intensive practice styles, is unknown" (Clement et al., 1994, p. 1491).

A recent study provides another perspective on the use of specialty physicians and practice site. No "meaningful differences" were found among nonelderly patients with either hypertension or non-insulin-dependent diabetes who received care from either generalist or specialist physicians in an HMO, individual practice association (IPA), or fee-for-service setting (Greenfield et al., 1995). The authors concluded that (with respect to physiologic, functional, and mortality outcomes measures) there was "no evidence that any one system of care or physician specialty achieved consistently better 2-year or 4-year outcomes than others" (p. 1436) for the conditions studied.

Carlisle and colleagues (1992) compared elderly HMO and fee-for-service patients who had been hospitalized with acute myocardial infarction to evaluate the quality of care for this condition provided to Medicare beneficiaries. The study showed no significant mortality differences between HMO members and fee-for-service beneficiaries, although HMO compliance with process criteria was greater in three of five outcomes measures (Carlisle et al., 1992).

A randomized trial of elderly Medicaid beneficiaries found that enrollment in prepaid plans had no adverse effect on poor, elderly Medicaid beneficiaries during the year that the patients were evaluated. Although the enrollees in prepaid plans used significantly less care, there was no indication that they experienced poorer health as a result (Lurie et al., 1994).

Although the studies noted above are examples of evidence that HMOs have satisfactorily treated older or chronically ill patients, there is also evidence in the research literature that finds this model wanting with respect to vulnerable populations. The following describes several studies that point up concerns.

Safran and colleagues (1994) compared staff/group model HMOs, IPAs, and traditional fee-for-service plans to determine the extent to which each of five core dimensions of high-quality primary care (accessibility, continuity, comprehensiveness, coordination, and accountability) were received by chronically ill patients[3] The results showed that neither prepaid systems nor fee-for-service plans provide primary care optimally. The prepaid plans (HMOs and IPAs) provided increased financial access and coordination and "reduced patient-physician continuity and comprehensiveness of care and, in many cases, . . . diminished organizational access and interpersonal treatment" (p. 1583).

The authors examined access from two perspectives, financial and organizational. Financial access was a greater barrier in fee-for-service plans because of requirements for higher out-of-pocket costs. However, organizational barriers were greater in some, although not all, HMOs studied. In the cases in which organizational access was a barrier, patients reported difficulties in receiving medical care on short notice and longer waits for emergency treatment. The authors observed that organizational barriers to access are disruptive to the continuity of care (which might be of particular significance to those with chronic

---

[3]To qualify, a patient had to have at least one of five conditions: hypertension, diabetes, congestive heart failure, recent myocardial infarction, or major depressive disorder—all conditions known to affect functional status and well-being.

conditions). With respect to continuity, the results showed some overlap on scores on the high end among the three types of plans studied, but showed that the prepaid plans produced a range of scores that extended much lower than those for the fee-for-service plans. The lower comprehensiveness of care[4] score for HMOs may reflect "organizational access barriers and/or HMO referral practices" (p. 1584). The authors suggest that HMO patients may opt to see other providers rather than wait to see their own providers. Also, HMOs rely on primary care providers more than IPAs or fee-for-service plans do. Thus, in that study HMO patients were less likely than their IPA and fee-for-service counterparts to see a specialist for primary care. (Less than 5 percent of HMO patients received primary care from a specialist.[5])

Shaughnessy and colleagues (1994) found most home health care outcomes in fee-for-service plans to be better than those in HMOs. (There were no differences in outcomes for wound patients and patients receiving intravenous therapy.) Schlenker (forthcoming) found that HMO home health care costs are "significantly lower" than those in fee-for-service plans, even after controlling for case mix, demographic characteristics, region, and agency factors. Despite reduced expenditures for home health care, HMOs did not substitute other services for home health care services. Shaughnessy and colleagues (1994) observed that "relative to the fee-for-service sector, it appears that HMOs tend to approach some aspects of home health care with more of a 'maintenance' philosophy than a rehabilitative or restorative philosophy" (p. 219). If true, this would have enormous implications for the vulnerable populations under discussion here, whose very quality of life could depend on achieving or maintaining maximum function. Shaughnessy and colleagues noted that the findings were most pronounced among HMO patients whose care was contracted out to home health agencies. Thus, the ways in which managed care plans organize the provi-

---

[4]"Comprehensiveness" measured the total number of health care visits and the number of visits during the preceding 6 months.

[5]Some analysts believe that primary care provided by primary care physicians rather than specialists improves continuity and comprehensiveness and does not compromise quality of care or outcomes (Franks et al., 1992).

sion of services has implications for patient care as well. Shaughnessy and colleagues further observed that the HMOs may not be aware of the "potential value of home health care in terms of service integration, patient preference, quality of life, and patient benefits in terms of functioning" (p. 219). These conclusions should be of particular concern to Medicare beneficiaries because "home health care has provided a 'safety net' for major reductions in institutional care. . . . In fact, reductions in home care are likely to lead to increased uses of and expenditures for other services" (Schlenker, forthcoming, p. ii).

Outcome studies of HMO patients with serious mental illness show conflicting findings (Christianson and Osher, 1994). In a literature review of studies of patients with severe mental illness, Christianson and Osher cited the RAND medical outcomes study that reported no significant difference in the recognition and treatment of depression by psychiatrists in HMOs, group practice, and solo practice settings. However, HMO patients "receive a less intensive style of care than comparable persons under fee-for-service coverage." Still citing the RAND study, Christianson and Osher noted that HMO patients were less than half as likely as fee-for-service patients to be seen by a psychiatrist. The RAND study indicated that there is some evidence that among patients of psychiatrists, some HMO members with depression experience worse outcomes than those in fee-for-service plans (Rogers et al., 1993). However, depressed patients of general clinicians or nonphysician mental health specialists showed no differences in clinical or functioning outcomes by type of payment. Lurie and colleagues (1992) conducted a randomized controlled trial to determine the effect of type of payment on the health outcomes of Medicaid enrollees with chronic mental illness and found that there were no significant differences between prepaid and fee-for-service patients, at least in the short run.

The RAND Health Insurance Experiment examining the health outcomes of individuals randomly assigned to HMOs and fee-for-service plans concluded that there were different effects for high- and low-income HMO enrollees who entered the experiment with health problems (Ware et al., 1986). Compared with their fee-for-service counterparts, HMO enrollees with high incomes showed "significant improvement," while low-income sick HMO enrollees reported "significantly more bed-days per year due to poor health and more serious symptoms" than those in fee-for-service plans. The authors observed that the "results suggest that high and low income groups may realize different benefits from prepaid group practice and fee-for-service" (p. 1021).[6]

Patient Satisfaction

In general, surveys of the satisfaction of HMO members indicate that they are more satisfied with the out-of-pocket cost of care and the reduced paperwork burden in managed care than those in fee-for-service but that they are less satisfied with access to care, including availability of specialist referrals and restrictions on the choice of physicians. These findings are consistent across several surveys (e.g., Clement et al., 1992; The Commonwealth Fund, 1995; U.S. Department of Health and Human Services, 1995c). A 1994 study of Medicare HMO enrollees found that 84 percent remained in the same plan, 6 percent switched to another HMO in their area, 6 percent disenrolled for reasons unrelated to the plan, and 4 percent returned to fee-for-service plans (Group Health Association of America, 1995c).

A recent survey of enrollees in managed care plans found that nonelderly sick enrollees reported more problems getting the health services that they or their providers believed that they needed and more difficulty getting to see specialists than those in fee-for-service plans (The Robert Wood Johnson Foundation, 1995). Compared with sick or disabled patients in fee-for-service plans, enrollees in managed care plans also reported that they waited longer for appointments, that managed care physicians failed to explain what they were doing during visits,

---

[6]It should be noted that these conclusions have been challenged by Wagner and Bledsoe (1990), who argue that "the correct interpretation of associations between the quantity and quality of health care and changes in these nonspecific health status indicators (i.e., bed-days and serious symptoms) for a heterogeneous low-income population remains uncertain at best. In the absence of corroboration, the most compelling explanation for the differences in health outcomes is chance."

and that the medical care that they provided was not correct or appropriate. Sicker HMO members also complained about specialist care. Compared with fee-for-service patients, more managed care enrollees thought that specialist care was incorrect or inappropriate, the examination that they received was not thorough, and that the time that the physician spent with them was inadequate. The sick or disabled managed care enrollees also reported lower out-of-pocket costs than their fee-for-service counterparts.

Disenrollment

The findings from disenrollment studies are also instructive. In 1993, although the majority of Medicare beneficiaries surveyed by the Office of the Inspector General (OIG) of the U.S. Department of Health and Human Services reported they received the services they needed, 20 to 25 percent of those who disenrolled claimed that they failed to receive primary care, referrals to specialists, and HMO coverage of emergency care (U.S. Department of Health and Human Services, 1995c). Another OIG report indicated that among HMOs with higher disenrollment rates, more enrollees reported service access problems (U.S. Department of Health and Human Services, 1995b). Disenrollees rated their health status lower than enrollees rated their health status and reported a greater decline in health status during their HMO enrollment. Disenrollees who were disabled or who had ESRD reported difficulty getting access to care more often than beneficiaries over the age of 65 did. HMOs with more experience in the Medicare risk HMO program showed the largest decreases in their disenrollment rates over time.

Other studies of disenrollment from Medicare HMOs have found that disenrollees "have characteristics usually associated with high use of services" (Porell et al., 1992). They were poorer, more likely to be disabled, and more likely to report a problem requiring hospitalization. However, an earlier look at disenrollment in the Medicare Competition Demonstrations found that, "among the variables that indicate an association between health status and disenrollment, only the amount of Part B Medicare expenditures prior to joining the HMO approached a level of significance that indicated a relationship may exist" (Langwell and Hadley, 1989, p. 71). Also looking at the Medicare Competition Demonstrations, Retchin and associates concluded that "although disenrollees were more likely to experience functional declines (in one or more ADLs), at follow-up, these declines were of marginal statistical significance and most likely due to baseline differences" (Retchin et al., 1992, p. 665).

SERVICE DELIVERY

Several years ago, Fox and colleagues (1991) recognized that there was a dearth of research about the delivery of services to older persons in managed care. They and others have proposed research agendas to fill this gap (e.g., Davis et al., 1994; Lewin/ ICF, 1990). Although interest in managed care research has grown considerably, results and conclusions remain sparse. Managed care is still evolving. Without firm and consistent evidence, it would be premature to make judgments about the effectiveness of current practices. The term "best practices" should be reserved for those that have been tested and evaluated on the basis of the quality and cost-effectiveness of the care provided.

Nevertheless, many managed care plans are actively involved in demonstrating different approaches to the provision of care of their vulnerable populations (see, e.g., Group Health Association of America, 1995a; Health Care Financing Administration, Division of Policy and Evaluation, Office of Managed Care, 1994). These might be called "promising interventions" or "models of care" (Teresa Fama, Deputy Director, Chronic Care Program, Washington, D.C., personal communication, November 1995). As Medicare enrollment continues to increase, plans that have heretofore had few older, disabled, or chronically ill members will be confronted with the greater diversity of needs of such individuals. Undoubtedly, they will look to current practices, as well as experiment with other interventions to care for their Medicare enrollees.

Pawlson (1994) has suggested that the "acute disease paradigm" (an isolated event with a single, proximate cause) that has been the hallmark of the U.S. health care system is no

longer appropriate for large numbers of the population. Instead, a "chronic complex illness model" that involves a broader
range of variables appears more suitable in treating and assessing the quality of care for chronic illnesses. "The aim of therapy
must be multi-faceted, . . . modifying the rate of change of declining physiologic functions and concomitant functional impairments as well as addressing psychologic and social adjustment
to illness" (Pawlson, 1994, p. 37). Quality measurement should
include the patient's assessment of his or her illness and how
well different aspects of treatment (e.g., pain amelioration) have
been addressed.

It would seem that managed care plans are logical settings
for the implementation of "population-based medicine," "a strategy for designing and implementing an organized approach to
providing for the care of clinical problems, particularly chronic
problems, through the application of epidemiologic principles
and data" (Voelker, 1994; Wagner et al., 1995a, p. 12). For example, using computer algorithms, Group Health Cooperative
of Puget Sound identifies enrollees by such characteristics as
age, sex, health status, health complaints, and disease diagnoses. Once subgroups have been identified, specific services
and programs can be developed for them. By differentiating the
clinical needs of subsets of the health plan's population, more
effective planning can ensure that the unique needs of these
groups are met and that optimum outcomes are achieved.

The HMO Group Geriatric Interest Group (consisting of representatives from The HMO Group and Kaiser Permanente) has
identified the essential features of caring for elderly patients.
These include "unanimous agreement from provider and administrative staff that the elderly present unique issues and challenges; emphasis on independence, quality of life issues, and
prevention of acute illness; support systems and resources for
providers who care for elderly patients; a targeting mechanism
for early identification of health and related problems; a good
information system; ongoing collaborative efforts with organizations and universities specializing in geriatric efforts; and ability to maximally utilize community resources" (Wagner, 1993, p.
133).

Use of Geriatricians

Friedman and Kane (1993) studied the use of geriatricians by Medicare risk contractors. As of June 1991, 53 percent of the HMOs studied had one or more geriatricians. In 76 percent of the plans with such physicians, geriatricians provided primary care; they served as consultants in 61 percent of the plans. Friedman and Kane concluded that "geriatricians and many of the elements of organized geriatric practice are used [in HMOs] to a much lesser extent than experts recommend" (Friedman and Kane, 1993, p. 1144).

However, on the basis of randomized trial in an HMO, Epstein and colleagues (1990) recommended that "if geriatric assessment is to be used effectively in the ambulatory setting, tight targeting of the most severely ill or medically unstable patients may be necessary" (p. 543). Their study found that consultative geriatric assessment that involves only limited fol-low-up was not of benefit to most older, ambulatory enrollees in HMOs.

Practices of Some Medicare Managed Risk Program HMOs

Kramer and associates (1992) have described the geriatric care provided by group/staff model Medicare HMOs. On the basis of their visits to seven HMOs, they identified six strategies employed by these programs: (1) identifying high-risk patients, (2) assessing multiproblem patients, (3) treating multiproblem patients, (4) rehabilitating patients after acute medical events, (5) reducing medication problems, and (6) providing long-term and home health care. The authors noted that these strategies were often linked. For example, the presence of a system to identify high-risk patients usually indicated the use of an assessment tool as well.

Several of the HMOs screened or were planning to screen new enrollees to (1) determine patient status in areas such as functional disability, medication use, cognitive status, incontinence, and home safety or (2) to identify high-risk patients. In some plans, geriatricians provided referral guidelines to primary care physicians to help identify patients who would benefit from geriatric assessment. Once identified, patients were referred to multidisciplinary assessment teams or were provided with appointments or the screening information was forwarded to the primary care physician. Kramer and colleagues (1992) noted that geriatricians or those who had specialized training in geriatrics participated in most of the assessment programs.

Typically, the geriatric assessments included functional evaluation, mental status testing, medications review, a depression test, and a review of the member's social and home environment. Follow-up to the assessment varied by plan. In some cases, the assessment team was authorized to make the necessary changes in the patient's regimen; in others, the assessment team referred the patient back to his or her primary care physician.

There are those practicing in HMOs who suggest that a "geriatric focus" should include an interdisciplinary approach to coordinate multiple support and medical services (Calkins et al., 1995). However, Calkins and colleagues also note that plans need more information to implement this approach. Several of the plans studied by Kramer and associates (1992) coordinated the treatment of patients presenting several problems by integrating the activities of health providers with different specialties, sometimes at one site. Thus, for example, FHP integrated the care for such patients at particular sites, where physicians had smaller panels and were able to have longer visits with their geriatric patients.

Other methods observed on the site visits by Kramer and associates (1992) were the use of skilled nursing facilities for intensive rehabilitation and post-acute care, programs to profile medication use, and expanded coordination with social service providers. Widespread use of geriatric nurse specialists was also observed among the plans visited.

Primary Care Model for Chronic Care Illness

In considering a basic care model for chronically ill patients, Wagner and colleagues (1995b) have identified current deficiencies in the care of chronic illness: irregular or incomplete assessments, inadequate or inconsistent patient education, unintended deviations from accepted guidelines, and patient dissatisfaction because of inadequate information and psychosocial support. Wagner and associates have reported "real uncertainty as to whether to build integrated systems based in and supportive of primary care, . . . or to develop highly focused, specialized 'carve out' systems for various patient groups" (Wagner et al., 1995a, p. 27).

Group Health Cooperative of Puget Sound's Center for Health Studies has received funding from the Chronic Care Initiatives in HMOs to evaluate the primary care approach. The project will incorporate the elements that appear to be associated with good outcomes in chronic care illness: "systematic assessments, preventive interventions, effective education, psychosocial support, and consistent follow-up" (Chronic Care Initiatives in HMOs, undated; Wagner et al., 1995a). Frail elderly patients or patients with diabetes will be identified through disease registries to attend a chronic care clinic periodically. These patients will be followed by midlevel providers who will monitor patient compliance with a prescribed care plan and schedule follow-up visits. Care will be provided through existing primary care practices that will receive organizational support from the health plan. This support will include the development and dissemination of guidelines and information about treatments and services that have been shown to improve outcomes in the target populations, provider training, and so forth. Blocks of practice time will be devoted to the target population, periodically but regularly. At each miniclinic session: "planned assessments, visits, and a group meeting; standardized assessment of clinical and health status; development and execution of care plans constructed mutually with patients incorporating practice guidelines and reminders; continuous individual patient education; opportunities for group support; and systematic follow-up" are envisioned (Wagner et al., 1995a, p. 17).

Cooperative Health Care Clinic

The Kaiser Foundation Health Plan of Colorado has developed the Cooperative Health Care Clinic. This project is intended to integrate solutions to the physical, physiologic, and environmental problems of elderly patients with cardiovascular disease, lung disease, diabetes, or degenerative joint disease

(Chronic Care Initiatives in HMOs, undated; Scott and Robertson, 1995). The objective is to reduce the cost of care for these patients and to improve health status "through better preventive medicine, maintenance of independent living and improvement in access to care" (Scott and Robertson, p. 1) and improved patient and provider satisfaction. The model uses a multidisciplinary team that meets with groups of 12 to 30 patients every 4 to 6 weeks. The session provides "medical and functional assessment, group education, coordination of services between primary care and other health professionals, and an opportunity for the group to socialize with each other" (Group Health Association of America, 1995a; Scott and Robertson, 1995, p. 1).

Integration of Acute and Long-Term-Care Services

Patients needing chronic care services require a full range of treatment modalities that often span areas covered by acute and long-term-care insurance coverage. There have been several demonstrations to integrate acute and long-term-care services, most notably the Program of All-Inclusive Care for the Elderly (PACE)/On Lok projects and the Social Health Maintenance Organizations. These programs have tried to improve coordination by bridging through common financing, acute care benefits, and home and community-based long-term-care services.

The On Lok Senior Health Services was initially developed in 1971 as an adult day health center. It later received Section 1115 waivers that enabled it to receive capitation payments to provide comprehensive medical and social service benefits (e.g., primary medical and nursing care, day health, hospitalization, transportation, meals, and in-home services) through multidisciplinary teams to a nursing home-certified population. On Lok has since been replicated throughout the country through PACE. In general, although members of the On Lok/PACE projects have severe impairments, they are not as dependent in activities in daily living as nursing home residents (Weiner and Skaggs, 1995).

The Fallon Healthcare System is the first HMO to establish a PACE site, the Elder Service Plan (ESP) (Group Health Association of America, 1995a). Designed to enable frail elderly persons to remain in their homes, ESP focuses on preventive and rehabilitative services that permit enrollees to maintain maximum independence. It provides a full range of services, including physician and nursing services, home care, meals, recreational therapy, and transportation to and from the ESP center.

Even in the absence of full financial integration of coverage for acute and long-term care, some plans permit case managers to authorize services outside the covered range of benefits, thereby increasing the plan's ability to be responsive to the unique needs of individuals and, at the same time, saving through more efficient use of plan resources (Fama and Fox, 1995). Those authors noted that case management is being used to shorten hospital utilization by reducing the length of stay for acute episodes of chronic conditions and assisting patients in returning home instead of entering skilled nursing or long-term-care facilities. They point to Family HealthCare Services (a subsidiary of Sierra Health Services, which provides all post-acute and long-term-care services to Sierra Health Services enrollees), whose case management approach is to "maintain enrollees in the least restrictive and most safe and cost-effective setting. . . . Case managers consider the whole range of alternative care settings and services—from skilled nursing facilities to group homes and from skilled nursing services to home maker services" (Fama and Fox, 1995).

SeniorCare Options Program

The SeniorCare Options Program is sponsored by Allina Health Plans Group. Operating under the flexible benefits option of HCFA's Medicare Managed Risk Program, SeniorCare Options is a Medicare risk plan that offers Medicare beneficiaries "open access" to approximately 6,500 providers, including primary care and specialists. For a slightly higher premium, enrollees may self-refer directly to specialists. Upon enrollment, each new beneficiary is assigned a care advisor (either a geriatric nurse or a social worker) who assists the enrollee in navigating through the health plan. The care advisor performs a case management function and identifies low-, moderate-, and high-risk beneficiaries when they enter the plan by means of a health assessment tool that was developed with assistance from geriatricians at the University of Minnesota. Depending on the level of need, enrollees receive more or less intensive follow-up. A care plan is developed for individuals with multiple problems, that is reevaluated regularly (Olivia Mastry, Director, Center for Healthy Aging, Medica Health Plans, Minneapolis, Minnesota, December 1995).

Case Management

The Chronic Care Initiatives in HMOs studied the use of case management in 18 HMO Medicare risk contractors having more than 20,000 members and five other plans that did not meet this enrollment criterion. They concluded that "case management is currently being performed based on managerial judgment rather than on research findings" (Pacala et al., 1994, p. 2). According to that report, case management (including screening, assessment, care planning, the execution of a case management plan, and monitoring) is widely used in HMOs to treat older patients, but the plans do not carry out this function consistently. Nevertheless, the plans surveyed apparently are committed to using case management, and most reported that they are planning to expand its use. Most case management occurs in the hospital setting, and most patients are referred by providers for case management even if other screening mechanisms are in place.

All HMOs in the study were found to screen enrollees for case management, although they used different screening criteria. The criteria used most often were based on diagnoses (most commonly, congestive heart failure, chronic obstructive pulmonary disease, diabetes, stroke, and cancer), high use or cost, site of care (most often, hospitals), functional limitation, age, and living circumstance. One third of the plans used surveys to identify enrollees who met the targeting criteria. However, as noted above, most of those receiving case management were referred by providers.

Once identified, 80 percent of the plans conducted some form of assessment, and virtually all of those assessed were accepted for case management. Thirteen percent of the plans used a comprehensive geriatric assessment that was performed by a geriatrician and a multidisciplinary team. Most of the HMOs developed care plans, and most did so through multidisciplinary teams. However, in some cases, a case manager arranged care without a care plan and without consulting the enrollee or the provider. The plans reviewed cases at various intervals, depending on the site of the case management program.

Pacala and colleagues (1994) developed a typology to describe the case management activities of the HMOs studied. They found that the programs fell along a continuum based on the intensity of contact with the patient. At the highest levels of intensity, case management resembled the activity in social health maintenance organizations, whereas at the lowest intensity, it resembled "an elaborate utilization review model" (Pacala, undated, p. 21).

PROTECTING THE PUBLIC INTEREST

Even without the impetus of federal legislation, managed care in the Medicare program will continue to grow. To protect beneficiaries, HCFA has a fiduciary responsibility to hold its managed care contractors publicly accountable for the cost and quality of care that they provide. As the nation's largest purchaser of managed health care, HCFA has acknowledged that "it is not just like any private sector purchaser"—it must hold its contractors to "a higher standard" (Vladeck, 1995, p. 2). Accordingly, careful and comprehensive oversight coupled with consumer protections are critical to ensuring that the services provided are accessible and meet quality standards. To be effective, HCFA must take several steps.

National, Uniform Standards

National, uniform standards must apply to the plans that Medicare offers to beneficiaries. At a minimum, these standards should address fiscal solvency, access and availability of services, quality of care, marketing and enrollment practices, physician credentialing, utilization review, data collection, and grievance and appeals processes. HCFA needs such standards to monitor contractor performance and to serve as a basis for its enforcement and sanction activities.

Useful, Reliable Information

As Medicare expands the choice of plans available to beneficiaries, the importance of useful, reliable information about the availability, quality, and outcomes of services will grow. If consumers are given choices, they must be given the tools to exercise informed choice. Because there is evidence that consumers are most interested in receiving information from people like themselves, patient-reported information will play an important role for vulnerable populations, especially as better methods are developed to survey and report specific information about subpopulation groups.

The methods used to collect the data that are then reported to consumers are also important. Information should be collected in a manner that will ensure comparability across health plans. Consumer satisfaction data should be standardized and collected and audited by an external entity. Consumers may be legitimately wary of data that have been collected by the plans themselves. Research is needed to learn more about the kinds of information that different consumers will find useful and the best ways to disseminate such information. It is necessary, however, to begin at once with the best information that is currently available. Different dissemination strategies should be used to ensure that all segments of the beneficiary population will find the information understandable.

Quality Assurance and Improvement and External Quality Review

Some aspects of health care delivery cannot be ensured adequately through information alone. Managed care plans must demonstrate and document the ongoing effectiveness of their internal quality review processes through performance measurements and external reviews. New performance measurement systems should include measures of access to and timeliness of care, the appropriateness of the setting and treatment, and premature hospital discharges. For the chronically ill, it is particularly important to track the continuity of care across multiple settings, including home health and other long-term-care settings, and to assess the interpersonal aspects of care, such as patient-physician communication.

Managed care plans must also be subject to the ongoing review of professional external quality review and improvement organizations. There are those who would substitute accreditation for external review (Balanced Budget Act of 1995). Indeed, many private purchasers rely solely on accreditation as a means of distinguishing among managed care plans. However, the fact that a plan is accredited merely is an indication that it has the systems in place to produce high-quality care. This represents just a point-in-time description of the plan's capabilities. Beneficiaries need assurances not only that systems are in place but also that there are processes to determine whether the structures and systems are actually working in practice. Therefore, there is a need for ongoing external quality review to detect problems that may not be revealed through an accrediting process.

Grievance and Appeals

Inevitably, in a system that restricts choice and limits care to "medically necessary services," there will be disagreements between the health plan and its enrollees. A critical beneficiary protection is a grievance and appeals process that enables enrollees to receive timely and clear information about the specific reasons for denials of a service or payment and the right to appeal a denial. For vulnerable populations, it is especially important that the methods of communicating information about the grievance and appeals process be tailored to meet their specific needs.

Beneficiaries must retain the right to a review by an independent decision maker outside of the managed care plan, using medical expertise when appropriate, and then access to the federal courts. Of critical importance to vulnerable populations is an expedited review process that includes specific deadlines for situations in which failure to receive care or referral for specialized treatment promptly could jeopardize the patient's health or preclude optimal outcomes. These protections are so essential

to beneficiaries that a plan's failure to comply with requirements, including rules that pertain to timeliness, should result
in automatic approval of the disputed service or claim.

CONCLUSION

For the employed population under age 65, the U.S. health
care system has shifted to managed care. As this trend continues, it is possible to contemplate the disappearance of "pure"
fee-for-service plans in the private sector. However, in the Medicare program, 90 percent of beneficiaries still receive their care
through traditional fee-for-service arrangements. Although this
may change over time, it is not yet certain whether enrollment
in managed care plans among older Americans will reach the
same level as that among individuals in the private sector.
There is no indication that HMOs will cease to attract younger
and healthier Medicare beneficiaries. The question is whether
the more vulnerable beneficiaries will also voluntarily enroll.

There are those who believe that current efforts to expand
managed care in the Medicare program may in the end result in
reduced rather than enhanced choices for beneficiaries, especially for those who are poorer or sicker. "One should not under-
estimate the importance of changes in Medicare's fee-for-service
reimbursement policy for the prospects of managed care. The
major revolution in commercial managed care has been driven
largely by pricing and restrictions on choice of indemnity coverage, not simply the availability of managed care alternatives"
(Lawlor, 1995, p. 16). If only the very sick remain in the traditional program, causing the Medicare fee-for-service risk pool to
deteriorate and eventually become economically unsustainable,
the cost of fee-for-service care could become so expensive that
only those with high incomes will be able to choose this option.
Then, the genuine choice between fee-for-service and managed
care plans would disappear. If this becomes the case, many
Medicare beneficiaries could find themselves in managed care
plans whether they want to be in them or not.

Those who do enroll in managed care plans are entitled to do
so with the confidence that their health and related needs will
be met by these plans—that is, that services will be available,

accessible, and affordable. Today, would such confidence be justified?

Medicare beneficiaries are substantially different from those who have typically enrolled in managed care organizations. Several of the researchers whose works were cited in this paper observed indications that the plans studied lacked experience dealing with particular types of chronically ill patients or did not understand the importance of certain treatment modalities that are of importance to those with chronic care needs (e.g., Clement et al., 1994; Shaughnessy at al., 1994). Furthermore, the research evidence is inconclusive. Some studies indicate that older individuals and/or those with chronic conditions have fared well, whereas others indicate that the experiences of older, sicker populations have been less than satisfactory. Moreover, the studies that have been conducted have been hampered by the absence of well-defined norms to adequately evaluate plan performance, particularly in the treatment of chronic conditions. It would be imprudent to generalize from the findings because the reported results may have been peculiar to the model type of the plans investigated, the payment arrangements, or the particular market in which the plans were situated. Clearly, a great deal of research is needed before it will be possible to make unequivocal statements, in either direction, about the experiences of vulnerable populations in managed care plans.

Regrettably, waiting for research results will not be an option for today's beneficiaries. The U.S. Congress is poised to expand managed care and other options in Medicare in the short term. At the same time, Congress is also intent on achieving "savings" from the Medicare program. These savings will be realized in both the traditional and managed care programs. Unfortunately, the present payment methodology used to reimburse HMOs is widely recognized as flawed (U.S. General Accounting Office, 1995b). The adjusted average per capita cost methodology does not contain an adequate risk adjuster, thereby giving plans an incentive to "cherry pick" the healthiest risks. The U.S. General Accounting Office (GAO) has identified several promising efforts in the area of risk adjustment but predicts that an effective risk adjuster is not likely to be available in the near future (U.S. General Accounting Office, 1994). This means that plans will not be properly compensated for their vulnerable members, encouraging them either to avoid enrolling high-cost, high-risk individuals or to refrain from serving such members adequately, if they do enroll. The absence of an adequate risk adjuster underscores the importance of oversight on the part of HCFA to ensure that financial incentives that do not interfere with the provision of appropriate care and to help minimize any perverse incentives the reimbursement methodology might permit. A standardized benefit package would also help to mitigate risk selection.

Although many factors may influence physician decision making (e.g., the plan's quality assurance system, the physician's personal ethics, malpractice concerns, and the desire to retain patients [Gold and Reeves, 1987]), recently, the role of financial incentives on physician behavior has been receiving widespread coverage in the media. Several years ago, GAO recognized that, in the absence of proper controls, incentive payments to physicians had the potential to have a negative impact on the quality of care provided to Medicare beneficiaries. At that time, GAO suggested that "the closer financial incentives are linked to decisions about individual patients, the greater the potential threat to quality of care" (U.S. General Accounting Office, 1988). GAO identified four features that were most likely to affect quality adversely: shifting HMO risk to physicians by holding physicians responsible for the cost of all services, distributing incentives on the basis of individual physician cost performance, paying a percentage of HMO savings on patients as incentives, and measuring physician cost performance over a short period of time. It is disturbing that these practices are still commonly found in physician incentive programs of managed care plans.

Many are advocating for the disclosure of the financial incentives used by managed care plans. Although this is a start, it is doubtful that most consumers will comprehend the complex arrangements in use. To avoid the possibility of financial incentives interfering with the quality of services provided, HCFA must identify and ban practices that can be detrimental to patients.

In spite of these reservations, it must be said that managed care does have great potential to serve vulnerable beneficiaries. Managed care plans can provide more effective management, coordinate multiple medical and social problems, and exercise greater flexibility to provide the care that beneficiaries might require (Fama and Fox, 1995; Retchin et al., 1992; Tanenbaum and Hurley, 1995). However, as Schlesinger and Mechanic (1993) have noted, "the capacity of a prepaid plan to provide appropriate treatment to enrollees with persistent and severe illness depends to a considerable extent on the way the plan is organized" (p. 129). Those who are vulnerable must be assured that a comprehensive package of safeguards that includes rigorous standards for public accountability, accessible grievance and appeals mechanisms, and skilled professional oversight will be put in place and maintained by HCFA. Better-integrated and better-organized systems of care promise potentially-high quality and effective care, but only if a commitment is made at the outset to strong quality assurance, a service ethic that cares for the whole person, and outreach to those in the community who are most in need.

REFERENCES

Adler, G. S., and M. Phil. 1995. Medicare beneficiaries rate their medical care: New data from the MCBC. Health Care Financing Rev. 16(4):175-187.

American Association of Retired Persons, Administration on Aging, U.S. Department of Health and Human Services. 1995. A Profile of Older Americans. Washington, D.C.: The Association.

American Association of Retired Persons, The Urban Institute. 1995. Coming Up Short: Increasing Out-of-Pocket Health Spending of Older Americans. April. Washington, D.C.: The Public Policy Institute.

American Society on Aging. 1992. Serving Elders of Color: Challenges to Providers and the Aging Network. San Francisco, Calif.: The Society.

Armstead, R., P. Elstein, J. Gorman. 1995. Toward a 21st century quality measurement system for managed care organizations. Health Care Financing Rev. 16(4):25-37.

Bates, E. W., and B. S. Brown. 1988. Geriatric care needs and HMO technology. Med. Care 26:488-498.

Braveman, P., and T. Bennett. 1995. Let's take on the real dragon: Profiteering in health care. J. Public Health Policy 6:261-268.

Brown, R. S., J. W. Bergeron, D. G. Clement, J. W. Hill, and S. M. Retchin. 1993. The Medicare Risk Program for HMOs. Final Summary Report on Findings from the Evaluation. Final Report. February 18. Princeton, N.J.: Mathematica Policy Research, Inc.

Calkins, E., D. Dempster, and T. Kroll. 1995. Progress in geriatric care. HMO Pract. 9:27-31.

Callahan, C. M., H. C. Hendrie, and W. Tierney. 1995. Documentation and evaluation of cognitive impairment in elderly primary care patients. Ann. Intern. Med. 122:422-429.

Carlisle, D. M., A. L. Siu, E. B. Keeler, E. A. McGlynn, K. L. Kalin, L. V. Rubenstein, and R. H. Brook. 1992. HMO vs. fee-for-service care of older persons with acute myocardial infarction. Am. J. Public Health 82:1626-1630.

Christianson, J. B., and F. C. Osher. 1994. Health maintenance organizations, health reform, and persons with serious mental illness. Hosp. Community Psychiatry 45:898-905.

Chronic Care Initiatives in HMOs. (undated). Project summaries. Washington, D.C.: Chronic Care Initiatives in HMOs.

Clement, D. G., S. M. Retchin, M. H. Stegall, and R. S. Brown. 1992. Evaluation of Access and Satisfaction with Care in the TEFRA Program. Final Report. October 28. Princeton, N.J.: Mathematica Policy Research.

Clement, D. G., S. M. Retchin, R. S. Brown, and M. H. Stegall. 1994. Access and outcomes of elderly patients enrolled in managed care. JAMA 271:1487-1492.

The Commonwealth Fund. 1995. Executive Summary. In Patient Experiences in Managed Care. New York: The Commonwealth Fund.

Congressional Budget Office. 1995. Memorandum. The effects of managed care and managed competition. Congressional Budget Office, Washington, D.C.

Davis, K., K. S. Collins, and C. Morris. 1994. Managed care: Promises and concerns. Health Affairs 13:178-185.

Epstein, A. M., J. A. Hall, M. Fretwell, M. Feldstein, M. L. DeCiantis, J. Tognetti, C. Cutler, M. Constantine, R. Besdine, R. Rowe, and B. J. McNeil. 1990. Consultative geriatric assessment for ambulatory patients—A randomized trial in a health maintenance organization. JAMA 263:538-544.

Fama, T., and P. D. Fox. 1995. Beyond the benefit package. HMO Pract. 9:179-181.

Families USA Foundation. 1995. Managed care: Serving the chronically ill and disabled. States of Health 5(6):1-5.

Fox, P. D., L. Heinen, A. M. Kramer, and S. Palsbo. 1991. Initiatives in Service Delivery for the Elderly in HMOs. February. Princeton, N.J.: The Robert Wood Johnson Foundation.

Franks, P., C. M. Clancy, and P. A. Nutting. 1992. Gatekeepers revisited—protecting patients from over treatment. N. Engl. J. Med. 327:424-429.

Frederick/Schneiders, Inc. 1995. Analysis of Focus Groups Concerning Managed Care and Medicare. Prepared for The Henry J. Kaiser Family Foundation. Washington, D.C.: Frederick/Schneiders, Inc.

Friedman, B. R., and L. Kane. 1993. HMO medical directors' perceptions of geriatric practice in Medicare HMOs. J. Am. Geriatr. Soc. 41:1144-1149.

Friedman, E. 1995. The power of physicians: Autonomy and balance in a changing system. Paper presented at National Health Policy Forum, George Washington University. May. Washington, D.C.

Gabel, J. R., T. H. Dial, J. Hobart, L. Pan, C. Bergsten, A. Bernstein, M. Opanga, H. Whitmore, C. Barnes, and S. Palsbo. 1994. Industry Profile. Washington, D.C.: Group Health Association of America.

Ginzberg, E. 1995. A cautionary note on market reforms in health care. JAMA 274:1633–1634.

Gold, M., and F. Reeves. 1987. Preliminary Results of the GHAA—BC/BS Survey on Physician Incentives in Health Maintenance Organizations. November. Washington, D.C.: Group Health Association of America, Research Department.

Greenfield, S., W. Rogers, M. Mangotich, M. F. Carney, and A. R. Tarlov. 1995. Outcomes of patients with hypertension and non-insulin dependent diabetes mellitus treated by different systems and specialties—results from the medical outcomes study. JAMA 274:1436-1444.

Group Health Association of America. 1995a. Innovative Answers for America's Health Care: Best Practices in HMOs. Washington, D.C.: Group Health Association of America, Research Department.

Group Health Association of America. 1995b. 1995 Sourcebook on HMO Utilization Data. Washington, D.C.: Group Health Association of America.

Group Health Association of America. 1995c. Medicare Beneficiaries Who Choose HMOs Stick with Them; Only 4 Percent Return to Fee-For-Service. June 8. Press release. Group Health Association of America, Washington, D.C.

Group Health Association of America. 1995d. Medicare at 30: An opportunity for all Americans. Discussion paper, July Meeting, 1995. Group Health Association of America, Washington, D.C.

Health Care Financing Administration. 1995. Medicare: A Profile. February. Washington, D.C.: U.S. Department of Health and Human Services.

Health Care Financing Administration, Bureau of Data Management and Strategy. 1995. 1995 Data Compendium. March. Baltimore, Md.: U.S. Department of Health and Human Services.

Health Care Financing Administration, Division of Policy and Evaluation, Office of Managed Care. 1994. A Collection of Best Practices of Managed Care Organizations. Washington, D.C.: Government Printing Office.

Health Care Financing Administration, Office of Managed Care (Operations & Oversight Team). 1995a. Medicare Managed Care Contract Report (data as of January 1, 1996). Baltimore, Md.: U.S. Department of Health and Human Services.

Health Care Financing Administration, Office of Managed Care (Policy & Program Improvement Team). 1995b. Analysis of age distribution of Medicare beneficiaries in fee-for-service vs. managed care risk plans. Health Care Financing Administration, Baltimore, Md. March 22. Internal memorandum.

Health Care Financing Administration, Office of Research and Demonstration. 1995. Health Care Financing Review, Medicare and Medicaid Statistical Supplement, 1995. Baltimore, Md.: U.S. Department of Health and Human Services.

The Henry J. Kaiser Family Foundation. 1995. Medicare and Managed Care. Menlo Park, Calif.: The Henry J. Kaiser Foundation.

The Kaiser Commission on the Future of Medicaid. 1995. Policy Brief— Medicaid and the Elderly. Washington, D.C.: The Kaiser Commission on the Future of Medicaid.

Kassirer, J. P. 1995. Managed care and the morality of the marketplace. N. Engl. J. Med. 333:50–52.

Kramer, A. M., P. D. Fox, and N. Morgenstern. 1992. Geriatric care approaches in health maintenance organizations. J. Am. Geriatr. Soc. 40:1055–1067.

Kronick, R., Z. Zhou, and T. Dreyfus. 1995. Making risk adjustment work for everyone. Inquiry 32(Spring):41-55.

Langwell, K. M., and J. P. Hadley. 1989. Evaluation of the Medicare competition demonstrations. Health Care Financing Rev., Special Rep. 11(2):65-80.

Lawlor, E. F. 1995. Is Managed Care the Answer? The Public Policy and Aging Report 6(5/6): 1995. Chicago: Center on Aging, Health and Society, University of Chicago.

Lewin/ICF. 1990. A Research and Demonstration Agenda on Health Services Delivery to Older Persons in HMOs. A report on a workshop convened by the Robert Wood Johnson Foundation and the National Institute on Aging, November 15, 1990. Fairfax, Va.: Lewin/ICF.

Lurie, N., I. S. Moscovice, M. Finch, J. B. Christianson, and M. K. Popkin. 1992. Does capitation affect the health of the chronically mentally ill? Results from a randomized trial. JAMA 267:3300–3304.

Lurie, N., J. Christianson, M. Finch, and I. Moscovice. 1994. The effects of capitation on health and functional status of the Medicaid elderly. Ann. Intern. Med. 120:506–511.

Mashaw, J. L., and T. R. Marmor. 1995. Real talk about Medicare. Washington Post. December 5, p. A19.

McNeil, J. M. 1993. Americans with Disabilities: 1991–92, Data from the Survey of Income and Program Participation. Current Population Reports, Household Economic Studies, P70-33. December. Washington, D.C.: Bureau of the Census.

Meyer, J., S. Silow-Carroll, and M. Regenstein. Forthcoming. Managed Care and Medicare. Washington, D.C.: American Association of Retired Persons/The Public Policy Institute.

Miles, S. H., E. P. Weber, and R. Koepp. 1995. End-of-life treatment in managed care: The potential and the peril. West. J. Med. 163:302–305.

Millman, M., ed. 1993. Access to Health Care in America. Committee on Monitoring Access to Personal Health Care Services, Institute of Medicine. Washington, D.C.: National Academy Press.

Pacala, J. T., C. Boult, and K. W. Hepburn, L. Morishita, R. Reed, R. A. Kane, F. G. Kane, and J. K. Malone. 1994. Case Management in HMOs. Final Report. Washington, D.C.: Chronic Care Initiatives in HMOs.

Pawlson, L. G. 1994. Chronic illness: Implications of a new paradigm for health care. J. Quality Improvement 20:33-39.

Pope, A. M., and A. R. Tarlov, eds. 1991. Disability in America: Toward a National Agenda for Prevention. Washington, D.C.: National Academy Press.

Porell, F. W., C. Cocotas, P. J. Perales, C. P. Tompkins, and M. Glavin. 1992. Factors Associated with Disenrollment from Medicare HMOs. Findings from a Survey of Disenrollees. Waltham, Mass.: Health Policy Research Consortium, Brandeis University.

The Public Policy Institute/American Association of Retired Persons. 1995. Memorandum from K. B. Wu to Legislation and Public Policy Division. November 13, 1995. The Public Policy Institute, Washington, D.C.

Retchin, S. M., D. G. Clement, L. F. Rossiter, B. Brown, R. Brown, and L. Nelson. 1992. How the elderly fare in HMOs: Outcomes from the Medicare competition demonstrations. Health Services Res. 27:651-669.

The Robert Wood Johnson Foundation. 1995. Sick people in managed care have difficulty in getting services and treatment, new survey reports. June 18. Press release. The Robert Wood Johnson Foundation, Princeton, N.J.

Rogers, W. H., K. B. Wells, L. S. Meredith, R. Strum, and A. Burnam. 1993. Outcomes for adult outpatients with depression under prepaid or fee-for-service financing. Arch. Gen. Psychiatry 50:517-525.

Rolnick, S. J., J. Garrard, L. Luepke, K. Hogan, and R. Heinrich. 1994. Self-reported depressive symptons in a HMO seniors population: The process of case identification. Pp. 811-819 in Conference proceedings from Navigating Reform: HMOs, Managed Care in a Time of Transition. Washington, D.C.: Group Health Institute.

Safran, D. G., A. R. Tavlov, and W. H. Rogers. 1994. Primary care performance in fee-for-service and prepaid health care systems. JAMA 27:1579–1586.

Schlenker, R. E. Forthcoming. Home health payment legislation: Review and recommendations. Washington, D.C.: American Association of Retired Persons/Public Policy Institute.

Schlesinger, M., and D. Mechanic. 1993. Challenges for managed competition from chronic illness. Health Affairs Suppl. Managed Competition 12:123-137.

Schneider, E. L., and J. M. Guralnik. 1990. The aging of America: Impact on health care costs. JAMA 263:2335-2340.

Scott, J. C., and B. J. Robertson. 1995. Kaiser Permanente Medical Care Program, Denver, Colorado—Cooperative Health Care Clinic. Project summary presented at the Robert Wood Johnson Invitational Conference on Chronic Care Initiatives in HMOs, Washington, D.C., April 27-28, 1995.

Shaughnessy, P. W., R. E. Schlenker, and D. F. Hittle. 1994. Home health care outcomes under capitated and fee-for-service payment. Health Care Financing Rev. 16:187–222.

Smyer, M. A. 1993. Testimony at the Forum on Mental Health and the Aging before the Special Committee on Aging, U.S. Senate. 103d Cong., July 15, 1993, Serial No. 103–10.

Sulmasy, D. P. 1995. Managed care and managed death. Ann. Intern. Med. 153:133-136.

Tanenbaum, S. J., and R. E. Hurley. 1995. Disability and the managed care frenzy: A cautionary note. Health Affairs 14(4):213-219.

U.S. Congress, Senate, Special Committee on Aging, the American Association of Retired Persons, the Federal Council on the Aging, the U.S. Administration on Aging. 1991. Aging in America—Trends and Projections. Washington, D.C.: U.S. Department of Health and Human Services.

U.S. Department of Health and Human Services. 1995a. Medicare Beneficiary Interest in HMOs. October. OEI-004-93-00142. Washington, D.C.: Office of the Inspector General, U.S. Department of Health and Human Services.

U.S. Department of Health and Human Services. 1995b. Medicare Risk HMO Performance Indicators. October. OEI-06-91-00734. Washington, D.C.: Office of the Inspector General, U.S. Department of Health and Human Services.

U.S. Department of Health and Human Services. 1995c. Beneficiary Perspectives of Medicare Risk HMOs. March. OEI-06-91-00730. Washington, D.C.: Office of Inspector General, U.S. Department of Health and Human Services.

U.S. Department of Health and Human Services. 1995d. Vital and Health Statistics, Trends in the Health of Older Americans: U.S., 1994. DHHS Pub. No. (PHS)95-1414. Public Health Service, Centers for Disease Control and Prevention. Hyattsville, Md.: National Center for Health Statistics.

U.S. Department of Health and Human Services, Public Health Service. 1995. Health United States 1994. Centers for Disease Control and Prevention. DHHS Pub. No. (PHS)95-1232. May. Hyattsville, Md.: National Center for Health Statistics.

U.S. General Accounting Office. 1988. Medicare: Physician Incentive Payments by Prepaid Health Plans Could Lower Quality of Care. Pub. No. GAO/HRD-89-29. December. Washington, D.C.: U.S. General Accounting Office.

U.S. General Accounting Office. 1993. Medicaid: States Turn to Managed Care to Improve Access and Control Costs. Pub. No. GAO/HRD-83-46. March. Washington, D.C.: U.S. General Accounting Office.

U.S. General Accounting Office. 1994. Medicare: Changes to HMO Rate Setting Method Are Needed to Reduce Program Costs. Pub. No. GAO/HEHS 94-119. September. Washington, D.C.: U.S. General Accounting Office.

U.S. General Accounting Office. 1995a. Medicare: Enrollment Growth and Payment Practices for Kidney Dialysis Services. Pub. No. GAO/HEHS-96-33. November. Washington, D.C.: U.S. General Accounting Office.

U.S. General Accounting Office. 1995b. Medicare Managed Care: Growing Enrollment Adds Urgency to Fixing HMO Payment Problem. Pub. No. GAO/HEHS 96-21. November. Washington, D.C.: U.S. General Accounting Office.

Van de Water, P. N. 1995. CBO Testimony on Federal Entitlement Spending before the Committee on the Budget, U.S. Senate. February 1. Washington, D.C.: Congressional Budget Office.

Vladeck, B. C. (Administrator, Health Care Financing Administration, U.S. Department of Health and Human Services). 1995. Statement before the U.S. Senate Special Committee on Aging, August 3, 1995.

Voelker, R. 1994. Population-based medicine merges clinical care, epidemiologic techniques. JAMA 271:1301-1302.

Wagner, A. 1993. Geriatric care in HMOs. HMO Pract. 7(3):133–135.

Wagner, E. H., and T. V. Bledsoe. 1990. The RAND Health Insurance Experiment & HMOs. Med. Care 20:191-200.

Wagner, E. H., B. T. Austin, and M. Vonkorff (Center for Health Studies, Group Health Cooperative of Puget Sound). 1995a. Improving outcomes in chronic illness. Paper presented at the Robert Wood Johnson Invitational Conference on Chronic Care Initiatives in HMOs, Washington, D.C., April 27–28, 1995.

Wagner, E., J. Scott, N. Euchner, and D. Reuben. 1995b. New models for the delivery of primary care for people with chronic conditions. Paper presented at the Robert Wood Johnson Invitational Conference on Chronic Care Initiatives in HMOs, Washington, D.C., April 27–28, 1995.

Ware, J. E., W. H. Rogers, A. Ross Davies, G. A. Goldberg, R. H. Brook, E. B. Keeler, C. D. Sherbourne, and J. P. Newhouse. 1986. Comparison of health outcomes at a health maintenance organization with those of fee-for-service care. Lancet 1(8488):1017–1022.

Weiner, J., and J. Skaggs. 1995. Current Approaches to Integrating Acute and Long-Term Care Financing and Services. Washington, D.C.: The Public Policy Institute/American Association of Retired Persons.

Williams, S. J., R. L. Seidman, J. A. Drew, B. L. Wright, J. P. Elder, and M. E. McGann. 1995. Identifying depressive symptoms among elderly Medicare HMO enrolless. HMO Pract. 9(4):168-173.

Winslow, R. 1994. HMO quality is rated similar to other care. Wall Street Journal. May 18, 1994.

H

Reaching and Educating Medicare Beneficiaries About Choice

Carol Cronin[*]

INTRODUCTION

Every month approximately 225,000 Americans turn age 65 and become eligible for Medicare, the largest health insurance program in the country. Traditionally, although the financing of beneficiary health insurance changed at age 65—from the private sector to the public sector—the actual delivery of health care services was little affected. With the introduction of managed care over the last 10 years, Medicare beneficiaries are increasingly faced with choices about the way in which they will receive their health care. Recent and proposed legislation will further increase the options available to beneficiaries by allowing additional types of health care arrangements such as preferred provider organizations, point-of-service plans, and provider service networks. The introduction of managed care as a choice in the public sector reflects the growth of managed care offerings to active workers by many private sector employers. According to an annual survey of employers, the number of employees enrolled in some form of managed care rose from 52

[*]*Health Pages*, New York, New York.

percent in 1993 to 63 percent in 1994, the largest increase seen in the 9-year history of the survey (Foster Higgins, 1994).

With the changing options available under the Medicare program comes the need to clearly inform and educate beneficiaries about their choices in order for them to make a decision that best meets their personal needs. This paper focuses on communicating with Medicare beneficiaries over age 65 about their health plan options, with an emphasis on communicating about the topic of managed care. Information on reaching and educating disabled beneficiaries under 65 is not addressed in this paper.

The paper first reviews the literature with reference to communicating with older adults in general, including an analysis of the preferred media. The literature on communicating with older adults about health care, and managed care in particular, will then be presented. The balance of the paper includes case examples of different communications channels, including print, telephone, broadcast, video, electronic, and person to person, approaches used to disseminate information about health, managed care, or health plan choices. Wherever possible the examples given pertain to Medicare beneficiaries or older adults; however, in some cases they apply to all health care consumers.

The case examples, largely drawn from telephone interviews and a review of program materials, are organized by information source including public agencies (such as the Health Care Financing Administration or public libraries), nonprofit organizations, private companies, employers, and health plans. The paper is not meant to be a complete description of what these organizations do, nor is it meant to be a comprehensive review of all of the organizations that use these types of media, but rather, it is meant to highlight the range of organizations communicating with older adults about health care and the types of media that they use.

COMMUNICATING WITH OLDER ADULTS: MEDIA APPROACHES

A discussion of the literature on communicating with older adults includes two bodies of work. The first deals with the literature relating to the use of various media to educate older adults about a topic and the second deals with marketing to the "mature market," a relatively new aspect of business interest that has emerged with the growing size and potential purchasing power of older adults.

In the context of health care choices, the purpose of education is generally to assist an individual in making an informed choice, often through the presentation of complete and easy-to-obtain information (Davidson, 1988). This is particularly important in the context of Medicare beneficiary choices about health care, because the consequences of a poor choice can be particularly devastating. On the other hand, marketing generally involves four major elements, known as the four P's: product (the good or service being offered), place (the location where it can be purchased), price (the value to the consumer), and promotion (the ways in which potential purchasers are made aware of and encouraged to buy the product) (Dychtwald et al., 1990). A good definition of marketing, particularly in the context of Medicare managed care, can be found in the Health Care Financing Administration (HCFA) policy manual regarding marketing conducted by health maintenance organizations (HMOs) and competitive medical plans (CMPs) with Medicare contracts: "Marketing includes activities undertaken by an HMO/CMP to generate good will, encourage individuals to enroll in or remain in a prepaid health plan, or to provide information on plan benefits or costs and membership rules" (Health Care Financing Administration, 1992a).

The following review of the literature focuses primarily on the use of media preferred by older adults rather than the content of the media or its purpose (educational versus marketing). However, as further discussed in the conclusion, the question of content and purpose are key issues that will need to be addressed in the context of public policy discussions.

Older adults are active users of mass media of all types. Television is the most widely used medium among adults age 55 or older (Moschis, 1992). A special report for American Association of Retired Persons' (AARP's) *Modern Maturity Magazine* conducted by the Roper Organization (Modern Maturity/The Roper Organization, 1992), indicated that adults over age 50 spend a median of 161 minutes per day watching television, four to five times more than the time spent with any other media. Older adults' television viewing increases dramatically around prime time but is also high during the daytime hours (National Council on the Aging, 1985). Entertainment and relaxation are the chief reasons for watching television (36 percent); this is followed closely by news (32 percent) (Johnson & Johnson, 1988). In 1992, more than half of households with individuals over age 50 had cable television (53 percent) and owned a VCR (56 percent), up from 49 and 43 percent, respectively, in 1988 (Modern Maturity/The Roper Organization, 1992).

Proportionately fewer older adults than younger adults listen to radio, with approximately 20 to 25 percent of the adult radio audience comprising adults over age 55 (compared with 45 percent of adults ages 18 to 34) (Menchin, 1989). However, in this medium, station formats are varied and older audiences can be reached by carefully selecting the appropriate type of programming such as news or easy listening formats (FIND/SVP, 1993).

With reference to print media, older Americans are more likely to read newspapers on a daily basis compared with all adults (84 percent of adults over age 50 compared to 78 percent of all adults) (Modern Maturity/The Roper Organization, 1992), with readership remaining high even among those age 80 and older (Moschis, 1992). Newspaper magazine supplements, such as *Parade*, are noted to be particularly effective in reaching older adults, as are the growing numbers of newspapers for senior citizens which serve as "the trade journal of the retiree" (Menchin, 1989).

Most adults over age 50 (70 percent) are magazine readers (Modern Maturity/The Roper Organization, 1992), and households with subscribers over age 55 account for 40 percent or more of the subscribers to a large number of magazines such as *Prevention*, *Golf Digest*, *Southern Living*, and *Yankee* (FIND/SVP, 1993). Many women's magazines are widely read by older women and, similar to senior newspaper, senior magazines such as *Modern Maturity* and *Lears* are increasingly available (Menchin, 1989).

With reference to newer forms of media and communications vehicles, a recent study of on-line computer users indicated that only 2 percent of those age 65 and older and 9 percent of those ages 50 to 64 report ever having been on-line (Shannon, 1995). Looking at the entire population, barely 15 percent of the population can be considered on-line users, although 76 percent of the American public identifies on-line service use as "the wave of the future" and 50 percent of people who don't even own computers today see themselves on-line by the end of 1997.

The Modern Maturity/Roper survey indicated that adults over age 50 are generally quite positive toward both print and television advertising, with advertising that has verifiable claims and appeals to their intelligence and sense of fairness taken more seriously than those that rely on gimmickry. Of the different approaches, advertising that promises the security of a money-back guarantee if the customer is not satisfied is considered believable, whereas about half trust advertisements that carry the approval of well-respected health or medical organizations such as the American Medical Association. In contrast, older adults are skeptical of ads that carry celebrity endorsements and those that use slogans such as "new and improved" (Modern Maturity/The Roper Organization, 1992). Direct mail advertising and communication have also been described as effective in reaching older adults because they allow for a longer message and a presentation pace controlled by the reader and can reach older adults with timed precision (around when they need to make a decision) (Menchin, 1989).

Many writers on reaching and communicating with older adults note that mature consumers do not constitute a homogeneous age segment (Lumpkin et al., 1989). Education, age, income, and living arrangements have been related to communication channel selection, with elderly people who did not complete high school less inclined to select any communication channels and age, income, and living arrangements affecting the preferred type of communication channel used (Goodman, 1992).

A number of marketing efforts have been developed to segment the older population with reference to such factors as demographics, attitudes, values, and/or behaviors. Older adults are arrayed into distinct segments on the basis of such psychological factors as ability to cope with external changes/internal changes and their levels of independence/dependence or introversion/extroversion (FIND/SVP, 1993). For example, Strategic Directions, a Minneapolis-based consulting firm, has conducted research that has resulted in the definition of four segments of the older population specifically related to health: the proactive adult who seeks out a great deal of information about how to stay in good health, the faithful patient who relies on doctors and medication, the optimist who never gets sick, and the disillusioned who are least trusting of their doctors and seek out information (Morgan, 1993). Different communication strategies would then be used to reach each of these segments.

COMMUNICATING WITH OLDER ADULTS ABOUT MANAGED CARE AND MEDICARE CHOICES

Review of the Literature

A discussion about communicating with Medicare beneficiaries about their health care options, including managed care, should begin with a discussion of the extent of their knowledge about the Medicare program in general. If older adults do not understand the basic Medicare program, it is not likely that they can be informed enough to understand their health care options beyond the basic program. Several studies have shown that Medicare beneficiaries have limited knowledge of their Medicare benefits (Cafferata, 1984; LaTour et al., 1986), with beneficiaries generally more aware of the services most often used, such as physician care and prescription drugs, and less knowledgeable about less frequently used services, such as hospital and nursing home care (McCall et al., 1986). With regard to their knowledge of health insurance, Medicare beneficiaries are not that different from younger adults. A nationwide survey of more than 1,000 consumers in 1990 found that privately insured Americans have an uneven knowledge of their health coverage. They seem to understand basic elements of their health plans (hospital and physician coverage), but have less understanding of coverage for such items as mental health or long-term care (Garnick et al., 1993).

It is interesting to note, in addition, that all of the HMOs interviewed for this paper began their conversations with the author with the observation that a first task of the health plan in communicating with Medicare beneficiaries is to "educate them about Medicare." As will be further discussed in the conclusion, the finding that many Medicare beneficiaries lack basic knowledge about the Medicare program may have important implications for policy makers interested in communicating with beneficiaries about health plan choice.

When communicating specifically about health topics and choices to older adults, another more informal communication channel becomes important: family and friends. Although studies show that about half of adults over age 55 report awareness of medical and health information through magazines/newspapers and radio and television advertisements and programs, many also rely on friends/acquaintances and spouses (Moschis, 1994). With specific reference to communication with older adults about HMOs, one study that conducted structured interviews with 260 older adults concluded that only a relatively small number of people pay attention to brochures received in the mail, in contrast to the power of word of mouth by an HMO member (Titus, 1982).

Another study looked at both how beneficiaries learned about HMOs and the most influential sources of information in enrollment decisions about HMOs (Brown et al., 1987). The most often cited sources of information in learning about Medicare HMOs were the media (55 percent), a friend or relative (50 percent), personal contact with an HMO representative at an open house (48 percent), and direct mail (41 percent). With reference to which among the various sources of information was the most influential in their decision to enroll in an HMO, the most frequently cited sources were friends and relatives (31 percent), an open house (23 percent), direct mail (19 percent), direct contact with an HMO representative (11 percent), television (5 percent), and newspapers (4 percent). The researchers also found substantial differences in source of information and influential information among enrollees and nonenrollees and the level of previous knowledge about local HMOs.

A final study found similar results when surveying Medicare HMO and social/health maintenance organization (S/HMO) enrollees (a S/HMO is a health plan that combines Medicare HMO coverage with chronic care benefits and services such as personal care and homemaker services) (Newcomer et al., 1990). Among the HMOs, the vast majority of enrollees cited referrals from family and friends as being the most important source in learning about the health plan. The second most frequently cited source was health professionals; this was followed closely by direct mail contacts. In contrast, S/HMOs did not have the advantage of widespread communication through informal referrals such as family and friends. Instead, they appeared to have relied more on direct mail and telemarketing and on the dissemination of requested plan materials and advertising.

Another body of literature looks at communicating with Medicare beneficiaries about managed care from the perspective of the managed care plan. Because traditional HMO marketing targets employed populations and is characterized by marketing to groups, rather than the marketing approach to individuals required in the Medicare program (Prasad and Javalgi, 1992), HMOs need to change their organizational culture to address the specific needs of a mature population (Gilmartin, 1993). The importance of understanding and addressing the needs of older adults to help them make informed decisions about joining an HMO was the subject of a brochure developed by the Group Health Association of America (GHAA), the trade association of HMOs based in Washington, D.C. (Group Health Association of America, 1991). The brochure includes tips on conducting a thorough enrollment presentation and tips for talking to or writing for older adults, as well as outlining the perceived advantages of HMOs for older adults.

Focus Group Research

Another source of information about preferred sources of information about Medicare and health plan options comes from recent focus groups and structured interviews held with Medicare beneficiaries. A series of 15 focus groups conducted in the fall of 1993 for the Kaiser Family Foundation looked at a series of issues related to the overall Medicare program (Mellman, Lazarus & Lake, 1994). The focus group report concluded that the biggest problems with Medicare have to do with communication and coverage. When asked about specific ideas for improving communication about Medicare, focus group participants indicated the greatest interest in a toll-free number answered by a knowledgeable operator who could answer specific questions. They were also interested in seminars, again because of the opportunity to obtain answers to specific questions. Participants were mixed in their reactions to the use of videos and were less enthusiastic about a cable television show as a means of distributing information about Medicare.

Another series of focus groups, again held for the Kaiser Family Foundation, looked more specifically at issues related to managed care and Medicare (Frederick/Schneiders, Inc., 1995). This series of 14 focus groups held in eight locations in early 1995 explored the issue of how Medicare beneficiaries seek information, how they make their choices, and how they would prefer to receive information. A range of preferred information sources was mentioned by participants, including printed brochures, one-on-one sessions with HMO representatives, and meetings. Word of mouth was viewed as important by many of the participants with reference to the actual choice of an HMO, whereas there appeared to be less interest in videos.

The Setting Priorities for Retirement Years (SPRY) Foundation, a consumer-oriented, Washington D.C.-based nonprofit organization, conducted a series of 28 interviews for HCFA in June 1995. The purpose of the interviews was to seek insight into the views and preferences of older adults on their Medicare choices and to test their reactions to printed materials addressing these issues (Jorgensen et al., 1995). Among other things, the participants were asked where they would go if they wanted more information on Medicare managed care. The most common response was that they would call Medicare directly, although none of the respondents mentioned the HCFA toll-free hotline specifically (discussed below). Other preferred sources of information included seniors centers, public libraries, post offices, county aging service agencies, and Social Security offices. With reference to format, the majority of participants preferred a brochure printed on plain paper in large type with areas of white space to include some boxes and illustrations.

A final set of recent focus groups with Medicare beneficiaries was conducted by the Research Triangle Institute under contract for HCFA (Research Triangle Institute, 1995). Consistent with the findings obtained with other focus groups, when asked about different ways in which information for health plan choice could be presented to them, participants stated an overwhelming preference for personal presentations, either as a group presentation with opportunities for questions afterward or as a personal counseling session. Other participants recommended that written material be used in conjunction with the presentations. There was some interest in telephone hotlines, videos, and computer models, but concern was expressed over the technological aspects of each of these media. When asked about information sources, respondents noted that input from friends and relatives was seen as highly credible, insurance plan representatives were not likely to be trustworthy, and impartial information sources, such as *Consumer Reports*, were viewed as credible sources.

Additional focus groups that may shed further light on communicating with Medicare beneficiaries about their health plan choices are planned. A series of Medicare focus groups will be conducted by the National Committee for Quality Assurance (NCQA) in the course of a Commonwealth Foundation-funded project looking at consumer information. In addition, the teams of organizations funded under the federal Agency for Health Care Policy and Research's Consumer Assessments of Health Plans Study (CAHPS) are also planning to hold focus groups of adults (that may include Medicare beneficiaries) to look at the effectiveness of particular information strategies such as print materials and videos.

CASE EXAMPLES OF DIFFERENT MEDIA USED TO DISTRIBUTE INFORMATION ABOUT HEALTH PLAN CHOICE AND MANAGED CARE

Print Media: Pamphlets, Reports, and Guides

Public Agencies

To date, most of the information distributed to Medicare beneficiaries by HCFA about health care choices and managed care has been in a print format. Federal information dissemination about Medicare health care options is tiered. Approximately

3 months prior to turning age 65, the age of eligibility for Medicare and Social Security, an individual receives an initial enrollment package from the Social Security Administration consisting of an enrollment card, a letter, and pamphlets about Medicare ("What You Need to Know about Medicare and Other Health Insurance") and Social Security. The Medicare brochure includes a brief description about Medicare and managed care, Medigap insurance, and other private coverage that might be available to the beneficiary (employer coverage, workers' compensation) (Social Security Administration, 1994). The brochure's managed care narrative refers the reader interested in learning more to the Medicare Handbook (Health Care Financing Administration, 1995a) or to another HCFA brochure entitled "Medicare Managed Care Plans" (Health Care Financing Administration, 1995b), available through the Consumer Information Center in Pueblo, Colorado. The latter is a 15-page brochure that discusses how managed care works, enrollment issues, selection of doctors and hospitals, advantages and disadvantages of HMOs, disenrollment, and appeals.

In a separate mailing to the newly eligible Medicare beneficiary that occurs up to 3 months before or after the 65th birthday, HCFA sends the Medicare Handbook, currently a 57-page document available in English or Spanish, that covers all aspects of the program (Parts A and B, appeals, noncovered services, etc.). Two pages of the Handbook discuss Medicare managed care and the reader is given a toll-free number to call to see if there is an HMO in his of her area (currently, approximately 75 percent of Medicare beneficiaries have access to an HMO in their areas). The Handbook also includes all of the telephone numbers for state health insurance counseling programs (see below).

Current Medicare beneficiaries interested in managed care would probably only know about managed care options if they took the initiative to find out more themselves by calling the Medicare Hotline (see below), an HCFA regional or central office, or a senior counseling program or if they heard about HMOs through plan advertisements or family and friends.

There are several additional print materials that are available by request from HCFA on managed care and health care options including the following:

- Medicare Coordinated Care Questions and Answers, an 11-page report which includes 27 questions and answers about Medicare and HMOs (Health Care Financing Administration, 1992b).
- 1995 Guide to Health Insurance for People with Medicare, a 35-page report, developed jointly with the National Association of Insurance Commissioners, which covers a range of topics primarily related to what Medicare does not cover and private health insurance options for covering those gaps. Medicare managed care is described as one of the private health insurance options that covers Medicare gaps along with Medigap policies, continuation of employer coverage, long-term-care insurance, hospital indemnity policies, and specific disease policies (Health Care Financing Administration, 1995c).
- Medicare Managed Care Directory, which lists Medicare managed care plans by state including the telephone number, address, and counties covered (Health Care Financing Administration, 1995d).

In addition, HCFA Office of Managed Care staff interviewed for this paper mentioned several other initiatives related to the dissemination of print information for Medicare beneficiaries about their health plan options. The 1996 Medicare Handbook was revised to include a clearer statement on page 1 that Medicare beneficiaries have choices about the ways in which they can participate with the program. This new handbook was mailed to all Medicare beneficiaries during early 1996 (the last time that the handbook was sent to all beneficiaries, not just those who were newly eligible, was in the late 1980s). In addition, HCFA staff have developed a draft of a new brochure about Medicare choices discussing the pros and cons of fee-for-service and managed care systems. The agency hopes to include the brochure in the initial enrollment package mailed to beneficiaries by the Social Security Administration. HCFA also updated its current 15-page "Medicare Managed Care Plans" brochure for distribution primarily through the Medicare Hotline and the Consumer Information Center in Pueblo, Colorado. Finally, HCFA has hired a contractor to evaluate the effectiveness of publications for Medicare beneficiaries.

Another HCFA print initiative was developed by the California regional office and consists of a trifold 1995 HMO Benefits Comparison chart for each of three areas: Northern California, Southern California, and Arizona/Nevada (Health Care Financing Administration, 1995e). The charts briefly discuss considerations for beneficiaries thinking about enrolling in a Medicare HMO and then provide comparative information about the costs (e.g., monthly premium and copayments for doctor visits) and benefits (e.g., pharmacy and dental) offered by each of the plans in the three areas. The comparison chart is distributed primarily through Social Security offices and senior health insurance counseling programs and directly to approximately 1,500 beneficiaries who have requested it. HCFA is in the process of developing similar comparative charts for other regions that they plan to have available in disc format and on-line for regional offices and other interested organizations by early next year.

Libraries

Libraries are another potential public source of information for Medicare beneficiaries about their health plan choices. There are approximately 9,000 public libraries nationwide, with 16,000 outlets (G. Needham, Public Library Association, Chicago, Illinois, personal communication, 1995). A 1991 library public use survey indicated that approximately one third of adults over age 65 are library users (Scheppke, 1994). Some libraries, such as the Wheaton Regional Public Library in Montgomery County, Maryland, maintain Health Information Centers staffed by librarians. The Centers provide area residents with access to health books, journals, and pamphlets. Center staff report that they do get some questions requesting information about managed care, particularly information about the availability of HMO or preferred provider organizations (PPO) ratings. However, it appears to be a relatively small percentage of the almost 550 questions per week fielded by the staff (S. Unger, Wheaton Regional Public Library, Wheaton, Maryland, personal communication, 1995).

Non-Profit Organizations

Several non-profit organizations have developed educational print materials to help their members/constituencies understand more about Medicare managed care and their health care options. AARP has published a report titled *Managed Care: An AARP Guide* (American Association of Retired Persons, 1995a), a 21-page guide that discusses the differences between traditional insurance and managed care, the advantages and disadvantages of managed care, questions to ask, and a comparison worksheet that the reader can use to compare plan benefits. More than 80,000 copies of the guide were distributed in 1995. Several questions about managed care plans are also included in another AARP publication entitled *Healthy Questions: How to Talk to and Select Physicians, Pharmacists, Dentists & Vision Care Specialists* (American Association of Retired Persons, 1995b).

The Medicare Beneficiaries Defense Fund, a New York City-based nonprofit organization dedicated to ensuring the rights of seniors and people with disabilities, has developed a series of brochures about the Medicare program for consumers. Their Medicare managed care piece entitled "Medicare Health Maintenance Organizations: Are They Right For You?," is a 10-page pocket-size brochure that provides an overview of Medicare HMOs and that discusses how they work, what a beneficiary should consider before enrolling, enrollment/disenrollment procedures, and the complaints/appeals processes (Medicare Beneficiaries Defense Fund, 1994).

The Center for Health Care Rights has also developed print materials that provide an overview of HMOs for Medicare beneficiaries. In addition to a four-page brochure that describes the details of joining an HMO, the Los Angeles-based organization has also published and distributed 1995 Medicare HMO disenrollment data for Medicare HMOs in California (Center for Health Care Rights, 1995).

Employers

Increasingly employers are exploring the introduction of Medicare HMOs as an option for their retirees. For example,

Towers Perrin, an employee benefit consulting firm, has organized a consortium of large employers such as Nynex, Union Carbide, and LTV in a project to offer HMOs to their Medicare retirees (Winslow, 1994). Print information about Medicare HMOs available to corporate retirees is a key part of the communication effort used in the project, including a generic company announcement letter, an HMO highlights brochure, and a comparison grid that could then be customized to a participating employer's individual corporate needs (L. Guthridge, Towers Perrin, Los Angeles, California, personal communication, 1995).

Another employer, Bethlehem Steel, which introduced managed care for its retirees this fall, began its communication with an introductory letter to all eligible retirees from the chairman of the company; this was followed by additional information from the employee benefits department. The actual plan materials were sent directly to retirees by the plan; however, they were sent in a Bethlehem Steel envelope to increase the likelihood that they would be read. In addition, a key part of the communications strategy, coordinated by UltraLink—a network management company working with large employers—involved holding meetings in several states where retirees could learn more about the HMO option and have their questions answered by Bethlehem Steel employee benefits staff. A telephone hotline was also available to (and used by) retirees for questions or concerns (Howard Matsukane, UltraLink, Costa Mesa, California, personal communication, 1995).

Health Plans

Managed care plans that offer products for Medicare beneficiaries use print media in a number of ways to communicate with older adults about their products. All plans have brochures and marketing materials that generally describe how an HMO operates and provide information, often in a comparative chart format, about the specific benefits that they offer and how they compare to regular Medicare coverage.

The marketing materials used by health plans must be approved by HCFA before use. HCFA does not mandate a format or style for a plan's Medicare marketing materials; however, plans are instructed on the content of the pre-enrollment materials sent to a beneficiary. Materials must include an explanation of the plan's rules and other information sufficient for the beneficiary to make an informed decision about enrollment. This includes information on eligibility requirements, how and where to receive services, benefits, and premiums/copayments. Marketing materials must describe all restrictions on out-of-plan and in-plan service use, including an accentuated discussion of lock-in restrictions and clearly stated information about plan coverage of emergency and out-of-area urgently needed services. Prohibited marketing activities include any marketing attempts that discourage participation on the basis of actual or perceived health status (i.e., attempts to enroll beneficiaries from high-income areas, etc.); activities that mislead, confuse, or misrepresent; gifts or payments to induce enrollment (although plans may give gifts of nominal value—under $10.00—to all beneficiaries who attend a marketing presentation), door-to-door solicitation; and distribution of disapproved marketing materials.

Discussions with several Medicare HMO plans indicated that plans often use direct mail to disseminate printed marketing information about their products to older adults' homes. The direct mail material might encourage the recipient to send for more information, call a toll-free plan number for more information, or attend a meeting where additional information about the product will be presented by their representatives.

Print Materials: Newspapers and Magazines

Nonprofit Organizations

The Minnesota Health Data Institute, a nonprofit public-private organization created by the Minnesota State Legislature in 1993 with the overall goal of improving the quality of health care services available to Minnesotans, has recently released the results of a statewide survey of consumers on their satisfaction with health plans (Minnesota Health Data Institute, 1995). The results included the satisfaction of Medicare beneficiaries with the five Medicare HMOs available in the state. Survey results were distributed by using two unique dissemination methods: an insert in the major Minneapolis/St. Paul newspaper and affiliated papers and a series of three community meetings held throughout the state (further discussed below). The 16-page newspaper-sized insert was included in the October 6, 1995, edition of the *Minneapolis Star Tribune*, as well as 60 other newspapers statewide. The Minnesota Health Data Institute estimates that approximately 912,000 copies of the report were distributed to Minnesota residents. The Institute will be doing follow-up focus groups with various constituencies, including Medicare beneficiaries, to test specific reactions to the format and information.

Private Sector

Health Pages, a New York City-based consumer health magazine, provides both general information and community-specific information geared for the entire family. The magazine is published in eight areas nationwide: Atlanta, Cincinnati/Columbus/Dayton, Denver, Los Angeles, Miami/Ft. Lauderdale/West Palm Beach, Phoenix, Pittsburgh, and St. Louis. In five areas (Denver, Phoenix, Pittsburgh, South Florida, and St. Louis), the fall 1995 edition of the magazine included a six-page article on Medicare and the Managed Care Option. The article in the South Florida *Health Pages* for example, provided a four-page narrative overview of Medicare managed care and two pages of charts providing fairly detailed comparative information on the eight HMOs available to Medicare beneficiaries in that area (*Health Pages*, 1995). The magazine is primarily distributed to employees and retirees by large employers or business health coalitions in the cities. It is also available to the public at newsstands. In some cities, grants to health care coalitions have resulted in free copies being distributed to Area Agencies on Aging and their programs (including the senior health insurance counseling programs). The magazine is now exploring the on-line distribution of information.

Local senior citizens' newspapers are another potential source of information for Medicare beneficiaries about local health plan and managed care options. The April 1995 edition of *Arizona Senior World*, for example, included a comparison chart of HMOs available to Arizona residents (*Arizona Senior World*, 1995). There are over 100 senior citizens' newspapers throughout the country, with circulations ranging from 2,500 to more than 100,000 (Menchin, 1989).

Health Plans

Health Plans use print advertising to reach older adults, often advertising in metropolitan newspapers, senior citizens' newspapers, and other local print media. The purpose of the advertising is generally to build a positive image or reputation and to build name recognition (Harrington et al., 1988). Advertisements are generally upbeat, show older adults in active or intergenerational roles, or highlight the experience and credentials of the health plan. One advertisement for a Portland Medicare plan is built around an "Ask Helen" theme, Helen being an older woman experienced with Medicare HMOs who becomes the "personality" of the plan in their advertising efforts (Pickens, 1992).

Telephone

Public Agencies

HCFA staffs a Medicare Hotline (1-800-638-6833, TDD 1-800-820-1202) that is widely publicized to Medicare beneficiaries through most of their print materials. The Hotline is available from 8 a.m. to 8 p.m. EST Monday through Friday. The main purpose of the Hotline is to distribute information to callers on selected topics or to refer them to other resources. There are no live operators to answer specific questions on the Hotline. Callers with touch-tone phones are presented with a list of seven prerecorded options including an option for "information about health maintenance organizations or HMOs." Callers who press this option are asked to state their name and address, and information about HMOs and the plans in their areas will be sent to them. They then receive the "Medicare Managed Care Plans" brochure and the *Managed Care Directory*.

According to HCFA staff overseeing the Medicare Hotline, during the most recent 6-month period of April 1, 1995, to September 29, 1995, the Hotline received 265,406 calls, with 9,673 callers (4 percent) pressing the option on HMOs. The largest requests to the Hotline are for options dealing with "information about claims" and "general information about Medicare."

Senior Health Insurance Counseling Programs

Legislation passed in 1990 established federally funded, state-managed information, counseling, and assistance (ICA) programs for Medicare beneficiaries. The purpose of the program was to assist Medicare beneficiaries in making decisions regarding their health insurance coverage. The ICA programs are administered primarily through state Departments on Aging (two thirds) or Departments of Insurance (one third). In addition to basic funding, states with Medicare HMOs received additional funding to promote the availability and understanding of these health plan options.

A recent evaluation of the ICA program conducted by the Research Triangle Institute (McCormack et al., 1994) indicated that 45 states maintain telephone hotlines, although only 22 of these hotlines are operated specifically by the ICA program (the rest are maintained by their host state agencies). Some of the telephone hotlines provide actual counseling to Medicare beneficiaries with questions, whereas others are used primarily to make referrals to ICA program counselors for follow-up.

Health Plans

Although none of the plans interviewed for this paper mentioned using telemarketing—or cold calling—as a marketing strategy, it is not prohibited under the HCFA marketing guidelines. Many plans use the telephone to follow up with beneficiaries who have expressed interest by attending a plan presentation or sending for more information.

Health plans, or any other entity conducting telemarketing, would now be subject to Federal Trade Commission regulations prohibiting deceptive and abusive telemarketing practices under the 1994 Telemarketing Act. Among other things, the regulations limit the time of day that individuals may be called, requires disclosure that the purpose of the call is to sell goods or services, and prohibits unsolicited calls that are coercive or abusive.

Television and Radio

Public Agencies

HCFA is involved in a number of activities involving broadcast or cable television and radio, including the production of audio or visual public service announcements (PSAs) (Health Care Financing Administration, 1995f). Few of the PSAs or cable televsion programs appear to deal directly with information related to managed care; however, many refer viewers to local ICA programs where they can get information about managed care and their health care choices. Several of the radio efforts target specific ethnic communities including Spanish-speaking and Chinese-American Medicare beneficiaries.

The HCFA Office of Research and Demonstration is currently funding a contract to develop a beneficiary information, education, and marketing strategy to support a proposed demonstration on expanded choice of Medicare health plan options. Benova, a Portland, Oregon-based health communications company, won the contract to develop multiple prototype products for the pilot, including a suggested marketing/public relations strategy that is expected to include proposed scripts for radio and television PSAs. Benova is also exploring the use of cable television, as well as print materials.

Health Plans

Health plans also use TV and radio advertising, again as part of their marketing strategies to reach older adults. The purpose of the advertisements is to elicit interest and follow-up requests for information by calling a toll-free number or to encourage attendance at a presentation sponsored by the plan.

Videos

Public Agencies

Several years ago the HCFA Office of Managed Care produced a video on Medicare managed care. The 11-minute video, hosted by Hugh Downs, used a television anchor/guest expert format to discuss managed care. More than 1,600 copies of the video were distributed and used in a variety of settings including ICA program and HCFA presentations and in Social Security offices. The use of the tape has now expired.

As part of an HCFA-funded project titled "Information Needs for Consumer Choice," the Research Triangle Institute and its contractor, Benova, will be developing a video for Medicare beneficiaries that includes older actors in a shopping market making grocery selections and talking about consumer choice of health plans. The script also introduces the concept of managed care report cards. A similar video is also being developed for the Medicaid population.

Employers

The employee benefits consulting firm Towers Perrin, in conjunction with GHAA, has developed a 13-minute videotape as part of the multiemployer, multicity retiree project described above. The videotape uses an older female narrator speaking words from actual letters that senior citizens have sent to health plans. In addition, interviews with Karen Ignagni, President of GHAA, and physicians from managed care plans are also included. The video is primarily used by employers in presentations with retirees about managed care.

Computer/Electronic Media

Public Agencies

HCFA launched a home page on the Internet's World Wide Web approximately 1 year ago. The home page includes access to a wide range of information including an overview of Medicare, HCFA testimony, an HCFA staff phone directory, proposed regulations, and research. Several HCFA publications for Medicare beneficiaries are also available on-line, including the Medicare Handbook, the "Guide to Health Insurance for People with Medicare," and, of particular relevance to beneficiaries interested in managed care, the "Medicare Managed Care Plans" brochure and the *Managed Care Directory*. HCFA staff oversee-

ing the Web site report approximately 2000 people access the
site daily, though it is not possible to know what they are viewing or using.

Libraries

Libraries are increasingly making the Internet available to
an area's residents. For example, Sailor is a statewide, citizen
access project that provides Maryland residents with no-charge
access to Internet resources. The system, funded by the federal
and state Departments of Education, can be used either by going to a library branch equipped with the appropriate computers or by dialing into the system using a modem from home,
office, or school. Sailor maintains a listing of health and medicine resources that are primarily organized under general health
information topics (federal agency fact sheets, toll-free telephone
numbers) and by disease category. Managed care is not yet a
topic in the resource listing; however, through Sailor one could
use these words to search for information. The health and medicine information is a combination of references to other relevant
World Wide Web sites and Sailor-generated information (for
example, on breast cancer). The information on Sailor is developed by a group of volunteers who browse the Internet and cull
what is thought to be most useful to consumers.

Nonprofit Organizations

Several nonprofit organizations for senior citizens are involved in the dissemination of on-line health information to older
adults. One of the oldest is SeniorNet, a 9-year-old nonprofit
membership organization based in San Francisco. With 18,000
members, SeniorNet is designed to introduce adults over age 55
to the on-line computer world. The organization maintains sites
for older adults on two of the commercial on-line services:
America Online ($9.95/month allows unlimited access to
SeniorNet plus 1 free hour to the rest of the offerings) and the
Microsoft Network ($4.95/month for 3 free hours; additional
hours are $2.50/hour). SeniorNet also has a site on the Internet.
SeniorNet has a chat room available to members and also
provides access to a bulletin board where members can exchange

information. Users have a choice of seven topic areas, or forums, including the Health & Wellness Forum. Subtopics within
a forum are largely driven by SeniorNet members, who identify
areas of interest such as Alzheimer's disease, depression, exercise and fitness, or arthritis. The topic titled Medicare or managed care had more than 200 messages during a 5-month period
in 1995 (compared with topics such as Alcoholics Anonymous,
death and dying, or hearing, which had twice as many messages).

The Retirement Living Forum is an information resource
also designed for older adults available through another commercial on-line service, CompuServe. Since 1994, the forum has
been operated by the SPRY Foundation in Washington, D.C.
The forum is structured in three distinct parts: a message/bulle-
tin board, a library, and a conference center. A subscriber using
the message/bulletin board can leave a question to be answered
by an expert or leave a message for a private individual. Currently, there are several message sections dealing with health
including health and medicine, Medicare/Medigap, and medication management. In the library, subscribers can locate and
review information on any one of 19 topics including such topics
as health and medicine and Medicare. Information can also be
printed out for personal use. Finally, conferences are scheduled
periodically with experts in various subject areas. HCFA staff
participated in an on-line conference on managed care earlier
this year. The Retirement Living Forum currently has approximately 15,000 subscribers. CompuServe subscribers pay $9.95
a month, which includes 5 free hours of on-line access to a basic
package of information services. Additional hours are billed at
the rate of $2.95/hour.

Information Kiosks

Public Agencies

The Social Security Administration (SSA) has initiated a
pilot kiosk project in Albuquerque, New Mexico, which began in
the spring of 1995. The 13 kiosks provide information primarily
about the Social Security program. There is, however, a section
about the Medicare program, including information about how

to apply for Medicare, eligibility and benefit coverage, and Medicare HMOs in the area. The kiosks are located in public libraries, food stores, a national discount store chain, and state and federal public office locations. The kiosk text is available in Spanish, Vietnamese, and Navajo, in addition to English. An average of 40 to 50 people access each kiosk daily for information. The specific interest in Medicare information varies from location to location, with approximately 20 inquiries about Medicare of a monthly total of 3,335 (<1 percent) at the Wal-Mart kiosk, compared with 225 of 2,733 (8 percent) at the Social Security office kiosk. SSA staff will evaluate the kiosk program in 1996 for possible replication in other areas and are also talking about making the kiosk software available for replication to other states (Georgia and North Carolina) that maintain, or that are thinking of developing, their own kiosks.

Private Sector

Health*touch* is a touch-screen computer housed in a kiosk that contains a database on medications, health, and lifestyles. Health*touch* computer kiosks are located in about 1,500 retail pharmacies throughout the United States as a value-added service of Cardinal Health, a Columbus, Ohio-based pharmaceutical distributor. Using the touch screen to select a topic and specific files, a consumer can retrieve, read, and print out information on various topics. Most topics are in a question-and-answer format, and many are available in English and Spanish. Organizations such as the American Heart Association, the Centers for Disease Control and Prevention, and the SPRY Foundation contribute files to the database on topics of interest to older adults. Information on the topic of managed care is available under the category "health information." On the basis of research conducted by Health*touch* in the first quarter of 1994, consumers accessed the database 1.35 million times, printing out information to take with them in more than 60 percent of the cases. About 35 percent of the users were age 65 and over.

Community Meetings

Non-Profit Organizations

Under a 1985-1987 cooperative agreement with HCFA, HealthChoice, Inc. (HCI), which is the nonprofit arm of Portland, Oregon-based Benova, implemented a demonstration "independent broker" program at three sites: Los Angeles, Portland, and San Francisco. The demonstration was initiated to test the efficacy of having an independent broker work cooperatively with participating health plans to inform and educate Medicare beneficiaries about the health service options available to them. HCI coordinated HMO fairs, produced and distributed comparative information, and performed beneficiary counseling and enrollment and received remuneration from HMOs for beneficiaries who enrolled as a result of their efforts (Davidson, 1988).

In an evaluation of the demonstration at the Los Angeles and San Francisco sites, researchers found an increase in the level of knowledge of key HMO concepts among beneficiaries attending HCI health fairs; however, they had little or no impact on enrollment behavior (Langwell et al., 1989). Researchers also found differing objectives: the HMOs viewed HCI as a marketing tool, whereas HCFA perceived it as an educational program. They concluded that independent brokers were not effective in markets (such as the two evaluated) where HMO penetration was high, although they may be effective in markets where the HMO option is just being introduced.

In addition to disseminating information to consumers through the newspaper (referenced above), the Minnesota Health Data Institute also held a series of three community meetings to present the findings on consumer satisfaction with Minnesota health plans. The meetings, which were coordinated with the state office of AARP, were held in Duluth, Rochester, and St. Cloud, Minnesota, in October 1995. In St. Cloud and Rochester, information on health plan survey results was included on the agenda of already planned conferences, whereas in Duluth, the information was presented as part of a health fair sponsored by a local television station. According to staff involved in the meetings, attendance was good at the St. Cloud and Rochester meetings (200–400 attendees), whereas the Duluth meeting had a lower turnout.

Another example of a community education effort was a 1-day seminar entitled "Managed Care: What Is at Stake for Older Adults?" held on October 30, 1995, in Research Triangle Park, North Carolina. The seminar, cosponsored by the Leadership in an Aging Society Program of the Duke University Long Term Care Resources Program and the North Carolina Division of Aging, was attended by 100 older adult leaders, state officials, and other interested stakeholders. The topics discussed included quality, access, financing, and long-term care and included perspectives from other states.

Health Plans

Health plans extensively use community meetings as a way to interest Medicare beneficiaries in their HMO product. Often, these meetings are held at public sites such as restaurants or hotels. Plan representatives give a prepared presentation about their HMO product, often supplemented by print materials and in some cases a videotape. Representatives are also available to answer participants' questions. Some plans indicated that they use current plan enrollees in these community presentations as the best "ambassadors" for their program.

One-on-One Counseling

Public Agencies

As mentioned previously, Medicare beneficiaries have access in every state to an Information, Counseling and Assistance (ICA) program. In addition to telephone hotline counseling, the primary mode of delivering services to Medicare beneficiaries is through one-on-one counseling. In such a counseling session, the beneficiary usually goes to a central meeting place, such as a senior center, Social Security office, library, or Area Agency on Aging to discuss his or her questions or concerns with a trained counselor. According to a 1994 evaluation (McCormack et al., 1994), three fourths of all counties nationwide have at least one local counseling site. The program is primarily staffed by trained volunteers, with close to 10,500 individuals across the country volunteering with ICA programs.

The ICA program served approximately 192,212 individuals via phone or one-on-one counseling during a 1-year reporting period (April 1, 1993, to March 31, 1994), with more than 400,000 people participating in a presentation or seminar. This translates to a national average of 12 persons served per 1,000 persons over age 65, although there was substantial variation by state, with proportionately high numbers of older adults served in Idaho, Montana, and New Mexico and proportionately low numbers served in Alabama, Alaska, Hawaii, and South Carolina. Five percent of the total health insurance issues raised during counseling encounters dealt with managed care questions, although states with a high level of penetration into managed care, such as California, Massachusetts, and Oregon, had higher percentages.

Private Sector

The feasibility of a counseling program is being explored under an HCFA Small Business Innovation Research (SBIR) program that funds feasibility studies for small businesses. The project is being conducted by USHC Development Corporation, a for-profit subsidiary of the United Seniors Health Cooperative (USHC), a nonprofit organization that, since 1986, has helped older persons in metropolitan Washington, D.C., be informed consumers.

The project will specifically explore the feasibility of providing a counseling service and related products designed to provide unbiased consumer information to Medicare consumers who are in the process of choosing a managed care plan, as well as a self-assessment instrument and related publications. Included in the study is an investigation of potential markets for the counseling and related products, such as the ICA programs, employers, unions, professional and retiree associations, and managed care organizations.

Health Plans

One-on-one counseling with Medicare beneficiaries is also an important component of most health plans' marketing strategies. Under federal law, plans are prohibited from door-to-door marketing; however, they may go to a beneficiary's home if they are invited. Plans may also meet with interested beneficiaries in other settings such as plan offices.

CONCLUSION AND KEY FINDINGS

A review of the literature and case examples regarding communicating with Medicare beneficiaries about their health plan choices results in several key findings. A first finding is that any effort to communicate with beneficiaries about the choices that they now have or expanded future choices must be done in the context of low levels of Medicare beneficiary understanding of how the basic Medicare program works. Any discussion about the preferred communications channels for reaching older adults about their health plan options must therefore be preceded by a strategic understanding of what Medicare beneficiaries currently know.

Second, with reference to preferred media, older adults, as with their counterparts under age 65, are active users of media of all types. Television and print media, such as newspapers, are used by many older adults in general, although the literature also suggests that different segments of the older adult population may prefer different communications channels depending on sociodemographic and attitudinal factors. Focus groups and limited research seem to indicate that newer communications channels such as cable television, videotapes, and computer on-line services are less appealing to or used by older adults. However, market research has also indicated that the levels of ownership of VCRs and the numbers of cable television subscribers have increased among those over age 50. In addition, as adults age into the Medicare program, it can be expected that they will do so with a higher degree of exposure to newer forms of communication Finally, although not explored in this paper, the use of a variety of communications channels to reach the middle-aged children of current and future older adults who are asked to assist in Medicare choices might involve the use of different communications channels.

A third key finding is that there are a range of organizations now communicating with Medicare beneficiaries about their health plan choices. Some of the organizations, such as HCFA, public libraries, nonprofit organizations, newspapers and magazines, and the seniors' counseling programs, are attempting to educate beneficiaries generally, or specifically in the case of counseling, about their health plan choices. Other organizations, such as health plans with Medicare contracts, are attempting not only to educate but also to enroll beneficiaries in their plans. Given the growing number of HMOs with Medicare contracts and the relative resources that they will most likely devote to marketing to older adults, it is probable that many current and future Medicare beneficiaries will have their first contact with the idea of managed care and health plan choice through some type of plan marketing activity such as an advertisement or direct mail piece. As with reactions to marketing efforts for other types of purchases, it can be expected that some beneficiaries will completely ignore this information, whereas it may stimulate interest and awareness of choice with others. Some Medicare beneficiaries may want additional information, possibly from an unbiased source or from family and friends to evaluate the materials, and finally, others may only be confused or fearful about the information, particularly in light of recent media attention to Medicare "change," which may leave the impression that choice is being taken away, not expanded.

Unlike the purchase of other consumer goods and services, the choice of a health plan and the corresponding coverage and plan rules that they impose have significant consequences for the health and well-being of older adults and their families. This has important implications for public policy makers interested in expanding plan choice. Public oversight of marketing materials to ensure the accuracy of the messages presented is certainly one part of a strategy to ensure informed choice. Access to publicly available, objective, comparative information at both a broad level (i.e., the choice between having Medicare alone, Medicare with a Medigap policy, or a managed care plan) and a specific health plan level (the choice between Medigap plan A versus Medigap plan B or HMO plan A versus HMO plan B) must also be ensured.

The tenets of social marketing may be one approach used to address the tension between communicating for educational purposes and marketing to sell a specific product. Social marketing builds on the concept that social aspirations can be sold through the strategic use of marketing techniques. Used to address such public health topics as smoking and cardiovascular risk reduction, social marketing generally involves three broad principles: (1) the process of marketing is disciplined and objectives are clearly stated; (2) the consumer audience is understood along several psychosocial and demographic dimensions; and (3) the product is responsive on the basis of iterative research into consumers' wants and needs (Walsh et al., 1993). Application of social marketing principles to the objective of increasing a Medicare beneficiary's knowledge and understanding of health plan choices is probably a more complex task than application of those principles in campaigns targeted at changing a health behavior. The clear and unequivocal message in an antismoking campaign, for example, might differ substantially from the message in a campaign with the objective of increasing a Medicare beneficiary's knowledge about both his or her health plan choices and how those choices affect the individual's situation. The techniques, however, may still warrant further exploration.

A final key finding from the literature review, focus groups, and case example interviews is that older adults are particularly oriented toward communications channels that involve person-to-person exchange. Family and friends have been found to be a key means both of learning about health plan choices and in influencing selection. In addition, the opportunity to talk with informed others was also viewed as important. There are several implications of this finding. The first is that "family and friends" should probably also be the target of any information campaigns to help older adults make informed decisions about their health plan choices. Second, the person-to-person outreach widely used by Medicare HMOs in the form of group and individual meetings is probably particularly persuasive in interesting older adults in managed care. Given that these presenta-

tions are less conducive to public oversight, it is important that
older adults and their families have reasonable access to similar
person-to-person methods of providing more objective information about their choices, such as hotlines, group presentations,
or individual counseling, all staffed by individuals capable of
providing answers to general and specific questions.

A final implication of the significance of person-to-person
communications channels for older adults with reference to
health care is that if managed care plans and other emerging
health plans can reach, satisfy, and retain Medicare beneficiaries with their range of benefits and services, provider networks,
quality of care, and customer satisfaction, the word-of-mouth
value of their success will probably be their best marketing tool.

REFERENCES

American Association of Retired Persons. 1995a. Managed Care: An AARP
    Guide. Washington, D.C.: American Association of Retired Persons.
American Association of Retired Persons. 1995b. Healthy Questions: How to
    Talk to and Select Physicians, Pharmacists Dentists & Vision Care Spe-
    cialists. Washington, D.C.: American Association of Retired Persons.
Arizona Senior World. 1995. HMOs Which Assume Responsibility for Medi-
    care Coverage. Arizona Senior World, April, 1995, pg. 18.
Brown, R., K. Langwell, and A. Ciemnecki. 1987. Medicare Beneficiaries' Re-
    sponses to HMO Marketing in Single and Multiple HMO Markets. Pp.
    477-490 in Managing Quality Health Care in a Dynamic Era. Proceed-
    ings of the 37th Annual Group Health Institute. Washington, D.C.: Group
    Health Association of America.
Cafferata, G. 1984. Knowledge of Their Health Insurance by the Elderly.
    Medical Care 22: 835-847.
Center for Health Care Rights. 1995. HMO Members Vote With Their Feet.
    The Medicare Advocate 5: 2-3.
Davidson, B. 1988. Designing Health Insurance Information for the Medicare
    Beneficiary: A Policy Synthesis. Health Services Research 23: 686-719.
Dychtwald, K., M. Zitter and J. Levison. 1990. Implementing Eldercare Ser-
    vices: Strategies that Work. New York: McGraw Hill.
FIND/SVP. 1993. The Maturity Market. New York: FIND/SVP.
Foster Higgins. 1994. National Survey of Employer-Sponsored Health Plans.
    New York: Foster Higgins.
Frederick/Schneiders, Inc. 1995. Analysis of Focus Groups Concerning Man-
    aged Care and Medicare. Prepared for the Henry J. Kaiser Family Foun-
    dation. Washington, D.C.: Frederick/Schneiders.

Garnick, D., A. Hendricks, K. Thorpe, J. Newhouse, K. Doneland, and R. Blendon. 1993. How Well do Americans Understand Their Health Coverage? Health Affairs 12:204-212.

Gilmartin, J. 1993. Managed Care Providers and the Mature Adult Marketplace:Part 1—Changing the Frame of Reference. Medical Interface 6:71-75.

Goodman, R.I. 1992. The Selection of Communication Channels by the Elderly to Obtain Information. Educational Gerontology 18:701-714.

Group Health Association of America. 1991. Helping Older Adults Make Informed Decisions About Joining an HMO. Washington, D.C.: Group Health Association of America.

Harrington, C., R. Newcomer and T. Moore. 1988. Factors that Contribute to Medicare HMO Risk Contract Success. Inquiry 25: 251-262.

Health Care Financing Administration.1992a. Health Maintenance Organization/Competitve Medical Plan Manual. Transmittal No.8. Washington, D.C.: Health Care Financing Administration.

Health Care Financing Administration. 1992b. Medicare Coordinated Care: Q & A. Washington, D.C.: Health Care Financing Administration.

Health Care Financing Administration. 1995a. Your Medicare Handbook 1995. Washington, D.C.: Government Printing Office.

Health Care Financing Administration. 1995b. Medicare Managed Care Plans. Washington, D.C.: Government Printing Office.

Health Care Financing Administration. 1995c. 1995 Guide to Health Insurance for People with Medicare. Washington, D.C.: Government Printing Office.

Health Care Financing Administration. 1995d. 1995 Medicare Managed Care Directory. Washington, D.C.: Health Care Financing Administration.

Health Care Financing Administration. 1995e. Medicare Health Maintenance Organization (HMO) 1995 Benefits Comparison: Northern California, Southern California, Arizona and Nevada. San Francisco: Health Care Financing Administration.

Health Care Financing Administration. 1995f. Project Customer: A Listing of HCFA Consumer Service Activities. Washington, D.C.: Health Care Financing Administration.

Health Pages. 1995. Medicare and the Managed Care Option. Health Pages 1:52-57.

Johnson & Johnson. 1988. Aging Americans: Annual Audit of Attitudes. New Brunswick, N.J.: Johnson & Johnson.

Jorgensen, D., S. Maloney, and J. Finn. 1995. Consumer Reaction to Information about Medicare Choices. Washington, D.C.: SPRY Foundation.

Langwell, K., S. Nelson, L. Nelson, L. Bilheimer and L. Schopler. 1989. Evaluation of HealthChoice Inc. Independent Broker. Washington, D.C.: Mathmatica Policy Research.

LaTour, S.A., B. Friedman, and F.X. Hughes. 1986. Medicare Beneficiary Decision Making About Health Insurance: Implications for a Voucher System. Medical Care 24:610-614.

Lumpkin, J., M. Caballero, and L. Chonko. 1989. Direct Marketing, Direct Selling and the Mature Consumer. New York & Westport, Conn.: Quorum Books.

McCall, N., T. Rice and J. Sangl. 1986. Consumer Knowledge of Medicare. Health Services Research 20: 633-657.

McCormack, L., J. Schnaier, A.J. Lee, S. Garfinkel, and M. Beaven. 1994. Information Counseling and Assistance Programs: Final Report. Washington, D.C.: Health Economics Research.

Medicare Beneficiaries Defense Fund. 1994. Medicare Health Maintenance Organizations: Are They Right for You? New York: Medicare Beneficiaries Defense Fund.

Mellman, Lazarus & Lake. 1994. Medicare: Holes in the Safety Net—An Analysis and Report of Focus Group Findings. Prepared for the Kaiser Family Foundation. Washington, D.C.: Mellman, Lazaus & Lake.

Menchin, R. 1989. The Mature Market: A Strategic Marketing Guide to America's Fastest Growing Population Segment. Chicago: Probus.

Minnesota Health Data Institute. 1995. You and Your Health Plan: 1995 Statewide Survey of Minnesota Consumers. Saint Paul: Minnesota Health Data Institute.

Modern Maturity/The Roper Organization. 1992. Mature America in the 1990s: A Special Report from Modern Maturity Magazine and the Roper Organization. Washington, D.C.: Modern Maturity.

Morgan, C. 1993. Segmenting the Mature Market. Spectrum 7 (November/December): 11-15.

Moschis, G. 1994. Marketing Strategies for the Mature Market. Westport, Conn.: Quorum Books.

Moschis, G. 1992. Marketing to Older Consumers: A Handbook of Information for Strategy Development. Westport, Conn.: Quorum Books.

National Council on the Aging. 1985. Channels of Communication for Reaching Older Adults. Washington, D.C.: National Council on the Aging.

Newcomer, R., C. Harrington and A. Friedlob. 1990. Awareness and Enrollment in the Social/HMO. The Gerontologist 30:86-93.

Pickens, J. 1992. Power of Personality Markets Medicare HMO. Healthcare Marketing Report 10: 1,5-6.

Prasad, V.K., and R. Javalgi. 1992. Understanding Needs and Concerns of the Elderly Regarding Medicare Health Maintenance Organizations. The Journal of Consumer Affairs 26: 47-68.

Research Triangle Institute. 1995. Information Needs for Consumer Choice: Final Focus Group Report. Research Triangle Park, N.C.: Research Triangle Institute.

Scheppke, J. 1994. Who's Using the Public Library? Library Journal 119: 35-37.

Shannon, V. 1995. Inquiring Minds Want to Know the Secrets of Your On-Line Life. Washington Post, December 4, 1995, p. 20.

Social Security Administration. 1994. What You Need to Know About Medicare and Other Health Insurance. Washington, D.C.: Government Printing Office.

Titus, S. 1982. Barriers to the Health Maintenance Organization for the Over 65s. Social Science and Medicine 16:1767-1774.

Walsh, D.C., R. Rudd, B. Moeykens, and T. Moloney. 1993. Social Marketing for Public Health. Health Affairs 12(2):105-119.

Winslow, R. 1994. Employers Try to Get Retirees to Join HMOs. Wall St. Journal, December 16, 1994.

I

What Information Do Consumers Want and Need: What Do We Know About How They Judge Quality and Accountability?

Susan Edgman-Levitan and Paul D. Cleary[*]

INTRODUCTION

More than 25 years ago, Donabedian (1966) stimulated a still-burgeoning effort in theoretical and empirical work on quality assessment. Those who provide and finance health care, as well as the American public, are paying increasing attention to the quality of medical care (Berwick, 1989a,b; Bowen and Burke, 1988; Brook and Lohr, 1985, 1987; Caper, 1988; Cleary et al., 1991; Dubois et al., 1986; Hughes et al., 1987; Larson et al., 1988; Lohr et al., 1988; Meterko et al., 1990; Orient et al., 1983; Roper et al., 1988; Steffen, 1988). Numerous quality assurance and utilization review mechanisms have been developed to monitor and control the process of care in hospitals. In addition, a variety of new methods for monitoring and evaluating the outcomes of hospital care are being developed (Allen et al., 1994; American College of Physicians, 1988; Cleary et al., 1991b, 1992a; Ellwood, 1988; Lohr, 1989; McDowell and Newell, 1987; Patrick and Bergner, 1990; Patrick and Erickson, 1988, 1993; Schroeder, 1987; Thier, 1992; Wilson and Cleary, 1995). Many

---

[*]The Picker Institute and Harvard Medical School, Department of Health Care Policy, Boston, Massachusetts.

of these efforts, however, have two limitations: they rely only on medical or administrative records as sources of information, and they define "quality" in terms of a relatively narrow range of technical processes and physiological outcomes (Caper, 1988; Cleary and McNeil, 1988; Cleary et al., 1991a, b; Davies and Ware, 1988; Donabedian, 1988; Garvin, 1984; Lohr et al., 1988; Matthews and Feinstein, 1988; Meterko et al., 1990; Steffen, 1988). Interestingly, little of the systematic work to date on quality assessment and quality assurance has taken advantage of the information and perspective that only patients can provide.

Patient reports can be extremely useful in evaluating the quality of medical care. Many critical aspects of medical care, such as difficulty obtaining care, waiting time in an office, adequacy of communication, education, pain control, and emotional support, and whether patients were appropriately involved in important decisions about their care, are not recorded routinely by hospitals, health plans, or individual clinicians.

Furthermore, providers frequently have priorities different from those of patients and perceive events differently than patients do. In a Picker/Commonwealth Program for Patient-Centered Care-American College of Physicians study of 74 physicians and 814 patients, both groups agreed that clinical skill is most important, but patients ranked information and effective communication second in importance, whereas physicians ranked it sixth out of seven. The two groups differed substantially on 59 percent of the attributes in an item-by-item comparison of the ratings. Equally important, patients can provide information about important processes of care that is not available from other sources, for example, the length of waiting time in the doctor's office or the adequacy of pain control.

How Do Consumers Define High Quality Medical Care?

It often is assumed that consumers are particularly interested in knowing about other consumers' evaluations of health care providers or systems. Surprisingly little information is available on this topic.

Different types of consumers, for example, healthy persons

or those with chronic diseases have different informational needs. Not everyone has the interest or ability to evaluate detailed information, an issue of particular importance with an elderly population. Furthermore, to our knowledge, no one has distinguished the information needs of the general consumer from those of the health care decision maker in a family, that is, the person responsible for choosing the health benefits.

Information included in consumer reports can be selected on the basis of two related but independent criteria. First, users must be given the information they *say* they want and need. Second, reports also should include the information that best reflects the technical quality of care that health plans deliver.

Over the past several years, researchers have conducted hundreds of focus groups with different types of consumers to understand how patients define quality of care and which aspects of care should be measured, from the patient's perspective. Below, we summarize the results of some of those studies.

Patient satisfaction with medical care is perhaps one of the most commonly measured patient attitudes, and work in this field has increased markedly in the past decade or so (Allen et al., 1994; Cleary and McNeil, 1988; Cleary et al., 1991a, 1992a, 1993; Davies and Ware, 1988; Hall and Dornan, 1990; Hall et al., 1993; Hays et al., 1993; Rubin et al., 1993; Safran et al., 1994; Ware and Hays, 1988).

There is an extensive literature on both the determinants and the consequences of patient satisfaction (Cleary and McNeil, 1988; Davies and Ware, 1988). Almost all of the instruments used to assess patients' satisfaction with their care assess important aspects of care. However, many of the instruments used in earlier research studies were not based on careful assessments of how patients define and perceive quality and did not explicitly incorporate patient priorities during the development of measures. For example, many patient satisfaction scales place substantial emphasis on amenities (attractiveness of waiting rooms, parking, hospital food, etc.), whereas when consumers are asked to define the most important aspect of quality care, they do not place a high priority on those features of care.

An early activity of the Picker Institute was an evaluation of the existing measures and the development of a new instrument to assess the quality of hospital care, from the patient's perspective. The development process included a thorough review of the literature but placed a great deal of emphasis on eliciting directly from patients the ways in which they defined and evaluated care. For example, we conducted numerous focus groups with patients, their families, other laypersons, and health professionals.

We also conducted pilot interviews with patients and their families from different parts of the country. Subsequently, we had patients and health professionals critique the types of questions that we asked about the quality of health care and tell us about the priority that they gave to the different aspects of care that we asked about (Cleary et al., 1991a, 1992).

We conducted focus groups to find out more about the patients' experiences of illness and health care and the systems that do and do not work to meet patients' needs. What is it about their interactions with providers, systems, and institutions that patients say matters to them and affects them either positively and negatively (Gerteis et al., 1993). On the basis of that work, we defined several dimensions of care that we think describe how consumers define quality and reflect the most salient processes of care for which they might want comparative assessments. For hospital inpatients, the dimensions are as follows:

- respect for patients' values, preferences, and expressed needs;
- coordination of care;
- information, communication, and education;
- physical comfort and pain management;
- emotional support and alleviation of fear and anxiety;
- involvement of family and friends; and
- transition and continuity to the home or community.

The Picker Institute and its collaborators have conducted similar studies of ambulatory care. Focus groups have been used to identify the needs of ambulatory patients receiving care in emergency rooms, private doctor's offices, hospital outpatient clinics, community health centers, and managed care plans.

Ambulatory care patients are concerned about a somewhat different set of dimensions:

- access to care;
- coordination of care;
- information, communication, and education;
- respect for patients' values, preferences, and expressed needs;
- emotional support and the alleviation of fear and anxiety; and
- patients' experiences with specific processes of care: waiting times in the office, assistance from office staff, tests and procedures, and follow-up care and information.

Multiple focus groups conducted with Department of Veterans Affairs' (VA) patients from different geographic regions confirmed the dimensions of quality identified by earlier Picker Institute work as being most important to patients. The VA National Customer Feedback Center and Department of Quality have established them as the "customer standards" for all VA hospitals.

What Types of Information About Quality Do Consumers Want?

Learning about how consumers define quality medical care does not necessarily answer the question of what types of information consumers want to evaluate health care plans when making selections among plans. Health plans are increasingly making information about patients' evaluations of their care publicly available. Reports describing such information often are referred to as "report cards." Although we now know a great deal about how consumers define quality medical care, we know much less about what information consumers would like to see in such reports and how they interpret and evaluate such information.

The National Committee for Quality Assurance (NCQA) conducted research, in collaboration with the Picker/Commonwealth Program for Patient-Centered Care and the Agency for Health Care Policy and Reseach (AHCPR), to learn more about consumers' attitudes toward report cards. The work included a review of the literature and focus groups with a broad range of consumers.

This work and our review of summaries of focus groups conducted by other groups lead to several general conclusions:

- Consumers would use information on how a plan works, what it costs, the covered benefits, the quality of care, and overall satisfaction with care if it were available.
- Consumers are most concerned about costs of coverage, technical competence, the information and communication provided by physicians, coordination of care, and access.
- Consumers are savvy and are able to evaluate critically information about quality. In fact, they raise many of the same issues debated by experts in quality measurement. Every single focus group expressed concern, for example, about the source and quality of the data, the size of the population (denominator), the size of the survey sample, and the validity of the data.
- Consumers want to know how others "like them" evaluate care, and many trust patient evaluations more than any other source of data. Opinions about the appropriate balance between summary and detailed information varied.
- Consumers want an unbiased, expert source of judgment about health care quality. Many are skeptical about data collection or assessments performed by health plans, insurance companies, employers, and/or the government.

WHAT KIND OF INFORMATION IS OF PARTICULAR INTEREST TO MEDICARE BENEFICIARIES?

We have only limited data about how Medicare beneficiaries make decisions to join managed care plans and their needs for information to support those decisions. However, several organizations have conducted focus groups with Medicare beneficiaries about related issues that provide us with some insights, and inferences can be made about the kind of information that Medicare beneficiaries would want about managed care. We also conducted interviews with Medicare program managers in large managed care organizations, state insurance hot lines, and con-

sumer advocacy groups for the elderly. We describe below the
common themes that emerged from those efforts.

Focus Group Findings

Several organizations have commissioned focus group studies to examine attitudes and concerns of the elderly toward
Medicare managed care selections. Those studies are useful in
that the same themes emerge consistently. However, the findings are not necessarily representative for all Medicare beneficiaries, and those most in need of high-quality, comprehensive
care—the disabled, the chronically ill, and those who are cognitively impaired—may be the least likely to participate in focus
groups.

In a 1995 study conducted by Frederick/Schneiders, Inc., for
the Henry J. Kaiser Family Foundation (Frederick/Schneiders,
Inc., 1995), senior citizens expressed significant mistrust and
anger about managed care and believed that elders are being
forced to accept a lower standard of care to increase health care
profits and reduce the government's budgetary problems. The
study found that few consumers, especially the elderly, understand how managed care works except in areas with high levels
of penetration into the managed care market.

Focus group participants in that study, however, were interested in comparative data on benefits and quality of care and
descriptive information about how managed care plans function. They wanted information about how to choose a provider
and wanted to see specific information about primary and specialty providers, including information on training, a physician's
gender, location, and patient satisfaction information. They
were also concerned about how much choice they have with
respect to hospitals.

Much of the information that they requested is descriptive:
How does managed care work? What are their rights? How do
you pick a doctor? How do you switch physicians? What happens if you need experimental treatments? Where are centers
or clinics located, and what are their hours?

As for data, these focus group participants also were interested in satisfaction information, but they expressed concerns
about the utility of general satisfaction information. Most par-

ticipants talk about the need to understand the source of information: the value system, beliefs, and intelligence of the person or people from whom it was acquired. Word-of-mouth information, on the other hand, was seen as extremely valuable. Participants were much more interested in the opinions of their family members, friends, or neighbors than in those of their coworkers or other employees from their former places of employment.

In 1994, NCQA conducted focus groups as part of the Consumer Information Project that included Medicare recipients. Two of the groups who were composed of consumers who had chronic conditions or were retirees. The findings of that study—both for all consumers and for these two groups—were similar to the focus group findings described above. Participants were very interested in comparative information on costs, the benefits package, and how the plan worked. They also expressed dismay that no comparable information exists for fee-for-service coverage. They wanted assurances that the technical quality of care had been assessed and wanted information about other aspects of quality. They were primarily concerned with the quality of the physicians, their technical skill, their ability to communicate, and their accessibility, especially in the event of an emergency. Many found the typical information about how to pick a doctor confusing. Several participants said, "Just tell me if I can pick my doctor or not!"

Many elderly and chronically ill focus group participants made negative comments about the information provided to them about access. They did not want ratings, because they could not interpret another person's tolerance for waiting times for appointments or in the waiting room. They wanted to know the number of days or the time spent waiting in the office so that they could judge for themselves. Interestingly, they also wanted to know about access to information over the phone so that they could avoid an appointment, if possible.

Again, these consumers—some of whom were low-income patients with little education—were very able to critically evaluate the information provided to them. They wanted to know the source of the information, the size of the population measured, the sample size, and how the results compared with national norms. They also remarked that some Health Plan Employer Data and Information Set (HEDIS) measures (such as the percentage of women over age 50 who have had mammograms or the percentage of children who had been immunized) reflected personal behavior and social problems as much as the quality of a health plan.

Chronically ill and retired focus group participants had more concerns about the comprehensiveness of the coverage and the referral process for specialty care. They were also interested in the communications skills of their providers and in good access. They showed mixed loyalty to their physicians; for some, comprehensive coverage was more important than the ability to remain with their primary care provider.

These participants also expressed more interest in the ratings of satisfaction from family members and friends than from consumers in general. They also wanted detailed ratings of overall satisfaction rather than aggregate groupings of the "satisfied" versus the "dissatisfied."

The elderly were not interested in evaluations of services that they would not use, for example, pediatric immunizations. They wanted information that assessed and compared care that both genders were likely to receive and that was relevant to their age and health status.

The Research Triangle Institute is now conducting a study to develop and test prototype information materials for Medicare and Medicaid beneficiaries (Research Triangle Institute, 1995a,b). The findings from the focus group and case study components of that study are similar to the findings from other focus group studies and to those from interviews that we conducted with state health insurance counseling programs and advocacy groups. Consumers expressed interest in the following:

- structural measures, that is, the scope of benefits, premiums, and how the plan works;
- survey-based measures: access to care, communication/interpersonal skills, experiences with the physician/hospital/member services; and
- assurances that data have been collected and analyzed by an independent third party.

The report also suggests that Medicare beneficiaries would like more guidance to direct them toward a particular choice. It suggests that the development of composite measures or scores that synthesize concepts such as access, communication, and coordination of care might be helpful. Once again, participants found the information received from family members and friends to be more helpful and trustworthy than information received from other sources and also wanted to see more detailed information about the experiences of plan members "like them."

Literature on Health Care Consumer Decision Making

Berki and Ashcraft (1980) postulate that choice of plan will be a result of consumer characteristics, insurance characteristics (e.g., costs and benefits), and delivery system characteristics (e.g., access and quality). Acito (1978) emphasizes the role of information and satisfaction with care in the decision-making process, both the decision to enroll and the decision to remain in a given plan. There are surprisingly few empirical studies on how consumers, in general, or Medicare beneficiaries, in particular, make choices among health care providers.

Some studies suggest that a strong, satisfactory relationship with a health care provider will influence the decision to choose or remain in a plan (Lohr et al., 1991; Raymond, 1995). A 1993 study by Sofaer and Hurwicz tested a model of decision making that included the consumers' level of knowledge of available options and the most influential sources of information. The study found that 60 percent of Medicare beneficiaries switched managed care plans to preserve their preexisting relationship with doctors.

Beginning in 1993, the Office of the Inspector General of the U.S. Department of Health and Human Services began surveying Medicare beneficiaries enrolled in or recently disenrolled from health maintenance organizations (HMOs) to better understand enrollment procedures and service quality issues from the perspective of the beneficiaries. The intent of the study was to identify, from the beneficiaries' perspective, areas that need improvement and to suggest methods that the Health Care Financing Administration (HCFA) could use to monitor these areas in the future (Office of the Inspector General, 1995). Although that study was not intended to identify information that beneficiaries might use to select a plan, certain areas of performance or perceptions of service were strongly correlated with disenrollment. One could argue that comparative information about these areas might be helpful to beneficiaries in their initial selection of plans. The questions most predictive of beneficiaries' future disenrollment included the following:

- Were complaints taken seriously by the doctor? (Respect)
- Did their primary HMO doctors provide Medicare services, admit them to the hospital, or refer them to specialists when needed? (Access)
- Did they perceive that their HMOs are giving too high a priority to holding down the cost of medical care than to giving the best medical care?
- Did they perceive their health worsening as a result of the medical care that they received in their HMO?
- Did they experience long waits in their primary care doctors' offices? (Access)

Interviews with Decision Makers

To augment the literature about the informational needs of Medicare beneficiaries, we interviewed staff at state insurance counseling programs, consumer advocacy groups, HMO managers of Medicare programs, patient relations managers for large individual practice associations (IPAs), and prepaid group practice plans to learn more about the type of information most often requested and to find out what kind of information seemed most helpful to potential Medicare enrollees and/or their family members inquiring on their behalf. We also interviewed a benefits manager from a large national employer about how information is disseminated to retirees (personal interviews with: HealthPartners, Minneapolis, Minn.; Harvard Pilgrim Health Plan, Boston, Mass.; Fallon Health Plan, Worcester, Mass.; The Family Health Plan, Tampa, Fla.; state insurance information hotlines in Arizona, California, Florida, Massachusetts, Missouri, Texas; GTE, Waltham, Mass.; HCFA, Baltimore, Md.).

Those interviews suggest that Medicare beneficiaries have

many of the same concerns as most new enrollees in managed care plans. They often do not understand what managed care is and express concern that it represents "second-class care." Cost is a major concern, as is overall quality of care.

The managers of Medicare HMO programs confirmed focus group findings about beneficiaries' need for information. They report that the most frequent benefit questions focus on prescription benefits, home care and long-term-care coverage, dental and foot care services, and out-of-plan coverage, especially in plans in the Northeast or Midwest with large "snowbird" populations.

Many state insurance commissions have established free, long-distance hot lines, one-on-one counseling sessions, newsletters, and other types of educational presentations to provide Medicare beneficiaries with information. Our efforts to contact these services revealed several things:

• Many were extremely difficult to find; it required an assertive, determined person to locate many of the counseling or information services.
• Several insurance commission phone numbers required working through a maze of voice mail, only to end up with a recorded message asking the caller to leave a name and phone number.
• Many staff who we spoke with expressed concern about making subjective recommendations, or even providing helpful information about what to look for in a managed care option, for fear of "influencing" beneficiaries or of "being censored by health plans."

Interactive methods of presenting information are beginning to provide data about how consumers use "layered" information previously unavailable. Layered information allows the user to look at global information about a plan and then request more specific information about a plan, a center or provider, or specific patient populations, defined by demographic variables or diagnostic groups. Anecdotal information from our interview about the kiosk system reveals that the elderly are using the patient satisfaction information much more than expected now

that it is available. The first formal transaction data report
about the use of the kiosks designed by HealthPartners in Minneapolis may be available during 1996.

All of the individuals from managed care plans interviewed
indicate that their plans use a combination of written materials,
educational group presentations, face-to-face meetings, and benefits hot lines to inform and educate Medicare beneficiaries
about their plans. Some plans sponsor fairs and have support
groups for caregivers, as another way of providing information
and assistance to the elderly population. Those whom we interviewed commented on the importance of face-to-face meetings to
this population.

Although consumer advocates express concern about unfair
marketing practices that might occur in individual meetings
with Medicare beneficiaries, consumers seem to prefer to look
someone in the eye and decide whether they are trustworthy
and honest.

RECOMMENDATIONS

Our research and review of the literature confirm that a
great deal more needs to be known about the information needs
of all consumers, especially Medicare beneficiaries. Consumers
are much more sophisticated about data and information than
researchers or health care providers often give them credit for.
However, we have only a limited understanding about the kinds
of information consumers may ultimately find most helpful.

Many studies (Davidson, 1988; Hibbard and Weeks, 1987;
Sofaer, 1993a) have shown that Medicare beneficiaries need to
understand how Medicare works and need to have a basic understanding of managed care and their rights in managed care
plans before they can make informed choices about which plan
to choose. They need standardized benefit packages comparing
managed care and fee-for-service options that can be easily described and explained and standardized, clear information about
supplemental coverage. For example, Sofaer (1993b) estimates
that 10 to 15 percent of Medicare beneficiaries have duplicative
policies that entail significant out-of-pocket expenses to a population with limited means.

Consumers need comparative information about all health

care delivery options, not just managed care, to make educated decisions. Making an informed choice about managed care requires an understanding of the differences between managed care and fee-for-service plans and the availablity of comparable information about both types of plans on which an intelligent decision can be based (Sofaer, 1993a; Varner and Christy, 1986). The lack of objective comparative data about various types of health plans makes it even more difficult for Medicare beneficiaries to behave as informed consumers.

Many consumers say that they are not interested in overall satisfaction information because they do not know how to interpret it or what biases it reflects. Health care administrators and clinicians also told us this in early focus groups conducted by the Picker Institute/Commonwealth Program for Patient-Centered Care. Patient surveys should allow patients to *report* about their experiences with a plan's health care, as well as *rate* their overall satisfaction. Correlating patient reports about their experiences with satisfaction ratings can elucidate patient priorities for different aspects of care and predict which aspects of care will influence disenrollment. Combining these different evaluations of care in consumer information may increase the usefulness of these kinds of data to consumers.

Much of the available information about the informational needs of Medicare beneficiaries speaks to the need for providing a way to evaluate the trade-offs between cost, access, and quality for consumers. A Medicare manager from one of the largest and oldest managed care plans in the country talked at length about how value-conscious and shrewd potential Medicare enrollees have become, making almost actuarial-like decisions to compare how much they might save or lose, depending on their personal health needs and utilization history.

Consumers on fixed incomes pay close attention to their out-of-pocket expenses and would benefit greatly from a method of determining those costs that reflect their own health problems. The illness-episode approach developed by Sofaer and Davidson (1990) may be a way of providing information to Medicare beneficiaries and their family members that will allow them to make informed choices about the best plan for them, depending on their health status.

Focus groups conducted by the Picker Institute and NCQA suggest that consumers want information about how others like them fare in the health care system, with respect both to their experience and satisfaction with a plan's care and in terms of outcomes. The incorporation of patients' experiences with care, satisfaction, and outcomes data into the illness-episode approach could become a very useful way of providing information for people with chronic health problems.

Many Medicare beneficiaries may have few choices among plans, and the same plan may have different arrangements with physicians and hospitals and, in some instances, may even have differences in the services that they provide in the same geographic area. In the future, information that allows consumers to evaluate the care provided by different plan centers (clinics) or physicians may be the most valuable to consumers. We think that collecting and presenting these levels of data will become increasingly important. Devising cost-effective methods of collecting valid center- and physician-level data will be a major challenge in the future.

Below we present a typology of information that might be of most interest to Medicare beneficiaries. Some of the information is descriptive and would be presented in tabular or narrative format. Other information would require standardized data collection from a sample of Medicare beneficiaries receiving care across all types of delivery systems.

Typology of Consumer Information

PLAN/PROVIDER (FFS) INFORMATION (Structural Information)
1. Premium and copayments
2. Rating of hassle factor of paperwork
3. Brief summary of contractual arrangements with providers: incentives to reduce utilization
4. Medical/loss ratio of plan, if appropriate
5. Comparable information for fee-for-service plans
6. Description of grievance and disenrollment process
7. Percent disenrollment of Medicare beneficiaries

BENEFIT PACKAGE (Structural Information)
1. Description of the standard package

2. Coverage for special concerns of the elderly: prescriptions, foot care, home care, long-term care, other supplemental coverage.

QUALITY (Accreditation and Survey-Based Information)
1. Accreditation status
2. Percentage of board-certified physicians
3. Patient *reports* and *ratings* of care for all members and for members over age 65:
   a. Member services:
      i. member support
      ii. prior approval process
      iii. restrictions on referrals for specialty care, special services
   b. Access:
      i. appointment waiting times
      ii. visit waiting times
      iii. choice of primary care physicians and specialists
   c. Communication and interpersonal skills
   d. Coordination of care
   e. Information and education
   f. Respect for patient preferences
   g. Emotional support
4. HEDIS and other technical measures appropriate for a Medicare population.

Finally, we recommend that AHCPR's Consumer Assessment of Health Plans Survey project incorporate the informational needs of Medicare beneficiaries into the design of surveys and report formats. This effort to collect national comparative data for all other consumers could serve as the vehicle for capturing and presenting information to the Medicare population in the future. As all consumers become familiar and accustomed to using these kinds of data and information, there is no justification for recommending that they or the providers of care switch to a different survey or report format for the Medicare population. As we lay the foundation for collecting and disseminating consumer feedback now, we should develop a system that works for everyone. More important, why would we ask the Medicare population to shift to new surveys and report card formats at a time when it is most important for information to be clear and comprehensible?

WHY DOES ALL OF THIS MATTER: PERSONAL AND POLICY IMPLICATIONS

Making the right choice of a health plan is extremely important to older Americans. Older consumers need to establish a relationship with a physician and understand how to get the best care for their limited dollars. Their health care needs are likely to be more extensive than those of younger patients. Continuity of care and good communication with a doctor are likely to improve their subjective well-being and functional status.

From the perspective of the federal government, managing the costs of the Medicare program is extremely important. Helping Medicare beneficiaries make the right decision and making them comfortable with new organizational and financing arrangements will require providing them with the kind of information that they value and can interpret.

A recent Price Waterhouse study on the impact of disenrollment estimates that it costs plans close to $1,300 per Medicare disenrollee. Medicare enrollees may be less likely to change their choice of providers if they are initially given better information. They will also be better consumers in general if they understand their rights under managed care and how to make the plan work for them.

REFERENCES

Acito, F. 1978. Consumer decision-making and health maintenance organizations: A review. Med. Care 16:1.

Allen, H.M., H. Darling, D.N. NcNeill, and F. Bastien. 1994. The employee health care value survey: Round one. Health Affairs Fall:25-41.

American College of Physicians. 1988. Comprehensive functional assessment for elderly patients. Ann. Intern. Med. 109:70–72.

Berki, S.E. and M.L.F. Ashcraft. 1980. HMO enrollment: who joins what and why: A review of the literature. Milbank Quarterly 58:588.

Berwick, D.M. 1989a. Continuous improvement as an ideal in health care. N. Engl. J. Med. 320:53–56.

Berwick, D.M. 1989b. Health services research and quality of care. Assignments for the 1990s. Med. Care 27:763–771.

Bowen, O.R. and T.R. Burke. 1988. New directions in effective quality of care: Patient outcome research. Fed. Am. Health Systems Rev. Sept/Oct:50–53.

Brook, R.H. and K.N. Lohr. 1985. Efficacy, effectiveness, variations, and quality: Boundary-crossing research. Med. Care 23:710–722.

Brook, R.H. and K.N. Lohr. 1987. Monitoring quality of care in the Medicare program: Two proposed systems. JAMA 258:3138–3141.

Caper, P. 1988. Defining quality in medical care. Health Affairs 7:49–61.

Cleary, P.D., and B.J. McNeil. 1988. Patient satisfaction as an indicator of quality of care. Inquiry 25:25–36.

Cleary, P.D., M.C. Fahs, W. McMullen, G. Fulop, J. Strain, H.S. Sacks, C. Muller, M. Foley, and E. Stein. 1992b. Using patient reports to assess hospital treatment of persons with AIDS: A pilot study. AIDS Care 4:325-332.

Cleary, P.D., S. Edgman-Levitan, J.D. Walker, M. Gerteis, T.L. Delbanco. 1993. Using patient reports to improve medical care: A preliminary report from ten hospitals. Quality Management Health Care 2:31-38.

Cleary, P.D., S. Edgman-Levitan, M. Roberts, T.W. Moloney, W. McMullen, J.D. Walker, and T.L. Delbanco. 1991a. Patients evaluate their hospital care: A national survey. Health Affairs 10:254–267.

Cleary, P.D., S. Edgman-Levitan, W. McMullen, and T.L. Delbanco. 1992a. A national survey of hospital patients: The relationship between reported problems with care and patient evaluations. Quality Rev. Bull. 18:53–59.

Cleary, P.D., S. Greenfield and B.J. McNeil. 1991b. Assessing quality of life after surgery. Controlled Clin. Trials 12:189S–203S.

Daley, J., S. Jencks, D. Draper, G. Lenhart, N. Thomas, and J. Walker. 1988. Predicting hospital-associated mortality for Medicare patients: A method for patients with stroke, pneumonia, acute myocardial infarction, and congestive heart failure. JAMA 260:3617–3624.

Davidson, B.N. 1988. Designing health insurance information for the medicare beneficiary: A policy synthesis. Health Services Res. 23(5):685–720.

Davies, A.R., and J.E. Ware, Jr. 1988. Involving consumers in quality of care assessment. Health Affairs 7:33–48.

Donabedian, A. 1966. Evaluating the quality of medical care. Milbank 44:166.

Donabedian, A. 1988. Quality assessment and assurance: Unity of purpose, diversity of means. Inquiry 25:173–192.

Dubois, R.W., W.H. Rogers, J.H. Moxley, D. Draper, and R.H. Brook. 1986. Hospital inpatient mortality: Is it a predictor of quality? N. Engl. J. Med. 317:1674–1680.

Ellwood, P. 1988. Outcomes management. A technology or patient experience? N. Engl. J. Med. 318:1549–1556.

Frederick/Schneiders, Inc. 1995. Analysis of Focus Groups Concerning Managed Care and Medicare. Prepared for the Henry J. Kaiser Family Foundation. Washington, D.C.: Frederick/Schneiders, Inc.

Garvin, D.A. 1984. What does "Product Quality" really mean? Sloan Management Review 26:25–43.

Gerteis, M., et al., eds. 1993. Through the Patient's Eyes: Understanding and Promoting Patient-Centered Care. San Francisco: Jossey-Bass Publishers.

Hall, J., and M.C. Dornan. 1990. Patient sociodemographic characteristics as predictors of satisfaction with medical care: A meta-analysis. Soc. Sci. Med. 30: 811–818.

Hall, J., M.A. Melbourne, and A.M. Epstein. 1993. A causal model of health status and satisfaction with medical care. Med. Care 31:84-93.

Hays, R.D., C. Larson, E.C. Nelson, and P.B. Batalden. 1991. Hospital quality trends: A short-form patient-based measure. Med. Care 29: 661–668.

Hibbard, J.H., and E.C. Weeks. 1987. Consumerism in health care: Prevalence and Predictors. Med. Care 25(11):1019–1032.

Hughes, R.G., S.S. Hunt and H.S. Luft. 1987. Effects of surgeon volume and hospital volume on quality of care in hospitals. Med. Care 25:489–503.

Jencks, S.F., J. Daley, D. Draper, N. Thomas, G. Lenhart, and J. Walker. 1988. Interpreting hospital mortality data: The role of clinical risk adjustment. JAMA 160:3611–3616.

Larson, E., L.F. Oram and E. Hedrick. 1988. Nosocomial infection rates as an indicator of quality. Med. Care 26:676–684.

Lohr, K.N., ed. 1989. Advances in health status assessment: Overview of the conference. Med. Care 27(Suppl. 1):S1–S11.

Lohr, K.N., K.D. Yordy and S.O. Thier. 1988. Current issues in quality of care. Health Affairs 7:5–18.

Lohr, K.N., M.S. Donaldson, and A.J. Walker. 1991. Medicare: A strategy for quality assurance. III. Beneficiary and physician focus groups. Quality Rev. Bull. 17(8):242–253.

Matthews, D.A., and A.R. Feinstein. 1988. A review of systems for the personal aspects of patient care. Am. J. Med. Sci. 31:159–171.

McDowell, I., and C. Newell. 1987. Measuring Health: A Guide to Rating Scales and Questionnaires. New York: Oxford University Press.

Meterko, M., E.C. Nelson and H.R. Rubin, eds. 1990. Patient judgements of hospital quality. Med. Care 28(Suppl. 9).

Office of the Inspector General. 1995. Surveying Medicare Beneficiaries. Washington, D.C.: U.S. Department of Health and Human Services.

Orient, J.M., L.J. Kettel, H.C. Sox Jr, C.H. Sox, H.J. Berggren, A.H. Woods, B.W. Brown, and M. Lebowitz. 1983. The effect of algorithms on the cost and quality of patient care. Med. Care 21:157–167.

Patrick, D.L., and M. Bergner. 1990. Measurement of health status in the 1990's. Annu. Rev. Public Health 11:165–183.

Patrick, D.L., and P. Erickson. 1988. Assessing health-related quality of life for clinical decision making. P. 9 in Quality of Life: Assessment and Application. S.R. Walker and R.M. Rosser, eds. Lancaster, England: MTP Press Ltd.

Patrick, D.L., and P. Erickson. 1993. Health status and health policy. In Quality of Life in Health Care Evaluation and Resource Allocation. New York: Oxford University Press.

Raymond, A.G. 1995. Giving consumers the quality information they need. Quality Lett.

Research Triangle Institute. 1995a. Information Needs for Consumer Choice Case Study Report. Prepared for Office of Research and Demonstrations, Health Care Financing Administration. Research Triangle Park, N.C.: Research Triangle Institute.

Research Triangle Institute. 1995b. Information Needs for Consumer Choice: Draft Focus Group Report. Prepared for Office of Research and Demonstrations, Health Care Financing Administration. Research Triangle Park, N.C.: Research Triangle Institute.

Roper, W.L., W. Winkenwerder, G.M. Hackbarth, and H. Krakauer. 1988. Effectiveness in health care: An initiative to evaluate and improve medical practice. N. Engl. J. Med. 319:1197–1202.

Rubin, H.R., B. Gandek, W.H. Rogers, M. Kosinski, C.A. McHorney, and J.E. Ware, Jr. 1993. Patients' ratings of outpatient visits in different practice settings. JAMA 270:835-840.

Safran, D.G., A.R. Tarlov, and W.H. Rogers. 1994. Primary care performance in fee-for-service and prepaid healthcare systems: Results from the medical outcomes study. JAMA 271:1579-1586.

Schroeder, S.A. 1987. Outcome assessment 70 years later: Are we ready? N. Engl. J. Med. 316:160–162.

Sofaer, S. 1993a. Informing and protecting consumers under managed competition. Health Affairs 12 (Suppl.):76–86.

Sofaer, S. 1993b. Threats to consumers. Health/PAC Bulletin Spring.

Sofaer, S. and M. Hurwicz. 1993. When medical group and HMO part company: Disenrollment decisions in Medicare HMO's. Med. Care 31(9):808–821.

Sofaer, S., and B.N. Davidson. 1990. Illness-episode approach: Costs and benefits of medigap insurance. Health Care Financing Rev. 11(4):121–131.

Steffen, G.E. 1988. Quality medical care: A definition. JAMA 260:56–61.

Thier, S.O. 1992. Forces motivating the use of health status assessment measures in clinical settings and related clinical research. Med. Care 30:MS15–MS22.

Varner, T., and J. Christy. 1986. Consumer information needs in a competitive health care environment. Health Care Financing Review Suppl. Special No. 99–104.

Ware, J.E. Jr, and R.D. Hays. 1988. Methods for measuring patient satisfaction with specific medical encounters. Med. Care 26:393-402.

Wilson, I.B., and P.D. Cleary. 1995. Linking clinical variables with health-related quality of life: A causal model of patient outcomes. JAMA 273:59–65.

J

Medicare Managed Care: Protecting Consumers and Enhancing Satisfaction

*Patricia A. Butler**

INTRODUCTION

Although only about 10 percent of Medicare beneficiaries are enrolled in health maintenance organizations (HMOs), enrollment has been growing rapidly, more than 20 percent annually since 1994 (U.S. General Accounting Office, 1995c). Recent congressional proposals also would encourage even greater levels of participation in managed care plans, including provider networks and other arrangements. Any significant change in Medicare requires attention to the effects on its beneficiaries who may be unfamiliar with different delivery systems. Consumer protection is particularly important in a movement to enroll Medicare beneficiaries into capitated managed care organizations because of capitation's incentives to underserve and the greater health care needs of the elderly.

Understanding what managed care features and practices please or disappoint enrollees is important to both plans and policy makers contracting with them in a more competitive Medicare marketplace. The purpose of this paper is to examine sources of Medicare health plan enrollee satisfaction and dissat-

---

*Health care consultant, Boulder, Colorado.

isfaction and mechanisms to address consumer complaints through appeals processes and government oversight. The paper is divided into five sections. The next outlines current research evidence on Medicare HMO enrollee satisfaction. The the appeals processes available to Medicare health plan enrollees unhappy with plan coverage, payment, access, and other performance issues are then outlined. Current roles and standards of the federal and state governments in regulating managed care are then described. Consumer protection policy issues that arise in a competitive Medicare market are identified and the paper concludes with recommendations for further research and analysis.

MEDICARE MANAGED CARE: SOURCES OF SATISFACTION AND DISSATISFACTION

Like most Americans, the vast majority of Medicare beneficiaries enrolled in managed care plans respond positively to surveys of consumer satisfaction (Adler, 1995; Ferguson, 1995; Minnesota Health Data Institute, 1995; Rossiter et al., 1989; Ward, 1987). Working Americans enrolled in HMOs are about as satisfied with overall plan performance as people receiving care on a fee-for-service basis. Health plan enrollees, however, are more likely to rate highly their plan's premiums and cost sharing and are less likely than their indemnity plan counterparts to be happy with physician-patient interactions or general "quality" (Miller and Luft, 1994). People suffering from poor health or chronic conditions enrolled in managed care plans are more likely than those enrolled in fee-for-service plans to report problems (The Robert Wood Johnson Foundation, 1995). Analysts also have found that although Medicaid managed care improves access to care by several measures, enrollees are somewhat less satisfied than those in fee-for-service care, particularly if they do not remain with their personal physicians (Freund et al., 1989; Hurley et al., 1991).

Despite Medicare enrollees' overall high degree of satisfaction with managed care plans, it is important to understand the sources of complaints of those who are dissatisfied. Disenrollment is costly for plans and beneficiaries. Plans do not want to waste resources enrolling people who will not remain in the plan because marketing to individuals is very labor-intensive. Furthermore, as discussed below, unhappy enrollees sometimes have difficulty disenrolling quickly, and delays can both be costly (if they are liable for bills to nonplan providers) and adversely affect their health (if they are unable to obtain desired benefits). Furthermore, people may have given up their supplemental coverage and have difficulty resubscribing. This paper focuses on consumer reports of satisfaction and dissatisfaction rather than evaluations of HMO quality from other viewpoints. (The paper by Joyce Dubow synthesizes research on Medicare HMO quality on the basis of process and outcome measures.)

HMO Enrollee Satisfaction Surveys

Only a few studies, which vary in scope and methodological sophistication, have been published on the satisfaction of Medicare enrollees in risk-contracting plans. The Health Care Financing Administration (HCFA) does not routinely publish information on consumer complaints appealed through its formal process, through plan internal grievance systems, or to the local peer review organization (PRO), although HCFA uses such data in reviewing plan quality (U.S. General Accounting Office, 1995a). The information in this paper derives from a handful of recent surveys of Medicare plan enrollee satisfaction, which produce a reasonably consistent picture of what enrollees do and do not like about their plans.

Although useful, these surveys have limitations. First, they examined a voluntary market and might produce different results if there were greater incentives to enroll in HMOs. Second, even when defined by a series of specific survey questions, "satisfaction" is a subjective concept that measures the extent to which one's personal expectations are met. Furthermore, surveys may not include people most likely to use services, such as those with chronic or acute illnesses, who may experience greater problems with access or provider conduct than healthier enrollees.[1] Yet if financial incentives to enroll in managed care

---

[1]Regardless of whether Medicare HMOs currently receive favorable or adverse selection, which remains unclear, people with chronic illnesses and disabilities who are likely to use medical care represent a small proportion of the

are as strong as many policy makers hope, more people with such conditions are likely to be enrolled in managed care plans in the future. A limitation of studies of problems and complaints is that they generally do not compare HMOs with performance by providers in the fee-for-service Medicare program, making it difficult to determine whether these problems can be attributed only to HMO enrollment. Finally, current Medicare research has examined only HMOs, although HCFA is experimenting with other kinds of managed care organizations, which might raise different consumer protection issues.

Medicare HMO Enrollee Surveys

The first published study to compare Medicare enrollees in the "risk contract" (capitated HMO) demonstrations with those receiving care in the traditional fee-for-service system assessed satisfaction with technical and interpersonal aspects of care, convenience, and waiting times for appointments (Rossiter et al., 1989). The researchers found that about 80 percent of both groups were "very satisfied" with their health care overall. HMO enrollees, however, were considerably less satisfied that other Medicare beneficiaries with perceived professional competence and provider willingness to discuss problems and were more satisfied with waiting times and claims processing. Moreover, disenrollment rates were high. About 18 percent of enrollees disenrolled during the 12 to 15 months between study inter-views. Over one quarter of those disenrolling during the first 3 months apparently misunderstood the nature of the plan (limi-tations on physicians or covered services), and about half of those disenrolling later were dissatisfied with the plan (because of location, poor care, or lack of physician continuity).

Two recent surveys report that Medicare HMO enrollees are happier with their care than those in the traditional Medicare program. The Minnesota Health Data Institute found Minneso-tans enrolled in five Medicare HMOs statistically significantly more likely to be "very or extremely satisfied" with their Medi-

---

total enrollment and may be underrepresented in surveys if they are too frail to respond. If an objective is to understand sources of dissatisfaction, the people most likely to use health care should be oversampled.

care experience than non-HMO enrollees and much less likely to be dissatisfied (Minnesota Health Data Institute, 1995). This pattern held for several specific measures of satisfaction: adequacy of benefits covered, paperwork, satisfaction with specialists, practitioners' willingness to listen and explain, and thoroughness of examinations and treatment. HMO enrollees expressed levels of satisfaction and dissatisfaction comparable to those of nonenrollees on other measures, such as ability to obtain care when needed, scheduling appointments when they were sick, and getting telephone assistance.

Similarly, a study of Blue Cross/Blue Shield's Medicare HMO members found them to be statistically significantly more satisfied with overall quality of care, paperwork, cost, prescription coverage, and preventive and vision services but less likely to be satisfied with their freedom to choose physicians (Ferguson, 1995). The rates by which HMO and other respondents were "very satisfied" did not differ statistically significantly on issues such as physician and hospital quality, time with physicians and staff, or access to specialists, hospitals, emergency care, or technology. Respondents with various specific medical conditions or fair and poor health reported similar rates of satisfaction.

To identify sources of dissatisfaction among HMO enrollees who might be more likely to have complaints, a recent study compares Medicare health plan enrollees with those who had disenrolled (Office of Inspector General, 1995). Disenrollees were much less likely to have a full understanding of the restrictions on out-of-plan use. They were more likely to report (1) longer waiting times to get appointments with specialists or appointments with their primary care physicians when they were very ill; (2) dissatisfaction with telephone waiting time; (3) inability to obtain access to care that they felt they needed from their primary care physicians, referral to specialists, or payment for emergency care; (4) out-of-plan use; and (5) lack of sympathetic treatment by their physicians (not perceived as helpful and not taking complaints seriously). Disenrollees without prior experience in a managed care plan were much more likely to report negative perceptions or experiences. These differences were even greater after omitting from the analysis the 30 percent of disenrollees who left their plans for administrative reasons (who moved or whose physician left the plan).

Among current enrollees, 16 percent said that they would like to leave their HMO. A small share were leaving the service area, but the majority (more than 60 percent) felt that they could not leave because they felt that the HMO was the only way to afford needed care. Although this group represented only 10 percent of the total enrollees surveyed, it is important to understand their concerns. These dissatisfied HMO enrollees reported that disenrollment was not an option and appeared to feel trapped into delivery systems with which they were not satisfied.

One particularly troubling finding in the Inspector General's study was that compared with Medicare disenrollees who were elderly, those who were disabled or had end-stage renal disease were much less satisfied with their ability to obtain access to needed services and specialists and much more likely to report that physicians did not take their health complaints seriously, use out-of-plan care, believe that HMO physicians are motivated by cost rather than providing good care, and indicate that the HMO caused their health to get worse. The disabled disenrollees had shorter waiting times for appointments. Almost two thirds (66 percent) of disabled HMO enrollees, however, reported wanting to leave their HMO but feeling unable to do so because of the cost of the alternative. Similarities between these perceptions and those of commercial HMO enrollees who were ill and who responded to a recent survey (The Robert Wood Johnson Foundation, 1995) raises concerns about the ability of HMOs to serve people with disabilities and poor health status.

Focus Group Studies

The most recent research on Medicare health plan satisfaction comes from two organizations that held focus groups in several U.S. cities among current and former Medicare HMO enrollees as well as people who had never enrolled (Frederick/ Schneiders, Inc., 1995; Gibbs, 1995). In addition to noting some persistent impressions about HMOs (poor-quality doctors or long waiting times for appointments) that discourage people from enrolling, those studies found that the biggest obstacle to joining an HMO is the limited choice of physicians, especially if one must change from a current physician with whom one is satisfied. Other disadvantages cited by some enrollees were waiting time on the phone and in the office as well as delays in obtaining an appointment. The major advantages of HMOs cited by their enrollees are lower cost, certain valued additional benefits (particularly pharmaceutical benefits but also annual physical examinations), no paperwork, and the opportunity for coordinated care (Frederick/Schneiders, Inc., 1995).The authors of one study reported the negative impressions of HMOs and managed care in certain cities, such as Miami, where health plan reputations have not been good, compared with those in communities such as Minneapolis, where HMO penetration is high in commercial and public sectors and they are regarded favorably (Frederick/ Schneiders, Inc., 1995).

Study of Consumer Complaints

In contrast to surveys and focus group research that analyzed overall enrollee experiences, a 1993 study of Medicare enrollees in 10 risk-contract HMOs in California focused on consumer problems (Dallek et al., 1993).[2] It was designed to provide examples of problems, not to indicate their prevalence. Because it drew experience from only one state, it may not reflect overall Medicare HMO experience. (As noted above, Minnesota Medicare HMOs have received high satisfaction ratings.) This study is included because it represents the most detailed review of Medicare HMO consumer problems.

On the basis of information from HCFA, the California Department of Corporations (which licenses HMOs), health plan questionnaires, consumer advocacy organizations, and providers, the Medicare Advocacy Project (now the Center for Health Care Rights) cited instances of verified consumer complaints with plan marketing and care delivery. Stiff competition for Medicare enrollees seems to have led to marketing abuses. For

---

[2]Additional, more recent examples of similar problems in marketing, disenrollment delays, and access to services in California and New York were provided in congressional testimony in mid-1995 (Dallek, 1995).

example, some plans enrolled people who could not have been expected to understand the terms of enrollment because they did not speak English, could not see or hear, or had cognitive limitations such as senility. Because of commission structures, quotas, and lack of training, some sales representatives engaged in high-pressure sales tactics that were especially intimidating for older people in their homes. Some salespeople misrepresented the services available or did not explain plan requirements to use a limited network ("lock-in"), obtain specialist referrals from gatekeepers, or receive payment for emergency care in only narrowly defined emergencies. In a few instances, they forged signatures or lied about the significance of a signature on an enrollment form. State programs assisting Medicare beneficiaries choose health plans, and consumer advocates report that such sales practices remain current problems. These marketing abuses are similar to those in the Medicare Supplemental coverage market that led the U.S. Congress to enact consumer protections (U.S. General Accounting Office, 1991).

As analysts have suggested, disenrollment within 90 days of initial enrollment can indicate misunderstanding of the features and constraints of a managed care plan (Dallek et al., 1993; Rossiter et al., 1989; Office of Inspector General, 1995). In HCFA's Region IX, about 30 percent of disenrollment in the second quarter of 1995 occurred within 90 days, suggesting that a substantial portion of disenrollees did not understand the nature of the program that they enrolled in.

The California report noted the difficulty that some people have in disenrolling when they have been induced into enrollment by fraud, misrepresentation, or misunderstanding. Plans are required to provide enrollees information on disenrollment and to process disenrollment requests promptly, but they do not always do so. As the General Accounting Office (GAO) found, beneficiaries who continue to use their regular providers may be liable for these costs (U.S. General Accounting Office, 1995a). HCFA permits retroactive disenrollment for people misunderstanding the HMO lock-in requirements who have not used HMO services, in which case it will pay charges for services provided during the unintentional HMO enrollment (HCFA

HMO/CMP Manual Section 2002.3). It is not clear, however, that beneficiaries are aware of this opportunity.

The California study also identified examples of consumer complaints regarding access to and quality of care. One source of dissatisfaction is the HMO's network of primary and specialty physicians. Some enrollees, for example, did not understand that primary care physicians on the HMO's provider list may not be accepting new patients or a provider may have a limited contract (for example, a tertiary specialty center providing only selected services upon referral). The report raised three concerns about access to specialists: Is the panel of specialists sufficient to serve enrollees, are primary care physicians willing to refer patients to specialists when needed, and are restrictions on access to providers explained clearly? The Medicare statute prohibits HMOs from making specific payments to physicians to limit medically necessary care to an individual enrollee, but most HMOs place physicians at some financial risk to temper their use and authorization of care (Physician Payment Review Commission, 1995). Although patients and physicians may differ on the need for a referral to a specialist, this is a source of considerable dissatisfaction. Disputes over payment for nonplan providers and emergency care represent the majority of Medicare beneficiary appeals filed with HCFA (Network Design Group, 1995).

The California study reported enrollee complaints about access to rehabilitative services, particularly after hospitalization. For example, HMOs may deny authorization for short-term skilled nursing facility services; home health care;[3] physical, speech, or occupational therapy; or durable medical equipment (walkers and wheelchairs), all of which are Medicare-covered services when they are medically necessary or will improve functional status. If the HMO defines medical necessity or functional potential narrowly, disputes over needed care will arise.

---

[3]It is not clear from current research whether Medicare HMOs generally provide less access to home health care. The Mathematica study found a greater likelihood but lower numbers of visits (Brown et al., 1993), whereas Shaughnessy and colleagues (1994) found less use of home health care and poorer outcomes in Medicare HMOs than in the fee-for-service system.

In the fee-for-service realm, such differences of opinion often involve debate over who will pay for a service already provided. In a capitated health plan, however, these disputes generally occur before a service is rendered. Because the appeals process, discussed below, is often not understood and is always lengthy, an HMO's denial of coverage may result in the service not being provided. In some cases, by the time that an appeal is decided in favor of an enrollee, the service, such as short-term rehabilitation, may no longer provide benefit (U.S. General Accounting Office, 1995a).

Summary of Evidence of Medicare HMO Enrollee Satisfaction and Dissatisfaction

Research on what makes Medicare HMO enrollees happy enough to stay in their plans or unhappy enough to desire to leave them reveals the following:

• Most people are satisfied with their managed care plans (Ferguson, 1995; Minnesota Health Data Institute, 1995; Rossiter et al., 1989), but a substantial fraction (perhaps 20 percent) are dissatisfied and some plans have experienced annual turnover of up to 20 percent (Dallek et al., 1993), although disenrollment rates vary widely and may be lower in mature HMOs.

• Although instances of deliberate misrepresentation are probably rare, even marketing information approved by HCFA can be confusing to some Medicare beneficiaries and sales tactics can be intimidating (Dallek, 1995; Dallek et al., 1993). Salespeople may not spend enough time answering questions thoroughly or satisfing themselves that each enrollee fully understands the HMO's features, limits, and procedures for use.

• People who do not understand the nature of the HMO, its limited network, its gatekeeper restrictions, its process for referral to care, the actual availability of primary care physicians, how they can change providers, and limits on out-of-area and emergency care appear likely to be unhappy and disenroll quickly, particularly if they are satisfied with their personal physicians outside the HMO (Office of Inspector General, 1995).

• Although the vast majority of enrollees are happy, some

who understand and accept the general limitations of an HMO still report problems, whose prevalence is not well documented but which can be grouped into four categories:

—*poor provider technical quality*, such as thoroughness of exams (Rossiter et al., 1989);

—*poor provider interpersonal quality*, such as unwillingness to discuss problems and explain diagnoses and treatments or lack of sympathy toward the patient (Rossiter et al., 1989; U.S. Department of Health and Human Services, 1995);

—*inconvenience*, such as the time required to obtain an appointment or the time that one must wait on the phone or in the office (U.S. Department of Health and Human Services, 1995); and

—*access*, including geographic proximity to offices, ability to see specialists, disputes over emergency care (in and out of the plan), and access to posthospital recovery and rehabilitation services or durable medical equipment (Dallek, 1995; Dallek et al., 1993; U.S. Department of Health and Human Services, 1995; U.S. General Accounting Office, 1995a).

•   Persons eligible for Medicare because of disability who disenroll from HMOs report considerably less satisfaction than elderly disenrollees on measures such as obtaining referrals to specialists or obtaining covered services, suggesting that HMOs may not all meet the needs of people with chronic illness and other serious health problems. Most disabled Medicare HMO enrollees report that they want to leave the HMO but are unable to do so because of inability to afford needed care under the fee-for-service system (Office of Inspector General, 1995).

•   Although fewer studies have attempted to discover what HMO enrollees really like about their plans that keep them enrolled, it appears that Medicare enrollees, like those in commercial plans, prefer HMOs for their cost containment and preventive orientation. They especially value additional services such as prescription drugs. They also seem to appreciate the opportunity that HMOs offer to coordinate care—the positive side of a gatekeeper requirement (Ferguson, 1995; Frederick/Schneiders, Inc., 1995; Gibbs, 1995; Minnesota Health Data Institute, 1995; Rossiter et al., 1989).

MEDICARE HEALTH PLAN ACCOUNTABILITY: MECHANISMS FOR DISPUTE RESOLUTION

One mechanism that can be used to correct, if not prevent, consumer dissatisfaction is a well-functioning dispute resolution system. Two types of appeals processes are available to Medicare HMO enrollees: one for disputes involving coverage of services within the basic Medicare HMO benefits package and one for other grievances.

Disputes over Medicare-Covered Services

Enrollee complaints are processed through Medicare's traditional five-step dispute resolution process if they involve (1) an HMO's refusal to pay for emergency or urgently needed services, (2) services rendered by out-of-plan providers that the enrollee believes are covered by Medicare and for which the enrollee believes the HMO should pay, and (3) an HMO's refusal to provide services an enrollee believes that Medicare covers and the that HMO should furnish (42 C.F.R. Section 417.606–417.638).

If an enrollee requests a service or payment for a service in one of these categories and the HMO denies the request, it must notify the enrollee within 60 days of receiving the request (24 days if the claim is complete [HCFA CMP/HMO Manual Section 2403]), specify the reasons for the determination, and notify the enrollee of the right to request reconsideration of the decision. Because some plans had not provided timely responses to enrollee requests, regulations issued in November 1994 permit a beneficiary to appeal without a formal written denial notice from the HMO. The enrollee or a representative may request reconsideration from the HMO within 60 days of the initial determination and must be allowed to present evidence in person or in writing. The reconsideration must be conducted by a person not involved in the initial determination. If the HMO recommends an action that is adverse to the enrollee's interest, it must forward the appeal to HCFA for reconsideration. HCFA has contracted with a private firm, the Network Design Group (NDG), to process these requests. Notice of the reconsidered determination must be mailed to all parties.

If the amount in controversy is $100 or more, any party dissatisfied with the reconsidered determination may have a hearing before an administrative law judge (ALJ) of the Social Security Administration by filing a written request within 60 days of the date of the notice of the reconsideration. An enrollee may present oral evidence at a hearing. Any party to a hearing dissatisfied with the ALJ's decision may appeal to the Social Security Administration's Appeals Council and thereafter, if the amount in controversy is at least $1,000, to a federal district court.

An analysis of reconsiderations processed by NDG in 1993-1994 revealed that just over half (55 percent) of plan decisions were upheld (Network Design Group, 1995). The two most common categories of disputes are the use of out-of-plan practitioners for which the HMO refused to pay (27.5 percent) and emergency room services (26.8 percent). The remaining 45 percent of disputes included durable medical equipment or medical supplies, inpatient hospital coverage, ambulance bills, laboratory or X-ray bills, nursing home care, whether a benefit was covered by Medicare, home health, special therapies, mental health services, and hospice care. The annual rate of reconsideration requests per 1,000 Medicare plan enrollees filed with NDG ranged widely across plans, from none to more than 19 (Network Design Group, 1995). The meaning of such variation is unclear; plans that encourage enrollees to file appeals might appear to have more complaints than those whose enrollees are unaware of their appeal rights.

HMO Grievance Process

Medicare regulations and HMO licensure laws in all states require HMOs to have a grievance system to resolve disputes other than those that can be pursued through the Medicare appeals process described above [42 C.F.R. Section 417.436 (a)(7)]. Consequently, disputes involving optional supplemental services, appointment waiting times, or insensitive treatment by staff must be accepted through a plan's grievance system. Although HCFA requires plans to inform enrollees about this system and monitors the types and numbers of complaints, no federal standards prescribe how it must be structured or administered.

Issues in the Medicare HMO
Dispute Resolution Process

As the GAO and others have recently noted, the Medicare appeals process poses several problems for HMO enrollees (Dallek et al., 1993; U.S. General Accounting Office, 1995a). First, it is not designed to provide prompt responses to disputes over whether a service should be provided. Regulations require requests that HMOs take no more than 60 days to reconsider initial determinations (42 C.F.R. Section 417.620), but the GAO reports that some take two to three times as long. Even if plans meet HCFA standards, a reconsideration request may not be forwarded to NDG for 6 months. Although NDG attempts to decide most cases within 30 days, only 38 percent of appeals are decided within that period (45 percent required 3.5 months and others took NDG more than 6 months in 1993 [U.S. General Accounting Office, 1995a]). Such a delay may pose less of a problem in the case of disputes over payment for a service already provided, although it may be difficult for an elderly person to resist demands for payment from providers or collection agencies while pursuing an appeal. Delay, however, can mean denial of care if the dispute involves an HMO's refusal to authorize access to a service, such as a diagnostic specialist, physical therapy, or medical equipment, that may be needed promptly (for example, after a hospital discharge) in order to be effective (Dallek et al., 1993; U.S. General Accounting Office, 1995a).

Furthermore, it appears likely that many beneficiaries do not understand their appeal rights. One-quarter of the respondents to the survey (Office of Inspector General, 1995) indicated that they did not know that they could appeal denials of service or payment. A study of the Medicare HMO experience in California concluded that beneficiaries themselves, hospital social workers, and other providers were unaware of the statutory appeals system or the HMOs' internal grievance processes, even though HMO enrollment materials described these systems in accurate detail (Dallek et al., 1993). Some HMOs do not give enrollees the required written explanation of their appeal rights when denying a service or payment, and some do not process appeal requests promptly. For example, some fail to forward reconsideration requests to NDG or to process appeals that should be decided under the Medicare system as internal health plan grievances (Dallek et al., 1993).

These problems result in some beneficiaries being denied potentially valuable care, facing out-of-pocket costs (at least pending resolution of their disputes), and disenrolling from the HMO. For example, GAO reports that about one quarter of Medicare enrollees appealing coverage disputes disenrolled within 90 days of the reconsidered determination and that more than 40 percent disenrolled within 2 years of the date of the disputed services (U.S. General Accounting Office, 1995a).

GAO found that HCFA recognizes these problems and has addressed some of them. For example, in 1994 HCFA adopted regulations allowing HMO enrollees the same opportunities available to nonenrollees for expedited review by PROs of disputes over hospital discharge, and it has authorized enrollees to file appeals without a formal written notice from the plan denying service. HCFA also is considering expedited appeals for urgently needed services and exploring how to educate beneficiaries about their appeal rights (U.S. General Accounting Office, 1995a).

MEDICARE HEALTH PLAN ACCOUNTABILITY: PUBLIC OVERSIGHT

Federal Medicare HMO Contracting Standards

The Medicare statute and regulations prescribe contract standards for risk-bearing plans: either federal HMO qualification or other similar federal standards (regarding solvency, minimum enrollment, and administrative capacity), state licensure, a minimum number of enrollees, coverage of all Medicare services and 24-hour emergency care, no more than 50 percent enrollment by Medicare and Medicaid beneficiaries, compliance with HCFA marketing standards, limits on physician incentive payments, an enrollee grievance system (including the right to file complaints with the local PRO), and a quality assurance program (42 U.S.C. Section 1395mm, 20 C.F.R. Section 417.1 et seq.). The statute also requires that plans contract with PROs for external review of quality and appropriateness of services.

The 1995 Budget Reconciliation Conference Bill would have permitted provider-sponsored organizations (PSOs) to accept risk contracts to enroll Medicare beneficiaries without meeting requirements of state HMO solvency standards if they meet standards developed by the Secretary of the U.S. Department of Health and Human Services. Furthermore, PSOs could seek an exemption from other state licensure standards. The bill also would have changed several provisions of current law. For example, it provided more detailed requirements for internal quality assurance systems (requiring that they monitor high-volume and high-risk services and evaluate continuity and coordination of care). The bill also would have exempted plans accredited by private organizations from ongoing PRO external review, would no longer prohibit offering gifts to induce enrollment or door-to-door sales, and (after a 2-year transition period) would have permitted disenrollment after 90 days only at an annual enrollment period or if the plan substantially violates a material contract requirement. Policy issues raised by these provisions are discussed below.

GAO recently criticized HCFA's enforcement of Medicare HMO standards. It reported that HCFA does not routinely examine HMO compliance with internal quality assurance plans or limits on provider risk sharing, does not collect utilization data that could reveal patterns of underservice, and has been reluctant to use sanctions to enforce federal rules (U.S. General Accounting Office, 1995a). GAO also has recommended that because HCFA acts like an employer to select and monitoring plans, it should collect and distribute to Medicare beneficiaries information on plan performance, including patient satisfaction and process and outcome standards (U.S. General Accounting Office, 1995b).

State Regulation of Managed Care Organizations

HMO Regulation

States have traditionally regulated the solvency, marketing, grievance process, benefits structure, and rates of traditional insurers. Because HMOs perform the dual function of bearing risk and arranging for the delivery of services, they are regulated in most states under separate laws. The incentive inherent in a fixed per capita payment (capitation) to limit service justifies regulating not just financial solvency but also capacity to serve the enrolled population (network adequacy) and the quality of care provided. Although state laws differ, the laws of more than half of the states are drawn from the 1990 Model HMO Act of the National Association of Insurance Commissioners (NAIC). Only the District of Columbia has no law explicitly regulating HMOs. The NAIC model includes disclosure, rating standards, grievance procedures, "hold harmless" provisions, and insolvency protections (reserves, deposits, insolvency funds, and allocation of enrollees to other plans in the event of insolvency). It also requires that HMOs have a quality assurance program to ensure availability, accessibility, continuity, and quality of care and that they inform enrollees how to obtain care and provide notice if their primary care provider is terminated from the plan. NAIC is currently developing several other model managed care laws, for example, to expand the requirements for health plan quality improvement systems and to prescribe standards for health care provider contracting by plans with limited provider networks.

A recent analysis of the HMO licensure statutes and regulations in all 50 states concluded that most states regulate marketing activities and require basic benefits, protections against insolvency, consumer grievance systems, quality assurance plans, and external quality audits (Dallek et al., 1995). That study also pointed out, however, the wide diversity in state HMO licensure laws and found that few states set explicit standards for access (such as provider-to-enrollee ratios, referral requirements, or maximum distance or appointment waiting times), limit provider risk-sharing arrangements, survey enrollee satisfaction, prohibit self-dealing, establish specific quality standards, or require a consumer role in plan governance. GAO also has noted the variation in state health insurance regulation. Not only do statutes vary but so do the resources devoted to their enforcement. Such variety results from political and regulatory philosophy, the state's economy, business climates, and historical trends (U.S. General Accounting Office, 1993a).

Several state HMO licensure laws address common Medicare health plan enrollee complaints (Dallek et al., 1995) and could serve as models to strengthen Medicare risk-contracting standards. Some involve enrollee information, which could be especially useful in view of the fact that as many as 25 percent of Medicare HMO enrollees do not seem to understand plan constraints and procedures. For example, Florida requires that an HMO employee not in the marketing department verify that each new enrollee intends to enroll and understands the HMO's restrictions. (One of the Medicare plans whose administrator was interviewed for this paper contacts each Medicare enrollee by telephone after receiving HCFA confirmation of enrollment to discuss lock-in, appointment procedures, and other plan features and requirements.) Minnesota requires HMOs to explain that the listed providers may not be accepting new patients. Arizona requires plans to provide enrollees information on how to obtain referrals and whether provider compensation programs include incentives or penalties to encourage withholding of services or referrals.

Few state laws regulate health plan features that make obtaining care more convenient, but several require that appointments be available within a "reasonable" time. Florida law requires that patients be seen within an hour of their scheduled appointment times except when delay is "unavoidable." Several states address issues of access to care. About half have a general requirement that HMOs have a sufficient number of physicians to serve enrollees. California, Delaware, Pennsylvania, and South Dakota establish specific primary care physician-to-enrollee ratios. Because access to specialists involves both network capacity and the willingness of gatekeepers to refer, Minnesota requires that referrals be made in accordance with accepted medical practice standards. Several states prescribe maximum travel time or distance. For example, Minnesota requires that primary care providers and general hospitals be located within the lower of 30 miles or 30 minutes from enrollees and that other providers be available within 60 miles or 60 minutes.

Because of the confusion surrounding the definition of emergency services, California requires plans to pay for out-of-plan emergency care unless an enrollee reasonably should have known it was not an emergency. Minnesota law provides that plans consider several factors in deciding when to pay for emergency care, including an enrollee's reasonable belief that the condition required immediate care, time of day, symptoms, efforts to follow the HMO's procedures, and other circumstances that might preclude following them.

PPO Regulation

Preferred provider organizations (PPOs) emerged in the 1980s as networks of providers serve enrollees of health plans or self-funded employers (Rolph et al., 1987). They generally encourage enrollees to use network providers by imposing higher cost sharing on out-of-network use. To overcome uncertainty about whether such delivery arrangements could be authorized, about half of the states have adopted PPO enabling legislation to permit selective contracting with and channeling business to a limited set of providers. Because PPOs typically do not bear risk (those that do are licensed under HMO or other insurance standards), these state laws are less prescriptive than those licensing HMOs. Yet even without bearing risk, limited networks raise issues of whether consumers have adequate access to appropriate quality care (Rolph et al., 1987). Consequently, most include consumer protections, such as requirements that plans inform consumers about network providers or offer adequate access to care. Some state laws also require participation of any willing provider in PPOs or set limits on cost sharing or payment differentials for out-of-network use.

New Types of Delivery Arrangements

State policy makers are currently exploring the extent to which new types of managed care organizations that share risk with providers should be regulated under traditional insurance regulatory principles. Among the organizations emerging in the fast-evolving health care marketplace are integrated provider networks, such as provider-sponsored organizations, created to contract with employers and other health care purchasers. To the extent that they are independent from insurers or HMOs but bear risk (for example, accepting a monthly capitation payment to provide various categories of care to enrollees), these new entities raise consumer protection issues. According to a recent survey of state regulators, organizations bearing even partial risk must be licensed as HMOs in half of the states, but the regulatory situation in other states is less clear (Group Health Association of America, 1995). Many insurance regulators assert that a provider organization that bears any risk should be regulated as an HMO to protect consumers against insolvency, misinformation, access capacity, and poor-quality care. Opponents of state regulation of new types of integrated provider organizations argue, however, that application of traditional HMO licensure law, with its high reserve requirements, solvency provisions, and access standards, will stifle delivery system innovation and increase purchaser health care costs and that limited provider risk arrangements ought to be permitted without requiring HMO licensure.

Minnesota has tried to strike a balance between consumer protection and health plan development in areas currently not served by HMOs. It permits the creation of "community integrated service networks" (CISNs) serving up to 50,000 people that have a governing body whose majority is residents of the service area. CISNs are subject to standards less stringent than those for other HMOs for cost sharing, net worth, insolvency protection, and quality assurance. For example, CISNs may partially satisfy capital requirements by guaranteeing that providers will care for enrollees if the plan becomes insolvent. To encourage integrated health care delivery, Iowa also has enacted authority for risk-bearing "organized delivery systems" that meet standards less demanding than those in the HMO law.

State Oversight of Medicaid Managed Care Plans

Because about 5 million Medicare beneficiaries are also eligible for Medicaid, they are affected by state regulation of Medicaid managed care plans (Saucier, 1995). Federal statute and regulations set out a few standards (generally consistent with those under Medicare) that states must follow when they pay health plans on the basis of capitation to serve enrolled Medicaid populations. States must ensure that plans do not discriminate on the basis of health status; provide evidence of ability to deliver services efficiently, effectively, economically, and promptly; make any emergency services covered available 24 hours per day, 7 days per week; provide an internal grievance system and quality assurance system; use only acceptable physician incentive payments; and enroll no more than 75 percent of their members as Medicare or Medicaid beneficiaries (42 C.F.R. Section 434.20 et seq.). Medicaid agencies also are required to conduct periodic medical audits to evaluate plan quality and accessibility and to contract with outside agencies such as PRO or private accreditation bodies to review quality of care. Within these broad federal guidelines, state standards vary considerably.

For example, the Office of the Inspector General of DHHS examined states' use of 13 types of quality assurance measures (Office of Inspector General, 1992). Its 1992 survey of Medicaid agencies in 25 states revealed that all states included patient education, procedures to ensure access to care, and enrollee grievance systems; most required written quality assurance (QA) plans and provider credentialing and either conducted patient satisfaction surveys or required HMOs to do so; about half required HMOs to report patient care data, review enrollee complaints, review utilization, and review medical records. Few states, however, require HMOs to use clinical practice guidelines; monitor patient outcomes; control physician practice through selection, education, or payment; or report problems with physician performance.

Both the Office of the Inspector General and GAO have concluded that most Medicaid QA standards are structural or process-oriented and do not measure actual patient health outcomes (Office of Inspector General, 1995; U.S. General Accounting Office, 1993b). A recent joint federal-state effort has developed new quality assurance protocols for managed care, combining standards from the National Committee for Quality Assurance (NCQA), the National Association of Managed Care Regulators (NAMCR), and HCFA (Booth and Fuller, 1995). In addition to structural and process measures, QARI (the Quality

Assurance Reform Initiative) tested the use of outcome-oriented standards through focused studies in clinical areas such as prenatal care, immunizations, asthma services, and diabetes care in Minnesota, Ohio, and Washington State. This approach offers an opportunity for improved state oversight of managed care plan performance.

Experience with public agency regulation of health plans through licensure or contracting authority suggests the following:

- Standards tend to focus on health plan structural capacity (such as credentialing or written policies) and processes (such as patient education or use of internal QA programs) rather than enrollee outcomes. Some state Medicaid programs, however, are developing outcomes standards, such as those used by commercial purchasers.
- Compared with some states' standards, HCFA has weak standards for access and quality of Medicare HMOs, and HCFA has not aggressively enforced its existing requirements.
- Legal standards as well as the capacity and willingness to enforce them vary among states. Just as HCFA can be criticized for lax enforcement of Medicare standards, some states regulate health insurers, including licensed health plans, less actively than others. In a time of potentially rapid change in Medicare health plan enrollment, it is important to develop federal and state regulatory capacities to monitor plan performance.
- Several states have enacted HMO laws designed to address some of the problems experienced by Medicare beneficiaries related to marketing, access, emergency care, and plan capacity.
- States have focused on HMOs, but many license PPOs and a few are beginning to regulate new types of delivery arrangements, such as integrated provider networks.

MEDICARE HEALTH PLAN
CONSUMER PROTECTION POLICY ISSUES

The Role for Government in a
Competitive Medicare Marketplace

Although many policy makers prefer a limited role for government in a more competitive medical care marketplace, there are reasons that government should remain a forceful presence in Medicare. First, as trustee for billions of dollars, the federal government is responsible to taxpayers for prudent spending. Furthermore, it acts in a fiduciary capacity as the primary health care purchaser for millions of elderly and disabled people, many of whom face language or cultural barriers, are in poor health, are unsophisticated buyers of medical care, or are unfamiliar with integrated delivery systems.

To meet these responsibilities, the federal government performs functions ranging from facilitating the operation of a fair market to a more active regulatory role. As the foundation for a functioning market, the government should, at least, set standards for information that health plans must make available to prospective and current enrollees. The complexity of comparing plans suggests that the government should go further to compile and distribute accurate and detailed, yet simple and useful information to Medicare beneficiaries[4] and support counseling programs that assist beneficiaries in using such data.

Like an employer that buys health coverage for employees, the federal government's interest in access to high-quality care for its Medicare beneficiaries justifies setting and enforcing health plan contract standards. Oversight is particularly important for capitated plans because of prepayment plans' financial incentive to underserve. Despite differences among policy makers on the content of such standards, there appears to be consensus on the need for government regulation of risk-bearing

---

[4]Omnibus Budget Reconciliation Act 1995 would have required the Secretary of DHHS to provide comparative information on plan benefits, premiums, and quality indicators such as disenrollment rates, enrollee satisfaction, enrollee outcomes, and compliance with federal requirements.

Medicare contractors. Retaining a strong role for government does not, however, diminish the potential for collaboration with private sector accrediting bodies, such as NCQA.

What Types of Managed Care Organizations Should Be Regulated?

Most analysts and policy makers agree that there is a public interest in ensuring that organizations agreeing to pay for or provide a service if an unpredictable future event occurs (i.e., to bear risk) are capable of meeting that obligation. Any health plan that accepts a premium to pay for future hospitalization that might occur is bearing a financial risk and must demonstrate a financial ability to meet that commitment. Health plans, like Medicare HMOs, that promise not only future payment but also a service delivery system must have both financial capacity and a system to meet enrollee needs for covered services. This additional responsibility justifies regulatory standards that include, beyond financial solvency, an adequate provider network, access assurances, quality standards, and expedited appeals processes.

There is no consensus on what standards should apply to the types of provider networks now emerging in the health care marketplace. Although agreeing that any organization bearing risk must demonstrate financial capacity, some state policy makers recognize that the level of protection could vary according to the level of risk assumed. The NAIC is developing model "risk-based" solvency standards, under which organizations bearing partial risk could maintain lower levels of reserves than full-risk HMOs. These standards must be developed with care: Although Medicare's proposed PSOs might be community based and more responsive to consumer needs, provider inexperience in the business of insurance may lead to capacity, access, and financial problems.

Overcoming Barriers to Satisfaction

As more Medicare beneficiaries enroll in HMOs and other kinds of managed care plans, it will be important to evaluate current contracting standards to determine whether they need to be strengthened, whether they may differ according to types of plan, and how they can be enforced to   protect consumers while encouraging innovation in health care delivery.

Accurate and Usable Information

A major source of dissatisfaction among Medicare HMO enrollees is the result of misinformation about or misunderstanding of the nature of managed care. A multivariate analysis involving Medicare enrollees in one HMO found that reported understanding of coverage and procedures to obtain care was the greatest predictor of enrollee satisfaction (Ward, 1987). Problems with marketing in the Medicare Supplemental coverage market suggest that ongoing review of materials and sales staff training and performance will be necessary (U.S. General Accounting Office, 1991). Dissatisfaction could be reduced by ensuring that marketing materials are not only accurate but also understandable to beneficiaries. Features as simple as typeface and reading level can make a difference in whether the information in a marketing flier or enrollment brochure is first read, then understood, and finally retained. Information must be developed with attention to the various levels of literacy, cognition, sophistication, and self-confidence of the Medicare population. Accurate and useful information will become more important as the variety of choices expands, for example, to include point-of-service plans, PPOs, and other delivery arrangements.

Although some potential enrollees are skeptical about sales promises, others may be misled by promotional advertising that paints an unrealistic picture and raises expectations about what the plan will offer. Training salespeople to ascertain whether prospective enrollees understand the plan's basic features and allowing them enough time to answer questions could minimize enrollee confusion. For example, a list of physicians in the network may be read as guaranteeing that a practice is accepting new patients. If having a particular physician is a *sine qua non* for a new enrollee, plans should help prospective enrollees determine whether that physician would accept the patient. Prospective enrollees should be helped to understand that because a specialist or tertiary institution is in the provider network does not guarantee that they will be referred to such providers. It also may be useful for prospective enrollees to understand how HMOs pay their physicians in order to evaluate disincentives to provide needed care (Stocker, 1995), although this information might be difficult to convey in a simple and comprehensible way.

It is not entirely clear what kind of information Medicare beneficiaries want in order to choose among managed care plans and other options. Research under way at NCQA to learn from focus groups and other sources what plan information consumers would like. Some Medicare beneficiaries not enrolled in HMOs who participated in two recent focus group studies were skeptical about consumer satisfaction ratings and indicated that this information would not be useful to them in choosing among plans unless the reports included specific questions of interest to them, information on who responded, and the sponsoring organization (Frederick/Schneiders, Inc., 1995; Gibbs, 1995). Medicare consumers appear similar to other prospective health plan enrollees recently surveyed by GAO who reported wanting more information on health plan outcomes and quality but expressed skepticism about reliability and validity of plan-generated "report cards" (U.S. General Accounting Office, 1995b).

Counseling and Advocacy Services

Even with better-trained and motivated plan sales staff and improved marketing and enrollment materials, prospective health plan enrollees may need the assistance of independent counselors to answer questions about the nature of managed care and specific plans. Although some people may be misled by plan marketing, others doubt that a plan's information will be objective and would value access to an outside source of information. Such assistance is provided by information, counseling, and assistance (ICA) programs funded by HCFA. Omnibus Budget Reconciliation Act 1990 provided federal funding for ICA programs (operating through a combination of paid staff and volunteer counselors at the state and local levels) to assist Medicare beneficiaries with obtaining appropriate public and private health insurance coverage (McCormack et al., 1994). Participants in a recent set of Medicare focus groups said that they trust and would use such organizations (Gibbs, 1995). Currently, all states have established ICA programs. Departments of Aging administer the grants in two thirds of the states, whereas Insurance Commissioners operate the remainder.

Through individual counseling, group presentations, and written materials, the programs provide information about Medicare, supplemental insurance products, long-term-care insurance, managed care plans, and eligibility for Medicaid and other public programs. They also can help Medicare beneficiaries complete claims forms and file appeals. Programs in half of the states have developed consumer guidebooks. An evaluation of the first year of ICA program experience reported that it provides a valued service and has attracted committed volunteers and in-kind support, although evaluators recommended increased publicity and outreach and more standardized data collection and sharing of materials. For many years, some states had developed a spectrum of senior information and counseling services financed with state funds (Davidson, 1988; U.S. General Accounting Office, 1991). California, for example, funds its counseling programs through an earmarked portion of insurance agent and broker licensure fees. Neither the ICA program evaluation nor the few assessments of earlier programs for providing health insurance information to Medicare beneficiaries has demonstrated a clear effect on knowledge, attitudes, or decision making (Davidson, 1988).

It is likely that most plans employ customer service representatives and other staff who can assist enrollees with access or other problems, but one plan providing information for this paper reported its intention to create a formal Medicare ombudsman position in 1996. An ombudsman can be either a neutral mediator or, as with long-term care ombudsmen, a patient advocate (Harris-Wehling et al., 1995). PROs in some states act as patient advocates. Wisconsin requires plans enrolling Medicaid beneficiaries to employ an independent enrollee ombudsman. ICA programs with sufficiently large paid or volunteer staffs function as mediators or patient advocates in some states.

Quality, Access, and Information Standards

In view of the types of problems reported by some Medicare

HMO enrollees, the U.S. Congress and HCFA should consider adopting some additional standards to ensure access to appropriate care. They could draw upon state HMO licensure laws and regulations in defining more precisely the adequacy of provider networks, definitions of medical necessity and emergency care, standards for specialty referrals, and time or distance standards. Requiring verification of new enrollment and including cautions about whether physicians with HMO contracts are accepting new patients also could prevent or eliminate some sources of dissatisfaction.

Which Level of Government Is Best Qualified to Set and Enforce Medicare Health Plan Standards?

The choice of the level of government that should regulate Medicare health plans raises several competing considerations. Unlike the federal government, states have historically regulated the insurance industry, authority sanctioned by the U.S. Congress in the 1945 McCarran-Ferguson Act. Furthermore, all states have experience regulating the "delivery system" aspects of managed care through their HMO licensure laws. Although managed care organizations are often national in operation, care delivery itself is inherently local, and state governments may be more responsive to local consumer concerns. Despite this state experience, however, the federal government should retain a significant role in Medicare health plan oversight. Medicare is a national program. As plans become more regional or national in organization, regulatory differences across state lines may complicate health plan operations. Model laws developed by NAIC can enhance the likelihood that state laws will be similar, although GAO points out the existence of many NAIC model laws does not guarantee that all states will adopt them (U.S. General Accounting Office, 1993a).

Each level of government has strengths and weaknesses. GAO has criticized both federal Medicare HMO oversight (U.S. General Accounting Office, 1995a) and insurance regulation and Medicaid HMO oversight by some states (U.S. General Accounting Office, 1993a, U.S. General Accounting Office, 1993b). Consequently, consumers might best be served by a federal-state partnership similar to that used to certify health care institutions' compliance with federal law. The Medicare statute sets standards for hospitals, nursing homes, home health agencies, and other providers that the states are primarily responsible for applying and enforcing. Because state HMO licensure is currently required for Medicare risk contracts, it forms a floor for solvency and other standards and provides jurisdiction for state managed care regulators to monitor compliance with consumer protection standards. As the number and types of Medicare risk-bearing health plans increase, this relationship could be formalized so that states monitor compliance with federally established standards. As it does for health care facility certification, the federal government could oversee state performance of this responsibility and accept consumer complaints. Government standards and periodic audits could be coordinated with private accreditation to the extent that private standards serve Medicare consumer interests.

Proposed Statutory Changes in Medicare Managed Care

As part of a restructured Medicare program, the U.S. Congress considered changes to current policy regarding enrollment in or standards for managed care organizations. Some of these proposals could have enhanced consumer protections. For example, as discussed above, the conference bill would have required the federal government to provide comparative plan information on benefits, premiums, and quality indicators. The U.S. Senate's version of the bill (but not the conference bill) would have required an expedited process of appeal to HCFA for disputes over services or payment that would result in "significant harm" to an enrollee.

On the other hand, several of these proposals would not benefit Medicare consumers. Door-to-door solicitation and gifts to encourage enrollment would no longer have been prohibited, which would likely lead to marketing abuses found in Medicaid managed care enrollment more than 25 years ago (D'Onofrio and Mullen, 1977) and Medicare Supplemental markets before 1990 congressional changes (U.S. General Accounting Office, 1991). Substituting accreditation (which typically involves review only every 2 or 3 years) for currently required annual external review would have eliminated a more frequent source of oversight of plan performance. Because quality problems early in the life of these Medicare market changes could undermine the program's future, federal policy makers should ensure that quality and consumer satisfaction are paramount objectives in any move to increase Medicare managed care enrollment and that policy development and enforcement are adequately funded.

Finally, permitting disenrollment only within 90 days after initial enrollment or at an annual open enrollment period, although increasing a plan's ability to budget and manage an individual's care, would eliminate an important safety valve for enrollees. In contrast to the current right to disenroll monthly, the conference bill would have permitted disenrollment after 90 days only if the plan misrepresented plan requirements or "substantially" violated a "material" contract provision. At least in the short term, the latter standard may be too restrictive. About 40 percent of Medicare beneficiaries filing appeals disenroll within 2 years of the disputed services (U.S. General Accounting Office, 1995a) and would not be able to disenroll under this standard.

RECOMMENDATIONS FOR FURTHER RESEARCH

Information on Enrollee Satisfaction

Additional research is needed on health plan enrollee sources of satisfaction and dissatisfaction. Of particular interest would be information from people recently disenrolled and from both enrollees and disenrollees who have actually used services and those who have poor health status. Satisfaction surveys can serve several functions and should be designed to meet multiple objectives. If they elicit information that prospective enrollees could use to compare plans, such as features that both satisfy and dissatisfy, they can enhance consumer choice. Surveys are also an important source of information for government monitoring agencies in deciding whether plans are meeting contract requirements and should be retained as contractors. Although regulatory sanctions would rarely seem appropriate for poor consumer ratings, survey responses (like other outcomes measures) could suggest patterns of poor care or access barriers that require further public agency investigation into actual care delivery or administrative systems. Multiple sources of information on satisfaction, such as routine enrollee surveys, targeted surveys of vulnerable groups, disenrollee "exit interviews," and information from appeals and grievance processes, are more likely than any single source to provide an accurate picture of reasons for satisfaction and dissatisfaction.

National and plan-specific data on the prevalence of complaints and problems could be important to government monitoring agencies as well as plans that want to improve their performance. Valid and reliable measures of the construct of consumer satisfaction are needed. NCQA has begun a study to determine what information Medicare consumers would like in order to choose among health plans. Some plans have developed their own Medicare enrollee assessment tools (Hanchak et al., 1996). Both HCFA and the Prospective Payment Assessment Commission are developing surveys for Medicare managed care enrollees and disenrollees. It would be useful to collect such information routinely over time. Under a grant from the Agency for Health Care Policy and Research, the Research Triangle Institute is developing survey modules on consumer satisfaction that will generate information that consumers can use in choosing among health plans. Although that project does not include Medicare beneficiaries, the instruments could provide models that could be tested on them in order to develop model Medicare consumer satisfaction survey tools. These current research efforts may be able to shed light on an issue not addressed in the literature, the cost to administer consumer satisfaction surveys and to compile and distribute their results.

HMO "Best Practices"

Perhaps because of the competitive nature of the current market, it was difficult to obtain information from Medicare HMOs regarding enrollee complaints and policies to solicit and address them. (Only three of seven plans contacted for this paper responded to a request for a telephone interview.) A few plan administrators, however, did report that their plans conducted Medicare member surveys (some as often as quarterly) that reveal very high levels of satisfaction. These plans use information from surveys, member forums, and their grievance processes to inform physicians about enrollee concerns, educate members about plan features, and change policy. For example, one plan uses the results of consumer surveys in determining physician incentive pay and another uses the results in determining management incentive pay. One requires each of its contracting physician groups to include as part of its annual work plan a means of addressing at least one consumer satisfaction problem identified in the survey responses. Another decided to provide additional coverage of out-of-plan use in response to enrollee complaints about limits on such payment.

Although competition creates incentives for plans to determine what makes enrollees happy or unhappy, information on the state of the art of Medicare HMO managed care could be useful to policy makers to set contract standards and promote innovation. It would be interesting to know, for example, whether more mature HMOs or those with more experience enrolling the elderly have more satisfied enrollees.

How Best to Provide Information and Facilitate Its Use

It also is important to determine not only what kinds of information Medicare beneficiaries say they want and will use (as discussed in other papers prepared for the committee) but also what channels of information are trusted and actually used. More research is needed on how plans should provide information. Because some enrollees will not avail themselves of even the most accessible outside information sources, it is imperative that plan sales staff provide accurate information in an atmosphere that fosters consumer trust, the opportunity to ask questions, and full understanding. Furthermore, it may be necessary to mandate that each salesperson use a checklist to disclose key information, such as lock-in restrictions, gatekeeper requirements (including in-plan and out-of-plan service use), referral procedures, and definitions of what emergencies will be covered.

Research on ICA programs and other senior information and counseling programs could reveal what programs are best able to provide information and facilitate its use. Of particular interest could be the advocacy/ombudsman role of these programs and whether a conflict exists between responsibilities to provide unbiased information and to assist enrollees in resolving disputes. It would also be useful to study whether these programs reach not only better-educated beneficiaries but also those with less education, experience, and sophistication, who need them most. For these more vulnerable elderly, additional resources, including representatives who can actively facilitate decision making, may be necessary.

If managed care enrollment increases as rapidly as some proponents expect, support for information and counseling services must grow as well. Consequently, research is needed on the costs of these programs and the levels of funding required to provide accessible and useful consumer information. It is difficult to measure the effectiveness and cost-effectiveness of these programs in affecting decision making. Yet such an assessment seems worth some effort, particularly to determine what features are associated with the most efficacious programs.

Effectiveness of
Government Consumer Protection Standards

Government contracting and licensure standards should be evaluated. It would be useful to know, for example, whether the quality and access standards in innovative state HMO laws and various enforcement strategies are effective in improving quality and enrollee satisfaction. Of particular interest is how to strike the appropriate balance between adequately protecting consumers while not unduly micromanaging health plans.

CONCLUSION

Policy makers need to understand the sources of satisfaction and dissatisfaction of Medicare health plan enrollees. Such information can be useful to help prospective enrollees understand plan features in order to enroll in plans most likely to meet realistic expectations, provide the basis for establishing Medicare contract standards, and monitor contract compliance. Because plan performance will not always meet expectations, it is important to establish mechanisms to accept and resolve enrollee complaints in a time frame that does not impede access to needed care.

In a more competitive health plan market, Medicare beneficiaries will be asked to be much more active consumers. Although consumer empowerment may be a laudable goal, policy makers should recognize that not all Medicare beneficiaries are equally comfortable with or able to perform such a role. Given adequate and well-presented information, some will be happy to make choices with little outside help. Others will have less confidence or ability to do so (because of age, education, or limited past experience with managed care) and will need independent information sources and possibly other assistance. It will be particularly important to monitor the health plan choice and enrollment experiences of the most vulnerable Medicare beneficiaries, especially those who are sick or frail, to determine whether a market system works for them.

Some of the confusion, concern, and dissatisfaction about Medicare managed care may subside as working Americans currently familiar with managed care plans age into Medicare. However, especially during the transition to a system very different from that which most elderly people have previously experienced, public agencies have a responsibility to set and enforce standards to protect Medicare beneficiaries and to ensure expeditious disenrollment and expedited grievance mechanisms.

REFERENCES

Adler, G. A. 1995. Medicare beneficiaries rate their medical care: New data from the MCBS. Health Care Financing Review 16(4):175-187.

Booth, M., and E. Fuller. 1995. Quality improvement primer for Medicaid managed care: Final report. National Academy for State Health Policy: Portland, Maine.

Brown, R. S., J. W. Bergeron, D. G. Clement, J. W. Hill, S. M. Retchin. 1993. The Medicare risk program for HMOs—Final Summary Report on Findings from the Evaluation—Final Report. Mathematica Policy Research, Inc.: Princeton, N.J.

Dallek, G., Testimony before the Special Committee on Aging, United States Senate, 104th Congress, 1st Session, August 3, 1995. Serial No. 104-6. U.S. Government Printing Office: Washington, D.C.

Dallek, G., A.. Harper, C. Jimenez, and C. N. Daw. 1993. Medicare risk-contracting HMOs in California: A study of marketing, quality, and due process rights. Center for Health Care Rights: Los Angeles, Calif.

Dallek, G., C. Jimenez, and M. Schwartz. 1995. Consumer protections in state
    HMO laws. Volume 1: Analysis and Recommendations. Center for Health
    Care Rights: Los Angeles, Calif.
Davidson, B. N. 1988. Designing health insurance information for the Medi-
    care beneficiary: A policy synthesis. Health Services Research 23(5):685-
    720.
D'Onofrio, C. N., and P. D. Mullen. 1977. Consumer Problems with Prepaid
    Health Plans in California. Public Health Reports 92(2):121-134.
Ferguson, G. 1995. BlueCross and BlueShield Association national Medicare
    surveys: Summary of findings. BlueCross BlueShield Association: Wash-
    ington, D.C.
Frederick/Schneiders, Inc. 1995. Analysis of focus groups concerning man-
    aged care and Medicare. Henry J. Kaiser Family Foundation: Washing-
    ton, D.C.
Freund, D. A., L. F. Rossiter, P. D. Fox, F. A. Meyer, R. E. Hurley, T. S. Carey,
    and J. E. Paul. 1989. Evaluation of the Medicaid competition demonstra-
    tions. Health Care Financing Review 11(2):81-97.
Gibbs, D. A. 1995. Information needs for consumer choice: Final focus group
    report. Research Triangle Institute: Research Triangle Park, N.C.
Group Health Association of America. 1995. PHOs and the assumption of
    insurance risk: a 50-state survey of regulators' attitudes toward PHO
    licensure. Group Health Association of America: Washington, D.C.
Hanchak, N. A., S. R. Harmon-Weiss, P. D. McDermott, A. Hirsch, and N.
    Schlackman. 1996. Medicare managed care and the need for quality mea-
    surement. Managed Care Quarterly 4(1):1-12.
Harris-Wehling, J., J. C. Feasley, and C. L. Estes, eds. 1995. An evaluation of
    the long-term care ombudsman programs of the Older Americans Act.
    Institute of Medicine. National Academy of Sciences: Washington, D.C.
Hurley, R. E., B. J. Gage, and D. A. Freund. 1991. Rollover effects in gate-
    keeper programs: cushioning the impact of restricted choice. Inquiry
    28(4):375-384.
McCormack, L. A., J. A. Schnaier, A. J. Lee, S. A. Garfinkel, and M. Beaven.
    1994. Information, counseling, and assistance programs: Final report.
    Health Economics Research, Inc.: Waltham, Mass.
Miller, R. H., and H. S. Luft. 1994. Managed care plan performance since
    1980: A literature analysis. Journal of the American Medical Association
    271(19):1512-1519.
Minnesota Health Data Institute. 1995. You and your health plan: 1995 state-
    wide survey of Minnesota consumers. Minnesota Health Data Institute:
    St. Paul, Minn.
Network Design Group. 1995. Special report of HMO/CMP Reconsideration
    Results (January 18, 1995). Health Care Financing Administration: Bal-
    timore, Md.
Office of Inspector General. 1992. Medicaid HMO quality assurance stan-
    dards (March 1, 1992). U.S. Department of Health and Human Services:
    Washington, D.C.

Office of Inspector General. 1995. Medicare: beneficiary satisfaction. No. OEI-06-91-0073. U.S. Department of Health and Human Services: Washington, D.C.

Physician Payment Review Commission. 1995. Annual Report to Congress. Physician Payment Review Commission: Washington, D.C.

Robert Wood Johnson Foundation. 1995. Sick people in managed care have difficulty getting services and treatment, new survey reports (June 28, 1995). Robert Wood Johnson Foundation: Princeton, N. J.

Rolph, Elizabeth S., P. B. Ginsberg, and S. D. Hosek. 1987. Regulation of Preferred Provider Arrangements. Health Affairs 6(3):32-45.

Rossiter, L. F., K. Langwell, T. T. H. Wan, and M. Rivnyak. 1989. Patient satisfaction among elderly enrollees and disenrollees in Medicare health maintenance organizations. Journal of the American Medical Association 262(1):57-63.

Saucier, P. 1995. Federal barriers to managed car for dually eligible persons. National Academy for State Health Policy: Portland, Maine.

Shaughnessy, P. W., R. E. Schlenker, and D. F. Little. 1994. Home health care outcomes under capitated and fee-for-service payment. Health Care Financing Review 16(1):187-222.

Stocker, M. A. 1995. The ticket to better managed care (October 28, 1995). New York Times.

U.S. General Accounting Office. 1991. Medigap Insurance: Better consumer protection should result from 1990 changes to Baucus amendment.. GAO/HRD-91-49. Government Printing Office: Washington, D.C.

U.S. General Accounting Office. 1993a. Health insurance regulation: Wide variation in states' authority, oversight, and resources.. GAO/HRD-94-26. Government Printing Office: Washington, D.C.

U.S. General Accounting Office. 1993b. Medicaid: States turn to managed care to improve access and control costs. GAO/HRD-93-46. Government Printing Office: Washington, D.C.

U.S. General Accounting Office. 1995a. Medicare: Increased HMO oversight could improve quality and access to care. GAO/HEHS-95-155. Government Printing Office: Washington, D.C.

U.S. General Accounting Office. 1995b. Health care: Employers and individual consumers want additional information on quality. GAO/HEHS-95-201. Government Printing Office: Washington, D.C.

U.S. General Accounting Office. 1995c. Medicare Managed Care: Growing Enrollment Adds Urgency to Fixing HMO Payment Problem. GAO/HEHS-96-21. Government Printing Office: Washington, D.C.

Ward, R. A. 1987. HMO satisfaction and understanding among recent Medicare enrollees. Journal of Health and Social Policy 28(4):401-412.

H

Medicare Managed Care: Current Requirements and Practices to Ensure Accountability

*Judith D. Moore**

BACKGROUND AND OVERVIEW OF MEDICARE REQUIREMENTS

From the beginning of the Medicare program in 1966 there were arrangements for coverage of beneficiaries through prepaid health care organizations. However, until passage of the Tax Equity and Fiscal Responsibility Act of 1982 (TEFRA), organizations that provided managed care to Medicare beneficiaries were few and far between. TEFRA simplified the contracting requirements.

The 1985 TEFRA regulations, implementing the 1982 changes, defined a system for Medicare contracting that was much more comparable to the processes that managed care organizations use to conduct their private sector, non-Medicare business. Thus, TEFRA provided the foundation for substantial growth of Medicare managed care arrangements. Various revisions in subsequent legislation (Consolidated Omnibus Budget Reconciliation Act in 1986, Omnibus Budget Reconciliation Act (OBRA) in 1985, OBRA in 1987, and OBRA in 1990) have not altered the basic statute but have usually added protections or modified requirements.

---

*Independent health care consultant, McLean, Virginia.

The extensive statutory provisions governing Medicare managed care are found in Section 1876 of the Social Security Act. The Secretary of the U.S. Department of Health and Human Services, acting through the Health Care Financing Administration (HCFA), administers these provisions of the statute, using lengthy regulations, guidelines, and contract procedures.

Number of Medicare Beneficiaries in Managed Care

HCFA data as of November 1, 1995, show a total of just over 3.7 million beneficiaries enrolled in prepaid care under 272 contracts.[1] The bulk of these beneficiaries—3,030,000—are in 182 plans with risk contracts. Between October 1 and November 1, 1995, enrollment in risk-based plans increased 2.1 percent, a rapid growth phenomenon experienced throughout 1995.[2]

Over the years, Medicare managed care enrollment has fluctuated greatly. In April 1985, for example, just before TEFRA regulations went into effect, risk-based plan enrollees totaled 300,000 and cost-based plan enrollees totaled more than 900,000. By December of that year, those figures were 440,000 in risk contracts and 730,000 in cost contracts. Since that time, the number of enrollees in cost contracts has stayed about level.

Initial growth after TEFRA regulations was rapid; by December 1986 the number of enrollees in risk contracts had almost doubled over the number in the previous year to 813,000. The next few years saw an additional 400,000 beneficiaries covered under risk contracts, with enrollment at 1.2 million in December, 1990. At the end of 1994 there were 2.2 million enrollees.

[1]Data reported herein are taken from internal monthly reports generated by and available from HCFA's Office of Managed Care, 7500 Security Boulevard, Mail Stop S3-022-01, Baltimore, MD 21244.

[2]The information in this paper will primarily address risk-based contracts, since that is the area of significant current and future growth. HCFA also enters into cost-based contracts, which must adhere to virtually all of the requirements that risk-based contractors follow other than peer review organization review. Another Medicare managed care variation is a health care prepayment plan (HCPP), usually a labor or employer organization that provides services exclusively for its members. There are currently fewer than 700,000 Medicare enrollees in cost-based plans and HCPP.

As noted, about 700,000 beneficiaries were added to risk-based contracts during the first 10 months of 1995. These HCFA figures are shown below:

Medicare Managed Care Enrollment in Risk Contracts

April 1985	300,000
December 1985	440,923
December 1986	813,712
December 1990	1,263,547
December 1994	2,268,364
November 1995	3,030,159

HCFA Organization and Approach

HCFA's Office of Managed Care (OMC) and the 10 HCFA regional offices are primary points of responsibility for administering Medicare managed care contracts. Regional offices receive and process applications and are the principal contact for HMOs after a contract is approved.

For new contracts, an extensive application is required. This application, supplemented by an initial site visit and monitoring activity following contract approval, contains the core accountability requirements for any managed care organization that wishes to contract with the government to cover Medicare beneficiaries. A detailed Medicare contract application, available in paper or diskette format from HCFA's OMC, must contain narrative descriptions in numerous areas, as well as accompanying documentation materials. An idea of the requirements can be seen by reviewing Appendix A, which contains the Table of Contents for the Documents Section and the Narrative Section for the Medicare Contract Application.

The key requirements for contractors, summarized below, are described in detail in the Medicare Contract Application itself.[3]

---

[3]The Medicare Contract Application: Competitive Medical Plans is available from HCFA's Office of Managed Care, 7500 Security Boulevard, Mail Stop S3-02-01, Baltimore, MD 21244.

Membership Requirements

To demonstrate its operational experience, a managed care organization seeking to contract for coverage of Medicare beneficiaries must have certain minimum numbers of commercial enrollees. For a risk-based contract, at least 5,000 prepaid capitated members must be covered, or 1,500 members must be covered in a rural HMO. This number may be met by the parent organization, but a minimum of 1,000 members must be in any subdivision or subsidiary that will serve Medicare beneficiaries.[4] In either cost- or risk-based contracts, the membership may not exceed 50 percent combined Medicare and Medicaid enrollees. This is referred to as the 50/50 rule, and this rule can be waived only for government entities or if the service area itself contains a general population that exceeds 50 percent Medicare and Medicaid beneficiaries (that is, if more than half of the residents of a county are covered by Medicare and Medicaid, the rule could be waived).[5]

Medical Services

Managed care organizations must be able to provide directly or through arrangements all Medicare Part A and Part B services available in their service area and must use Medicare-certified providers. The organization must provide 24-hour emergency services and make provision for payment of emergency services for out-of-area emergencies. All services must be available with reasonable promptness, and record-keeping must ensure continuity of care.

In addition to Medicare Part A and Part B services, non-Medicare services can be provided in several ways: as additional benefits, as optional supplemental benefits that a beneficiary can choose to purchase, through mandatory supplemental benefits that a beneficiary must purchase as a condition of en-

---

[4]To be eligible for a cost-based contract, there must be at least 1,500 commercial enrollees.

[5]Membership requirements are located in the Commercial Marketing and Medicare Marketing Sections of the Medicare Contract Application.

rollment (e.g., preventive benefits), or as benefits offered only to employer group retirees. Because of policy changes made in October 1995, point of service (POS) options may be offered under several of these approaches. These POS plans are subject to additional HCFA review and monitoring related to financial solvency, accessibility of care, quality, appeals processes, and marketing.[6]

Enrollment Requirements

Plans must have, at a minimum, an annual 30-day open enrollment and must also open their enrollment to Medicare enrollees from area plans that have not renewed or that have had their federal contract terminated, except that patients with end-stage renal disease and hospice patients must be denied enrollment. Open enrollment may be waived under a few special circumstances. Beneficiaries must be able to disenroll monthly, either through the plan or, at the beneficiary's option, at local Social Security offices.[7]

Marketing Specifications

Managed care organizations must market the Medicare plan throughout the service area that it specifies in its contract. All marketing material, including membership and enrollment material, must be approved by HCFA before use (HCFA has 45 days to review materials submitted by the organization). Certain marketing practices are prohibited, including door-to-door solicitation, marketing that is discriminatory (e.g., geographically targeted marketed is not acceptable), and marketing that misleads or misrepresents the plan.[8]

---

[6]Medical service requirements are located in the Organizational and Contractual and Health Service Delivery sections of the Medicare Contract Application.

[7]Enrollment requirements are located in the Health Services Delivery section of the Medicare Contract Application.

[8]Marketing specifications are located in the Commercial Marketing and Medicare Marketing sections of the Medicare Contract Application.

Financial and Administrative Requirements

HCFA carefully reviews the fiscal soundness of all applicants to determine financial viability and whether the organization has sufficient administrative capacity to carry out contract provisions. HCFA requires that certain financial records be submitted with the application and has the right to inspect any financial records; this inspection usually takes place during site visits. Data systems to record beneficiaries coming into and leaving the plan (referred to as "accretions and deletions") must be compatible with the HCFA system, or plans may submit data through two private sector contractors that HCFA uses. Plans must accept electronic funds from the Treasury Department on the first day of every month.[9]

Quality Assurance

A plan's internal quality assurance program must be the same for Medicare and commercial patients. The contract requirements center around traditional process measures, which call for systematic data collection of performance and patient results, peer review, and ongoing monitoring and evaluation with written procedures for remedial action.[10]

Since 1987, peer review organizations (PROs) have provided external review of inpatient and ambulatory care in managed care organizations. For both managed and fee-for-service care, the PROs are moving away from individual case review toward a continuous quality improvement model involving collaborative review of patterns of care. For example, in managed care, HCFA has begun a program to gather outcomes data and performance measures for the treatment of diabetes. In five states, PROs are working collaboratively with volunteer plans to abstract clinical data from medical records of diabetic beneficia-

---

[9]Financial and administrative requirements are located in the Organizational and Contractual and Financial sections of the Medicare Contract Application.

[10]Quality assurance requirements are located in the Health Services Delivery section of the Medicare Contract Application.

ries, looking at such measures as annual eye examinations and blood glucose control to determine how ambulatory care can be improved. This effort to develop outcomes measures for other clinical conditions will be expanded in the future.[11]

Beneficiary Rights

The beneficiary has the right to remain enrolled in a plan for the duration of the government contract, except for cause—which must have prior HCFA approval. Beneficiaries may appeal decisions about coverage or services. Through a contractor, HCFA reviews all decisions that are adverse to a member. Appeals to an administrative law judge and the federal court system may follow.[12]

The lock-in is one of the most difficult concepts for many beneficiaries who are used to fee-for-service medicine. Plans therefore are required to explain the lock-in to potential enrollees, and HCFA strongly recommends (but does not require) face-to-face discussion of this feature. HCFA itself provides an explanation of the lock-in when the beneficiary receives notice that he or she has been enrolled in a managed care plan.[13] As noted, beneficiaries can disenroll monthly, effective the first day of the month after request, either through the managed care plan directly or through a local Social Security office.

Ongoing Monitoring by HCFA

Both regional and central HCFA office staff monitor managed care contracts through monthly reports and biennial on-site visits. In 1996, HCFA will begin annual targeted on-site reviews. HCFA's overall ongoing monitoring involves the following:

---

[11]Interview with Paul Elstein, HCFA Office of Managed Care, November 30, 1995.

[12]Interviews with Gary Bailey and Rae Loen, HCFA Office of Managed Care, December 1995 and January 1996.

[13]Interview with Gary Bailey, HCFA Office of Managed Care, December 13, 1995.

- review of self-reported enrollment, financial, and other information, and
- targeted site visits and comprehensive monitoring to review insolvency arrangements, legal and financial requirements for plan, quality of care, marketing practices, enrollment and disenrollment, claims payment, and grievance and appeals procedures.[14]

HCFA reviewers follow a detailed, specific written protocol during on-site reviews. Two or three HCFA reviewers spend at least 1 week on site at the plan. They pull and check a sample of appeals, grievances, and correspondence. They review all internal processes, especially contracts. Following the site visit, they prepare a report, and the plan may be required to submit a corrective action plan. The corrective action plan is closely supervised.[15]

Protocol requires regional offices to follow up on all beneficiary complaints. These are handled in a case work fashion, working through the problem with the beneficiary and the health plan. When HCFA identifies a major problem, a full-scale on-site investigation is launched, with as many as 10 HCFA employees spending 2 weeks or more at a plan.[16]

Other HCFA Approaches to Medicare Managed Care Communications and Accountability

HCFA has under way a number of activities to help Medicare beneficiaries better understand that they may be able to choose different types of medical service arrangements.

---

[14]Interviews with Bruce Fried, Paul Elstein, Rae Loen, and Gary Bailey, HCFA Office of Managed Care, and Carlos Zaraboza, HCFA Office of Special Analysis, November and December 1995 and January 1996.

[15]Interview with Rae Loen, HCFA Office of Managed Care, January 18, 1996.

[16]Interviews with Bruce Fried, Rae Loen, Paul Elstein, and Gary Bailey, HCFA Office of Managed Care, November and December 1995 and January 1996.

Consumer Information for Beneficiaries

HCFA has begun an extensive program to revise and update Medicare publications. For example, a new section of the HCFA Medicare Handbook explains choices and managed care. A new HCFA publication currently under development has been reviewed by advocacy organizations and focus groups and is scheduled for publication in 1996. Finally, a brochure describing managed care choices to be sent out with the initial enrollment package[17] is being developed and will be tested in coming months.[18]

Information to Assist in Purchasing Managed Care

HCFA is developing comparability charts on a state-by-state basis to show in a standard format comparisons with plan benefits, copayments, premiums, geographic areas served, and so forth. It will also contain a general comparison to fee-for-service Medicare. Prototypes of this chart have been reviewed in focus groups; the publication goal is spring 1996. In Phase II of the comparability chart, targeted for spring 1997, consumer satisfaction data obtained from surveys of members in every Medicare contract plan will be included. In a final phase, scheduled for summer 1997, quality performance measures will be added.[19]

All of the basic information about managed care plans with Medicare contracts is available on the Internet. The comparison charts described above will likewise be available on the Internet when they are completed.

Insurance Counseling and Assistance Programs

The insurance counseling and assistance (ICA) grants pro-

---

[17]The initial enrollment package is a set of explanatory materials about Social Security and Medicare sent to beneficiaries 6 months before their 65th birthday.

[18]Interviews with Bruce Fried, Paul Elstein, and Gary Bailey, HCFA Office of Managed Care, November and December 1995 and January 1996.

[19]Interview with Gary Bailey, HCFA Office of Managed Care, December 13, 1995.

gram was created in OBRA 1990 to support state-based provision of insurance information to Medicare and Medicaid beneficiaries. States generally train senior volunteers to provide one-on-one or group counseling information via telephone, written materials, and presentations. Each state defines its own program, and HCFA has worked closely with many ICA program grantees to develop and provide information on managed care. Most states have trained their volunteers to answer questions about managed care choices. Many states have also developed written pamphlets and materials. For example, comparability charts have been developed by ICA program grantees in several geographic areas, including Chicago, to better explain features of Medicare managed care plans.[20]

HCFA Research and Demonstrations

HCFA's Office of Research and Demonstrations has under way a series of projects to learn more about effective Medicare managed care programs and to refine current program elements.

The Research Triangle Institute conducted focus groups under a research contract to assess the usefulness of three types of plan choice information: consumer ratings, quality of care measures, and cost comparisons. The Research Triangle Institute report notes that participants responded most favorably to samples of consumer ratings of plan performance. The focus groups were held to guide the development of information prototypes, which are now under way as the next phase of the contract. In the meantime, HCFA's OMC staff has used much of the information generated in developing its new publications and materials.[21]

Medicare Choices, a demonstration project just getting started, will waive some of the existing contract provisions (including, for example, financial solvency and 50/50 rules) for selected applicants. The project will test experience with several

---

[20]Interview with Eric Lang, HCFA Office of Beneficiary Services, November 30, 1995.

[21]Interview with Leslie Grunwald, HCFA Office of Research, November 30, 1995.

different types of plans—including provider sponsored networks, preferred provider options, and POS plans—to see if relaxed rules will produce more interest and higher levels of beneficiary satisfaction. Marketing, provision of information, quality, and beneficiary satisfaction will be carefully evaluated in these plans. In the area of quality, for example, the demonstrations will favor new continuous quality improvement models, using Health Plan Employer Data and Information Set, version 3.0, reports when they are available.[22]

Additional Future HCFA Plans

HCFA Online, an umbrella plan developed by the agency as a vision of state-of-the-art communications and data transmission for the 21st century, includes many features designed to provide more and better information about Medicare and choices to beneficiaries. This includes such features as toll-free telephone service, additional market research to better meet beneficiary needs, and more printed and database information about insurance, health care services, and managed care plans. Budget realities will limit some of these plans, but there has been a strong commitment to these activities on the part of HCFA leadership, even in the face of significant administrative cuts in the agency budget.[23]

POTENTIAL IMPACT OF RECONCILIATION LEGISLATION

Numerous provisions in the pending reconciliation legislation would affect Medicare managed care. Although the final outcome of ongoing negotiations is still quite uncertain, it appears that many of the basic regulatory processes and requirements related to Medicare managed care contracting would likely remain similar to the current processes. The addition of

---

[22]Interview with Leslie Grunwald, HCFA Office of Research, November 30, 1995.

[23]Interview with Kathy King, HCFA Office of the Administrator, December 1, 1995.

new types of plans would require new approaches, and quality of care requirements might be delegated to accrediting organizations. A major change would result if states rather than HCFA were involved in the regulatory process. Some observers close to the negotiations have suggested that the regulatory role of HCFA could be significantly more extensive under reconciliation provisions. Definitive judgments are impossible given the current inconclusive status of the legislative process.

REFERENCES

Research Triangle Institute. 1995. Information Needs for Consumer Choice. Prepared for the Office of Research and Demonstrations, Health Care Financing Administration. Research Triangle Park, N.C.

U.S. Department of Health and Human Services, Health Care Financing Administration. 1993a. Medicare Contract Application: Competitive Medical Plans.

U.S. Department of Health and Human Services, Health Care Financing Administration. 1992. Health Insurance Information, Counseling and Assistance Grants Program (program description).

Zaraboza, C., and J. LeMausurier. 1996. Medicare and Medicaid. Chapter 28 in Managed Health Care Handbook, Peter Kongspvedt, ed. Gaithersburg, Md.: Aspen Press.

L

What Should Be the Basic Ground Rules for Plans Being Able to Participate in the Medicare Managed Care Market?

Case Study: The California Public Employees' Retirement System

*Tom J. Elkin**

INTRODUCTION

As an increasing number of Medicare-eligible individuals enroll in managed care health plans, there is a growing concern about how health plans will be held accountable for providing Medicare patients with affordable, quality care. This paper describes how one large public purchaser, the California Public Employees' Retirement System (CalPERS), assures its active and retired members that they will continue to have access to quality service at affordable premiums.

Managed care has proven to be a cost-effective method of organizing and delivering health care. The dramatic increase in popularity of health maintenance organizations (HMOs) in recent years is the result of their ability to counteract the rising cost of fee-for-service medicine. Faced with escalating cost of care employers are turning to managed care to control costs and more effectively manage health care for their employees and

---

*Independent health care consultant, Sacramento, California.

338

retirees. In addition, increasing numbers of Medicare-eligible individuals are joining Managed Medicare Risk Plans to reduce their out-of-pocket costs and eliminate the added expense of purchasing supplemental policies. The success that managed care plans have had in reducing the cost of care has made them very attractive to purchasers. Yet there is a concern whether managed care can continue to reduce costs and still provide Medicare patients with access to quality health care. On the basis of the experiences of some large purchasers, a degree of oversight of the performance of health plans is necessary to ensure a balance between these two forces.

The primary focus of HMOs is on cost reduction through the control of both the price and the utilization of care. To curb the uncontrolled increases in the costs of fee-for-service medicine, employers have embraced managed care without clearly assessing the potential weaknesses of such a system. Purchasers are becoming aware of the impacts that these forces will have on the service and quality of care provided to members of managed care plans. There is a growing concern about the for-profit emphasis of many managed care plans. The pressure to show a profit every quarter and to generate dividends to the stockholders could erode an HMO's commitment to deliver quality care. Many clinicians, purchasers, and consumers have expressed concern that the economic and utilization incentives of capitated, managed care plans may result in the underutilization of care and the erosion of customer service.

To ensure the success of managed care as a viable health delivery system for the future, the needs of the members of health plans must be balanced with the need to reduce the cost and make more efficient use of our health resources. Some large employers and purchasing cooperatives have implemented monitoring and oversight requirements for HMOs to measure the services provided to their employees. These purchasers play an active role in assuring their employees, retirees, and their dependents that the health plans available to them provide access to affordable, quality care. The role of capitated, managed care is critical in reducing costs, effectively managing the utilization of care, and performing efficient enrollment and contractual tasks for purchasers. However, the individual member needs the support and, in some cases, the protection of an active, informed purchaser to hold health plans accountable (U.S. General Accounting Office, 1994, pp. 3-6).

BACKGROUND

The CalPERS Health Benefits Program purchases health care for 1 million California public employees, retirees, and their dependents. The primary goal of the CalPERS Health Benefits Program is to provide access to quality health care for its members. To achieve this goal the CalPERS Board of Administration has put into place various requirements to hold health plans accountable to the terms and conditions of their contracts. The success that CalPERS has achieved in cost containment, as well as in quality and service improvements, is the result of the active role that the Board plays in managing its Health Benefits Program. The Board believes that it has a responsibility to assist members and their families in navigating through the complex and confusing issues related to selecting a health plan and a primary care physician to ensure that the members receive a high level of service (U.S. General Accounting Office, 1993, pp. 1-4).

This is particularly critical for the Medicare population, which is enrolling in Managed Medicare Risk Plans in increasing numbers. The complex array of benefit options, copayment arrangements, marketing literature, and enrollment procedures can be confusing and, at times, misleading. This confusion can be overwhelming to a Medicare-eligible individual who is facing the transfer from a fee-for-service delivery system to a capitated, managed care plan for the first time in his or her life.

The independence of the 13-member CalPERS Board and the fiduciary responsibility it has to its members are essential elements in the success of the CalPERS Health Benefits Program. CalPERS was established in 1932 to administer the retirement program for California STATE employees. Six of the 13 board members are elected by specific membership groups and 7 are appointed or are ex-officio members. The Board has broad authority, specified in Article XVI, Section 17, of the California Constitution, to administer the system and is independent of the executive and legislative branches of government.

Board members serve 4-year terms of office on a nonpaid basis. They hold monthly public meetings and allow full participation by members of the system as well as the public at large.

Because six members are elected by various membership groups and three members are California state constitutional officers, the CalPERS Board has a strong commitment to public accountability and member service. The Board has historically had a strong member orientation and strives to provide a high level of service to its members. This orientation is the force behind its active role in managing its health benefits program (California Public Employees' Retirement System, 1994, pp. 5-6).

The health program provides medical coverage for active employees, retirees, and their dependents. One thousand California public employers participate in the program, representing 1 million covered lives. These employers include both employees and retirees of the State of California and the California State University System, as well as hundreds of smaller employers, including school districts, police departments, cities, counties, and special districts. More than 75 percent of the participating employers employ less than 100 workers. In recent years there has been a dramatic increase in the number of public employers joining the CalPERS Health Benefits Program because of the success in cost containment and improvements in service and quality standards (California Public Employees' Retirement System, 1994, pp. 349-382).

CalPERS contracts with 22 separate health care plans, which provide Basic Plan coverage to approximately 852,000 covered lives and supplement Medicare or Medicare Risk Plan coverage to approximately 135,000 covered lives, who are eligible for both Part A and Part B Medicare. Approximately 82 percent of the membership has chosen to belong to an HMO, whereas the balance belong to one of the two self-funded preferred provider organization (PPO) plans available. CalPERS spends $1.5 billion annually for health care.

Faced with double-digit premium increases during the 1980s, which threatened the stability of the program, and concern about the lack of accountability of health plans providing services to CalPERS members, the Board initiated numerous changes to increase the accountability of its managed care plans and to more aggressively negotiate premiums. These changes constituted a redefinition of the role of a purchaser in terms of negotiating premiums and measuring performance. By exercising its $1.5 billion purchasing power, CalPERS was able to improve service and quality, reduce costs, and increase the accountability of the plans contracting with CalPERS (LaRaja and Rosner, 1993, pp. 8-10).

BASIC REQUIREMENTS FOR PARTICIPATION

CalPERS requires its health plans to meet numerous standards and requirements to participate in their program. These requirements fall into five major categories: statutory and regulatory compliance, provider access, quality and cost data, uniform benefit design, and customer service. These major categories encompass contractual requirements, conditions of participation, monitoring systems, and internal procedures and policies that enable the staff to monitor the performance of the health plans and hold them accountable.

Statutory and Regulatory Compliance

To contract with CalPERS, an HMO must be licensed by the California Department of Corporations (DOC) to do business in California and must comply with the requirements of the Knox-Keene Health Care Service Plan Act of 1975, Section 1340 of the California Health and Safety Code. The California Commissioner of Corporations administers this statute and is responsible for ensuring that all HMOs doing business in California comply with the licensing laws and regulations. This law requires the plans to be financially stable, defines the basic benefits to be provided, ensures that patient protections are in place, and specifies enrollment and advertising standards and grievance systems. Provider access, credentialing, and tangible net equity requirements are also reviewed by DOC. For a plan to be licensed it must submit a detailed application and undergo a thorough review by DOC staff.

Provider Access

For an HMO to participate in the CalPERS Health Benefits Program, it must be licensed by DOC and must meet additional requirements mandated by the CalPERS Board. One critical requirement is that the plan must have adequate providers to serve members of specific geographic areas. In reviewing a proposal from a new plan or a proposed expansion of an existing plan into a new geographic area in California, CalPERS staff perform a careful analysis of provider access. Even though DOC examines network coverage as part of its licensure review, CalPERS staff verify the actual network coverage in detail to determine whether adequate primary care physicians, clinics, specialists, and hospitals are available to serve the enrollees. In one incident during the review of a proposed plan expansion, CalPERS staff discovered that physicians were not taking new patients from that plan; therefore, physician access was inadequate to meet the anticipated enrollment. The plan was notified and the expansion was suspended until the provider access problem was resolved.

Changes in contractual relationships between health plans and medical groups affect provider access by disrupting patient-physician relationships. CalPERS recognizes that contract disputes will occur in the evolving, competitive, managed care market. However, there must be a balance between the economic needs of the managed care company and those access needs of patients. A contractual impasse will occur when a health plan and a medical group cannot agree to the terms of their contract and the health plan terminates the contract. When this occurs the health plan notifies its members that they must select a new primary care physician from those still under contract. This causes disruption between patients and their physicians and generates dissatisfaction among the members of the plan.

In one incident a plan terminated its contract with a large medical group within 60 days of the close of the annual open enrollment period. CalPERS members who had just selected their health plan and primary care physician were informed by the plan that they had to choose another physician. It was too late for them to change plans. This resulted in angry complaints from members and physicians who felt that the timing and notification of the contract termination was not in the best interest of the patient. CalPERS sanctioned the plan, required that letters of clarification be sent to all members affected, and allowed members of the plan who wanted to change plans outside the open enrollment period to do so. Many members switched to other HMOs.

To minimize disruption to members who have selected a particular HMO and primary care physician, CalPERS requires health plans to inform members at least 60 days prior to any contract termination with a medical group and encourages health plans to minimize these contractual disputes during the contract year. Written communications to CalPERS members must be reviewed by staff prior to publication.

The balance between the value of managed care in organizing and controlling the use of medical resources and the patient's need for access to appropriate medical care is an issue that CalPERS actively monitors and manages.

Standard Benefit Design

In 1992, in an effort to improve consistency of health care and to assist members in making more informed health care decisions, CalPERS designed a standard benefit plan and required all HMOs to provide the benefits specified in the plan. Prior to standardizing the benefits, the complex array of benefit choices, the definitions of benefits, copayment charges, and limitations and exclusions were confusing and, in some cases, misleading to the members. The wide variation in copayment charges, as an example, had no relationship to the premiums charged by the HMOs. Plans that had low copayment charges, in some cases, were more affordable, whereas some plans that had high copayment charges had high monthly premiums. There was no basis for comparison; there were four different copayment charges for physician's office visits, nine different charges for mental health outpatient visits, and nine different charges for prescription drugs, with three different volume limitations. To make an informed comparison a member would have to perform a complex analysis of his or her projected use of various services and compare that with the differences in premiums between the plans available in his or her area. A daunting task!

The new benefit design used a standard definition for each benefit, the same copayment was to be charged for the same services, and many of the differences in exclusions and limitations were eliminated. By standardizing the benefit design, the members were better able to evaluate and compare the value of health plans and to be assured that they would receive the same level of benefits, regardless of the plan that they selected (U.S. General Accounting Office, 1993, pp. 8-10).

In addition to simplifying the plan selection process, standardizing benefits required all HMOs to provide the same level of benefits, which increased competition between plans. This heightened the importance of the premiums that the plans charged, for price became an important measure of value. Negotiations were more focused on price and performance than on the differences between benefit configurations. After adjusting for age, sex, and family size, the fact that the benefits provided by the HMOs were the same made variations in premiums more difficult to justify and improved CalPERS's ability to negotiate better prices.

CalPERS adopted a standard benefit design for Medicare Supplemental and Managed Medicare Risk Plans for the 1995-1996 contract year. To encourage CalPERS Medicare-eligible members enrolled in the PPO plan to enroll in Medicare Risk Plans, a standard benefit design was implemented with zero copayment charges for physician's office visits, durable medical equipment, emergency care services, home health services, hospice services, and blood and blood products. Prescription drugs required a $1.00 copayment. Standardizing the Medicare Supplemental and Managed Risk Plan benefits simplified the health plan selection process and assured Medicare-eligible CalPERS members that they would receive affordable, comprehensive services, regardless of the plan that they selected. The CalPERS Board believes that requiring HMOs to follow a standard benefit design has improved CalPERS' ability to hold its plans accountable, negotiate lower premiums, and simplify the plan selection process for its members (California Public Employees' Retirement System, 1995a, p. 16).

Cost and Performance Data

Collecting and analyzing cost and performance data are the most important changes that CalPERS has implemented. It is not possible to assure access to quality health care without basic information regarding cost, quality, and service. For decades purchasers, employees, and retirees have paid escalating prices for ill-defined, poorly quantified health care. Basic information regarding unit cost, comparative performance, and information on outcomes of medical interventions has not been available. In order to become a more informed purchaser and to hold health plans more accountable for the $1.5 billion annual premiums paid for care, CalPERS requires HMOs to provide basic cost and performance information on an annual basis.

Initially, HMOs were required to submit data on cost, rating methodology, and basic performance in an attempt to compare the cost of care provided by the health plans. (California Public Employees' Retirement System, 1996, pp. 16-38). By comparing the reported costs on a per member, per month basis for both inpatient and outpatient services for 22 HMOs, CalPERS staff were able to identify those plans that had excessive variations from the median cost for a specific benefit. The variation between the per member, per month cost for similar benefits was wide. In one example, one plan reported paying 100 percent more for drug ingredients than its competitor. In another case, a plan was paying 80 percent more for inpatient care than several of its competitors in the same geographic region. In addition to reporting benefit costs, the plans were required to report administrative costs, including marketing costs and profit. This information enabled staff to identify high-cost areas that health plans should more effectively manage and supported CalPERS's efforts to reduce the costs of annual premiums. This information was key to CalPERS's success at the negotiating table.

Once the standard benefit design was implemented, cost data became more meaningful, for all plans were providing the same benefits and charging the same copayments for each specific benefit to a similar demographic mix of CalPERS members. The comparisons were useful in evaluating the performance and value of each plan.

In subsequent years CalPERS expanded the data requirements to include information about organization and accreditation, access to care, customer service, quality assessment, practice patterns, and quality measurement. The goal was to develop a profile for each plan to determine the value that each plan offered in terms of price, quality, service, and innovation.

In 1994 CalPERS notified its health plans that it intended to provide its members with a Quality of Care Report Card in the spring of 1995 to assist them in making more informed choices. This marked the beginning of a major effort to independently collect and publish information by using 11 Health Plan Employer Data and Information Set (HEDIS, version 2.0) Quality Indicators developed by the National Committee for Quality Assurance.

Central to this initiative was the requirement that the data be collected and analyzed by an independent third party. It would not be plan-reported, self-reported data, as had been used in the past. CalPERS joined with the Pacific Business Group on Health (PBGH) to implement this initiative and formed the California Cooperative HEDIS Reporting Initiative (CCHRI) to serve as the managing group to implement the project. All HMOs contracting with CalPERS were required to participate in the project. As the scope and importance of this initiative became apparent, eight additional California HMOs joined the project bringing the total number of plans participating in the project to 24. These HMOs represented 85 percent of the state's commercial HMO membership.

CCHRI contracted with a health information consulting company to perform the data collection and analysis. The 24 HMOs funded the project and assisted in the successful completion of the initiative. A large random sample of patients was selected, and their medical charts were examined by a team of clinical reviewers to identify which specific preventive services had been performed. This information was compiled, analyzed, and reported to CCHRI, PBGH, and CalPERS.

On April 15, 1995, CalPERS mailed 500,000 Open Enrollment Information Packets to its members. Included in these packets was a Health Plan Quality/Performance Report, which presented the results of the quality survey of the HEDIS Quality Indicators. The report also included the results of a consumer experience survey conducted in 1994 (California Public Employees' Retirement Systems, 1995b, pp. 5-10). This was the first time that CalPERS had presented comparative quality information on health plans to its members. The report was well received and will be provided in subsequent years. As more sophisticated measures of quality become available, CalPERS will include them in its annual *Health Plan Quality/Performance Report*.

The combination of the standard benefit design and the report card have greatly enhanced the consumer's ability to make an informed decision when choosing a health plan. They have also been instrumental in helping CalPERS reduce the cost of care and enable members to continue to receive comprehensive services at affordable prices. At a time when cost containment is often achieved by reducing benefits and limiting coverage of dependents and retirees, CalPERS has achieved significant cost containment by becoming a more informed and assertive purchaser.

CUSTOMER SERVICE

One of the most important responsibilities of a purchasing cooperative is to manage and monitor customer service. The complex and very personal nature of health care requires a unique approach to service and customer satisfaction. Issues of choice, the requirement to use a primary care physician, and the use of network providers are key elements of the managed care environment. Learning to adapt to these new relationships and rules can be difficult for both active and retired members. For Medicare-eligible members who have been members of an indemnity or PPO for their entire working careers, moving into a managed care structure requires adapting to new and, at times, confusing rules. Many of the limitations of managed care generate member complaints about care or service when, in fact, nothing inappropriate has occurred. On the other hand, managed care companies must provide timely services and access to benefits and must not impede a member's ability to receive necessary and appropriate services.

CalPERS has established various requirements and systems

to assist its members in obtaining services within the managed care environment while attempting to balance the expectations and needs of the member with the discipline and structure of managed care.

In addition to the *Health Plan Quality / Performance Report*, CalPERS conducts a consumer experience survey to measure how members feel about the care that they receive. The results of the survey are published and mailed to all members of the program. The results are also analyzed and included in the annual rate renewal negotiations, providing information about how well the members rate their respective plans. This survey has proven to be an effective monitoring technique as well as a pubic comparison of the views of the members of particular plans. It is an important method of measuring service (Bay Area Business Group on Health, 1994, pp. 8-10).

Another survey that CalPERS initiated is an annual exit survey. Many individuals will not make formal complaints about their plan but, because of their dissatisfaction with the performance, will change plans during the annual open enrollment period. CalPERS determined that it would be useful to survey those individuals who changed plans and ask them basic questions about the reasons why they switched plans. The first exit survey was conducted in 1994, and the information was useful in monitoring the levels of service of specific plans. An improved exit survey was mailed to all members who changed plans during the 1995 open enrollment period, and the results will be used to identify problem areas.

Advertising and marketing practices is another area CalPERS closely monitors during open enrollment. With the highly competitive managed care market in California, HMOs aggressively seek new members and can be very creative in how they represent themselves to potential members. In past years some health plans were less than accurate when portraying themselves to CalPERS members during open enrollment. In response to these problems, CalPERS now requires its HMOs to submit their advertising text to CalPERS staff for review and approval. There are strict rules regarding the use of the name "CalPERS" and the representation of the results of surveys and comparisons.

In 1993 CalPERS implemented the Ombudsperson Program for the Health Benefits Program. The purpose of this new program was to provide specific assistance to those members who had extraordinary enrollment or benefit problems. There are times when a member is involved with an unusually complex enrollment change or embroiled in a dispute over a covered benefit and needs special assistance. The CalPERS Board believed that additional assistance was appropriate for these types of cases and implemented the Ombudsperson Program to address these unique problems. The ombudspersons have access to both eligibility information and health plan benefit data and are able to cut across the traditional lines of the organization to bring the issue to closure quickly.

The program has been very successful and is limited only by staff availability. Retired members who do not have the support and advice of peers at the work site have found this service to be particularly helpful in coping with the complexities of benefit and enrollment problems. The complex nature of enrollment systems and benefit policies can be confusing to consumers. The Ombudsperson Program is an attempt to provide additional support and assistance to those members who have difficulty navigating through the health care system. It is an example of the commitment that the CalPERS Board has made to customer service.

A major strength of the CalPERS Health Benefits Program is that members can appeal directly to the Board for review of their complaints once they have exhausted their appeal rights with their health plan. Members are informed of this option annually during the open enrollment period and are given the address and telephone number of the Member Service Unit, which is staffed by CalPERS Health Benefits Program employees. These staff members answer questions and advise members of their right to appeal an issue once it has been adjudicated by the health plan. This offers the members the opportunity to explain their problem to a neutral third party who can intercede on their behalf, when appropriate, or advise the members of their options.

The final element of customer service oversight is the development and distribution of information describing the eligibility rules and health plan options. CalPERS believes that the information distributed to its members prior to the annual open enrollment period should be clear, accurate, and free of marketing bias. The Health Plan Guide that is mailed to every member's home is prepared by CalPERS staff and clearly describes the process for making plan changes and enrollment changes as well the benefits, copayment charges, and deductibles for both HMO and PPO plans. Written text prepared by the health plans is reviewed and edited before it is inserted into the booklets so it complies with the Board's policy regarding the content of written material distributed to CalPERS members. This oversight of the development and distribution of procedures, policies, and health plan descriptions reduces confusion and assures the members, the Board, and the competing health plans that information will be presented fairly and accurately.

CONCLUSION

The CalPERS purchasing cooperative is a proactive model. Its use of purchasing power to achieve significant reductions in the price that it pays for health care has redefined the role and importance of the purchaser in the marketplace. Yet its active role in ensuring health plan accountability has had a significant impact on quality and service. Cost containment that is not balanced with measurements of service and quality is irresponsible. Value purchasing, something that the CalPERS Board is striving to achieve, means the effective balance of cost, quality, service, and patient satisfaction.

As more of the nation's Medicare-eligible population moves from a fee-for-service environment into a capitated, managed care delivery system, it is essential that basic monitoring systems be put into place to assure the members, the health plans, and the taxpayers that the elderly members of our society will receive compassionate, quality care at the lowest possible price. Providing a neutral, independent, third-party entity to act as an informed purchaser, ombudsperson, and in some cases, advocate for the Medicare-eligible population is critical to ensuring that enrollees receive the benefits that managed care has to offer. All of the requirements and systems used by CalPERS to ensure provider access, cost and quality data, uniform benefit design, and customer service, can be used to strengthen the purchase and delivery of managed health care to the Medicare-eligible population.

REFERENCES

Bay Area Business Group on Health. 1994. California Public Employees' Retirement System 1994 Employee Medical Plan Satisfaction Survey. San Francisco: Bay Area Business Group on Health.

California Public Employees' Retirement System. 1994. State Constitution extract. California Public Employees' Retirement Law. Sacramento: California Public Employees' Retirement System.

California Public Employees' Retirement System. 1995a. Health Plan Guide: Combined Information On: Basic, Supplement to Medicare and Managed Medicare Health Plans. Sacramento: California Public Employees' Retirement System.

California Public Employees' Retirement System. 1995b. Health Plan Quality/Performance Report. Sacramento: California Public Employees' Retirement System.

California Public Employees' Retirement System. 1996. 1995-96 Rate Renewal Questionnaire: Health Plan Administration. Sacramento: California Public Employees' Retirement System.

LaRaja, R., and J. Rosner. 1993. How managed competition controls costs: The CalPERS experience. Progressive Policy Institute Policy Brief, No.1. Washington, D.C.: Progressive Policy Institute.

U.S. General Accounting Office. 1993. Health Insurance: California Public Employees' Alliance Has Reduced Recent Premium Growth. Washington D.C.: U.S. General Accounting Office.

U.S. General Accounting Office. 1994. Access to Health Insurance: Public and Private Employers' Experience with Purchasing Cooperatives. Washington, D.C.: U.S. General Accounting Office.

Index

and satisfaction with care, 313-317
by states, 74
types of organizations, 313
Rehabilitation services, 71, 165, 298-299
Research recommendations
clinical effectiveness and outcomes,
155-156
communication of information, 321-
322
consumer protection standards, 322
enrollee satisfaction research, 319-
321
ICA programs, 321-322
Research Triangle Institute, 244-245,
254, 256, 278, 320, 336
Respite care, 52
Retirees
dissemination of information to, 280
education by employers, 95, 169-170,
249-250
information needs of, 278
Medicare services, 330
structuring choice for, 49-50, 163,
165-166, 168
Retirement Living Forum, 63, 258
Risk contract HMOs
beneficiary characteristics, 201
benefits, 16, 20
costs, 52, 53
enrollees, 4, 16, 18-19, 51, 196, 328
expenditures, 208
experience of Medicare beneficiaries
in, 51-54
geographic distribution, 16, 17, 52
incentives for enrollment, 16, 20
outcomes, 53, 208
point-of-service option, 15
profits, 15, 61
quality of care, 52-53, 69 n.38
satisfaction with care, 147, 293-295
service delivery for seniors, 52, 217-
218
standards for entry, 41, 304-305
Risk contracts/risk plans. *See* Private
health care sector
Risk selection
AAPCC methodology and, 227-228
adverse, 26-27, 45-46, 78, 146, 162,
176

by beneficiaries, 78
benefit plan standardization and,
184
conditions of participation and, 82
defined, 86-87
in FEHBP program, 146
and grievances, 86-87
importance, 7, 37, 84
measurement and adjustment, 83,
146, 161 n.1
number of plans offered and, 162
physician financial incentives and,
84
purchasing approach and, 152

S

Sailor, 257
Satisfaction with managed care. *See
also* Disenrollment; Quality of
care
assessment of, 186, 189, 272
consumer complaints, 296-299
with costs, 53, 65, 213
data sources, 170, 319-321
disenrollment and, 67-68, 293, 294
education of consumers and, 57-58,
66-67, 85, 299-300, 314-315
focus group studies, 66, 272, 273,
274, 276-277, 295-296
health status and, 213-214
HMO enrollees, 147, 292-293, 320-321
information accuracy and usability
and, 57-58, 314-315
information needs of consumers, 61,
274-275
Medicare HMO enrollee surveys,
293-295
overcoming barriers to, 313-317
overview, 65-67
with physician-patient interactions,
52-53
with quality of care, 52-53
rating system, 66-67
research recommendations, 319-320
sources of dissatisfaction, 65, 291-300
standardization of data, 224
survey results, 65-66, 67, 213-214